My Turn to Buy Gelato

My Turn to Buy Gelato

A Life Filled with Love and Food

———

Michael Savarese

Michael Savarese at nine months old.

Dedication

●

To my parents, who sacrificed every personal desire in order to see me achieve my goals.

To my children and my grandchildren, who inspired me to relate my story.

To my wife Joanie, who has been my sounding board throughout this adventure.

To Mariann De Barbieri and Anne Diaz, who gave me so much of their time to see that my work came to fruition.

To Alex Henderson, a fabulous writing coach who took my story to heart and showed me the way.

Preface

It's late September, 1978 at 192 Bleecker Street in Greenwich Village, New York City.

A neatly dressed man in his early thirties—white shirt, black tie—looks over the menu of daily specials while keeping one eye on the set up of the dining room tables for the day's business. Not far away, his partner—same clothes—inspects the flower arrangements that had just arrived. On a display table, Nicola, the chef, places a tray loaded with stuffed artichokes next to a huge half wheel of Parmigiano. Giorgio, the busboy, is playing with the radio to locate the correct station for the background music—a mix of international jazz and contemporary hits. A few weeks earlier, on August 14, Ennio Sammarone and Michael Savarese had finally fulfilled their longstanding dream—to open Ennio & Michael Ristorante.

Along with the staff, they were getting ready to open the door for the day. Mr. Guallini, the mailman, comes in and hands Ennio a stack of mail, along with a small box. Ennio looks at it, calls out: "Michael, there's a package for you. It's from Italy. Sign the return receipt." I look at the box and recognized my sister Sofia's hand writing. What could that small box contain that my family in Naples wants me to have? With trembling fingers, I open it. What I see inside makes me freeze and brings tears rolling down my cheeks. I sit on one of the chairs, take the ring out of the box, and slowly put it on my finger.

Table of Contents

x

Prologue:
The Big White Ship

The big white ship was there in front of us.

It was a sharply beautiful Italian autumn morning, and the time had come to go through document inspection and embark. After a few hugs from my family, I walked up the gangway and went down to my cabin to store my two suitcases—with the tortano dolce and the bottle of sweet vermouth for Aunt Teresina. I then went up on deck to try to find my people. The S.S. Atlantic sat tied to the dock with hawsers, with just a few feet of water separating the ship from the pier. The attendant crowd stood at the same height as the ship's main deck. I spotted where my family and friends were and took a spot by the rail closest to them. I leaned over the railing to better hear them over the noise of departure—I could almost touch them from where I stood. In typical Neapolitan fashion, they were all calling out loudly, occasionally screaming good-naturedly to get their farewells across. All the while, the big wharf clock ticked on the white wall across from the ship, and every time I glanced at it, its hands seemed to be spinning faster and faster.

It was hard to believe that all these people had shown up just for me. There stood my cousin Gennaro Grieco and his wife Giuseppina, who came with their baby in a stroller. My childhood friend Gigino, my sisters Antonietta and Sofia, and Antonietta's husband Giovanni (called Gianni by everyone who knew him) had all showed up earlier that day to drive me to the pier in their "new" used Fiat—a tight fit for five people and two suitcases. My aunt Giuseppina and her daughters Maria and Antonietta, Signora Pelillo and Dino. Don Tommasino was not there, he had to work. Don Gaetano and his son Alfredo. Titina, my brother Mario's fiancée, was there with her parents and her grand-mother. My cousin Michele, who would end up with my bike, and his wife, Assuntina. Vincenzo, the shoe shine man, was there too, along with few of my friends - two of whom were Salvatore Sorrentino and his brother Enzuccio. As it turned out, their father worked on one of the tugboats that were to pull my ship away from the pier. The evening before, when I went around to say goodbye, Mr. Sorrentino promised that he would be the last one to say goodbye to me with a double blow of the tug boat horn.

My father, wearing his Panama hat, was holding on to my mother with his left hand. With his right hand he kept wiping the sweat from his forehead, and most likely, also wiping away a few tears. My mother was holding on to him in a complete stupor, trying to hide her true emotions. She was no stranger to sad moments in her life; instead of showing tears, she had fallen very quiet, pouting her top lip tightly to the bottom one, in one tight squeeze. Earlier that morning, she had hung around my neck a thin gold chain with a crucifix, squeezed me close to her chest, and asked me to promise to her that I was not going to let America change me. Seeing her face pressed by the shifting crowd, first against my father's chest, then against Mrs. Pelillo's shoulder, made me think that my departure was adding another stab to her heart. My oldest brother Mario had left for Germany to work in the mines in Mannheim, and we rarely heard from him. It seemed that every male in her life had a certain fate, starting with her own father, who died when she was only six, to her second son Pierino, whom she had lost at the tender age of two-and-half, to her husband, who was totally destroyed by the war, and now *me*.

I couldn't help but think back to the previous day. My mother had asked me to visit our closest neighbors and friends to say goodbye. As I made the rounds, everyone was generally happy to see me off, giving me various reactions from "Why are you going?" to "Good for you! Get away from this misery!" However, the one response that struck me the most, and kept running through my head ever since, was when I said goodbye to the Cianos, a family who lived just above the Pelillos. Mrs. Ciano was a woman of few words who spoke only from the

2

heart. After taking a good drink of water, she looked up at me from the kitchen sink and said, "If you were my son, I would not send you to America."

I was surprised by her statement. Her son Pasquale had been a friend, though not as close a friend to me as Gigino or Dino. Even so, when walking by our door Mrs. Ciano never failed to call out praises to the aroma of our cooking, or of my singing in the shower. However, her husband Don Vincenzino now reprimanded her from his seat at their kitchen table.

"What is your problem? It's not your business! Stay out."

When I returned downstairs, my mother was about to dish out dinner. I hadn't even sat down when she said to me, "What's wrong?" She must have sensed something was bothering me. I told her what Mrs. Ciano had said, and she set down the ladle and cried, "What does *she* know? Does she think that I am happy to send you there? Doesn't she know what a sacrifice it is for me and your father?" She touched me on the shoulder for emphasis: "Your future is more important than anything. Don't listen to what other people say. Go make your life and don't look back!"

I looked in her eyes and saw her determination and thought: *She is the truth in my life.* Still, I wasn't sure I felt the same certainty she did. I sat down to eat my dinner, but Mrs. Ciano's words echoed in my head. They were the kind of words that, once they enter you, never really leave.

The next morning, on the car ride to the Port of Naples where the *S.S. Atlantic* was docked, no one said a word. All of a sudden, as we were about to pass the metal gate giving us access to the port, my sister Antonietta turned to me and blurted out, "You, look at me! Open your eyes. You are going to be by yourself in another world, so don't do anything stupid. And keep writing to us." I assured her that I would not repeat my brother Mario's behavior. Then it was time to take the suitcases out of the car and carry them onto the ship.

My eyes glanced back up at the clock, wondering how much time I had left until departure. Suddenly, three loud blows went off from the smokestack. The deck started to vibrate under my feet. We were ready to sail. The big vessel began at once to pull away from the pier, albeit at a very slow pace. I kept one hand on the rail and frantically waved with the other. With every minute that went by, the pier and the people on it became smaller and smaller.

Up until that point, I had managed to stay strong. I had successfully kept myself from breaking down emotionally. But as the ship slowly pulled away, everyone I had ever known and loved became one with the surrounding buildings, with the hills and Mount Vesuvius, until everyone and everything was all swallowed by the sea. Only then I tore myself from the railing and went to my cabin below and burst into tears.

Many years have gone by since then but I can still see that scene in my mind's eye and hear the echo of Mrs. Ciano's words.

Welcome To This World

The first time I tried tomato sauce, I was nine days old.

It was Christmas of 1945, the first holiday my family was able to celebrate in many years. My parents had lost almost everything during World War II—not just tangible things like their home, my father's electrical contracting business, or even the clothes on their backs, but things that can never be replaced. But now, they were no longer refugees, no longer homeless and no longer running from place to place. They had a place they could call home.

Sitting at the kitchen table, my mother said to my father, "Salvatore, the baby keeps looking at me when I eat."

My father told her, "Wet your pinky in the *Ragu* and put it to his lips."

As she did that, I began to lick my lips with many short strokes of my tiny tongue—I liked it.

Laughing, my mother, who was now sipping wine, held up her glass and said to my father, "Salvatore, look at him! Should I let him taste it?"

My father agreed, and there I had my first taste of wine too, which I quickly sputtered out. According to my parents, I had preferred the tomato sauce. I still do.

That tomato sauce wasn't supposed to be for me. I wasn't even supposed to have been born at all. To understand why I was here on this earth, you have to go six years earlier, to the afternoon that three army men came knocking on my parents' door.

It had been an uncharacteristically gloomy day in Naples. Three army men showed up at their doorstep and told my parents that they were there to collect on behalf of the Italian government—that it was their *duty* to inspect everywhere—and if my parents were smart they would give them everything they required. My father Salvatore let them in and allowed them to roam freely about the apartment and take whatever they wanted. Thanks to a tip off from Giuseppina, one of my mother's sisters, he'd had enough time to hide the massive amounts of copper supplies that he had been secretly hoarding ever since Mussolini lost his mind, as well as the family jewelry, including the expensive diamond ring that his jeweler had custom made for him. The attempted army collection was part of a national sweep to collect jewelry and precious metals from the populace. The men had no idea about my father's copper, or that the building featured a sub-basement. However, my parents must have known that the soldiers, whenever they came, wouldn't want to leave empty handed, so they had kept some of their jewelry up in the apartment, unprotected. This joined other possessions, silverware and a few copper pots, in the cloth bags the army men had brought with them, which they then sealed in front of my parents. As they were leaving, the youngest of the soldiers stepped back, and without saying a word motioned to my mother Maria to remove her wedding band, which she did, and for Salvatore to do the same. The man then put both rings in his pocket. My father looked him in the eyes.

"Young punk. If you were not wearing that uniform, I would chew you up right now."

The young soldier gave him a look of derision and left.

It was 1940, and the war was coming to Italy. Everything in Naples was becoming more difficult. Mussolini was making worse and worse choices, siding with Hitler, and allowing the Germans to do as they pleased. German troops, along with their artillery, hid inside monumental churches and historical buildings to surprise their opponents and to counterattack the British planes. It seemed only a matter of time before everything exploded. The area where my family lived lay a short distance from the port. Military activity abounded everywhere, with army trucks going in and out of the port, carrying artillery and tanks. Airplanes flew low, supervising everything. War was in the air.

Neapolitans, however, knew how to survive. For centuries, their city had been occupied by foreign powers. They knew that no war lasted forever. For all its violence and overwhelming destruction, they knew that one day this one too would end. However, things would get worse before they got better. In November 1940, the British RAF bombed the port of Naples, killing almost one thousand civilians in a single raid. For the next few months, the city was spared. Another one of my mother's sisters, Elvira, and her family took that opportunity to relocate to Sarno, a small town behind Mount Vesuvius, away from the big city. But my mother was pregnant, and my father Salvatore didn't want her to be running from place to place, so they decided to stay in Naples, hoping for the best. In June 1941, my mother gave birth to their third child, my older brother Pierino. With two boys and a girl, the family was now complete. And if all had gone as they dreamed, that would have been that.

When Pierino was five months old, Naples was bombed again. In three days several whole neighborhoods were destroyed, resulting in enormous casualties. Salvatore and Maria packed a suitcase and a few bags stuffed with what valuables they had been able to conceal from the militia, and left town. They had to get out of Naples; nothing else mattered. They locked the house and, at that point, Salvatore removed one of his shoe laces and slipped his diamond ring onto it and then tied it around Maria's neck.

They all left for the train station with Salvatore holding Mario's hand, Maria holding Antonietta's hand and carrying Pierino. They boarded a train for Salerno in the hope it would stop somewhere near Sarno or Pompeii. A few miles after leaving the Naples train station, the train came to a halt; the tracks had recently been hit by bombs, and the train was unable to proceed. All the passengers scrambled off the train and scattered into the woods. Salvatore and Maria, with the kids in tow and whatever else they could carry, started to walk in the direction the train had been traveling. They occasionally stopped to rest, away from the overpasses that the Germans were bombing. They reached Sarno on foot a few days later; however most of their valuables and belongings had been lost along the way.

They ended up staying in Sarno for two years. Salvatore landed a night job as a baker along with few electric repair jobs during the day. As Mussolini's fall brought Italy abruptly out of the war, housing projects began to spring up on the outskirts of the major cities, including Naples. They were principally built to house the thousands of people who had been displaced by the bombings. My father, Salvatore, applied for a home, eager to move his family back to Naples. In 1944, they finally did and settled in the section known as Barra.

In Barra, Salvatore and Maria settled in as well as they could. My father took on a few electrical jobs. They didn't have any furniture in the apartment—not even a bed, no pots to cook in, and hardly any clothing. But they still had the diamond ring—the ring my father had tied around my mother's neck at the start of their evacuation. They finally agreed they had to sell the ring to buy some cheap furniture and have cash to keep them going, in the hope of starting over again.

My mother stayed home to look after the two young kids, Mario and Antonietta and the toddler, Pierino. Like most wives, she did house chores, shopped, and cooked. Every day she took along Antonietta and Pierino and went shopping for bread, vegetables, pasta—food for the table.

One day on the way home from food shopping, my mother was carrying the grocery bags while Antonietta and Pierino ran ahead of her, laughing and playing. As small children do, they occasionally stopped to pick interesting objects off the ground, only for my mother to yell at them, "Drop that! Don't pick that up!" Suddenly, there was a concussive explosion. Some sort of bomb had exploded right there in front of them. Dirt and dust filled the air where Pierino and Antonietta had been running. My mother dropped her bags and ran to her kids. There was chaos everywhere, with people screaming and scrambling in every direction. She saw Pierino on the ground, dirty, with blood all over his small, beautiful face. He looked lifeless. She picked him up and ran toward her building, a block or two away.

In the meantime, my father, who had just come home from work, heard the explosion and ran out of the apartment to see what had happened. He realized that a bomb had exploded just hundreds of yards away. He ran towards that spot instinctively. He knew that was also the direction his wife and children were coming from. When he saw his wife running towards him holding Pierino in her arms, he realized that something terrible had happened. The little boy was still breathing, but with great effort, and a trickle of blood ran out of his ear. A long scream came out of him.

"Pierino! Pierino, oh God, no." He took the lifeless baby in his arms and held him close to his face. "Wake up. Please, oh God wake my boy up." Tears were streaming down his face. Dust swirled all around them, coating their clothes. "Please God, don't do this. Don't do this to me. We have survived so much already. Don't take my son."

My mother was in shock. The only thing that came out of her mouth was a faint sound, an almost lifeless tone: "Salvatore. I don't see Antonietta. *Where is Antonietta?*"

My father looked around with Pierino still in his arms. Antonietta was nowhere to be found. In the confusion of the explosion, she had gone missing. Our family was so new to the neighborhood—along with every other family—that no one knew who she was. After taking Maria and Pierino home and laying the injured child down on the family bed, Salvatore went to look for a doctor and at the same time to search for his missing daughter. He returned home with the doctor, but without the little girl.

Upon entering the bedroom, Doctor Sasso immediately saw the seriousness of Pierino's injuries. The little boy had suffered a trauma to his head, which was evident from the bleeding from his ears. Doctor Sasso suggested immediate hospitalization, but in war time that was not easy. The nearest hospital was about six or seven miles away, and with no local authorities or police to be found anywhere, everyone was left to fend for themselves. The city was a mess.

Instinctively, my father picked up his baby from the bed, determined to run the seven miles to the hospital if he had to. But his gesture was in vain. By that point, the little boy had stopped breathing. Pierino was dead.

As my parents looked at one another, the pain and the anguish they felt was too much to bear; still their love as well as their responsibilities as parents could not be diminished. They had another task at hand: finding Antonietta. With both hands, Maria grabbed her husband's face and said, "I'll stay with Pierino, you go find our little girl."

Salvatore searched the streets day and night, describing to everyone he met the clothes Antonietta was wearing and posting notes on the walls, on lamp posts, on store windows. Two days later, as Maria and Salvatore sat next to Pierino's body in the apartment, a man appeared at the door holding Antonietta's hand. Maria ran to her and clutched her to her chest. Salvatore and my brother Mario embraced them tightly, and stayed that way for a long time, afraid to let go. The stranger stood there watching with tears rolling down his cheeks. When Salvatore became aware that the man was standing there in tears, he went over and embraced him.

It was at this point that Maria realized Antonietta was not speaking. The man told them that the reason it took two days for him to find our family was because she was unable to communicate with anyone. He and his wife had cared for her until one of their neighbors told them about the man, my father, who had been searching for his lost daughter after the explosion. The gratitude and friendship that developed between my father and the other man, whose name was Don Eduardo, lasted well into the years that followed.

When Doctor Sasso examined Antonietta, he did not notice anything too serious. He explained that the shock of the explosion, and the fact that she had been lost had probably traumatized her, but that in a few days she would be talking normally again. Antonietta remained mute for several weeks, until the morning she saw a lizard crawling on the bedroom wall and gave a big scream. My mother ran into the room and saw Antonietta pointing at a spot on the wall while screaming loudly. She heard her saying, "Mama, mama there is a lizard on the wall, get it out of here!" Doctor Sasso had been correct. From then on, Antonietta started to talk again—even too much at times.

Although my mother would not give birth to me until December 1945, I always felt that I came into this world to replace my brother Pierino. My parents often talked of him. The depth of their sadness and yearning was a measure of their love for him. Telling stories about him helped them to bear their sorrow, and I always felt like I knew him.

My brother Pierino

He was a chubby boy who always smiled. Whenever someone offered him a candy, after grabbing it with one hand, he would open his other hand wide, expecting another, one for each hand. He had a deep contagious laugh. Just like me, his first steps on his own came when he was seventeen months old, and once they did, there was no stopping him. He loved to run, until the day when that running came to a sudden end.

Life in Barra

Pierino died before I was born, but I still had one brother—my parents' first born, Mario—whom I loved very much. He was nine years older than me, and I looked up to him as my champion. I remember one time when I was three he built a cart for me, which I pulled all around the neighborhood to my heart's content. My next door neighbor, a small, quick-witted boy named Gigino Pelillo, would spend hours with me, no, *days* playing with it. We loved that cart. From the garbage pile, Gigino and I would look for empty cans, fill them up with dirt, sticks, soda caps, and rocks. We would load them on the cart and bring them to different spots. We'd cart our cans everywhere. Gigino and I were an inseparable pair. If his mother called him to go in, I'd go with him, and if my father called me, he'd come in with me. One thing about living in the projects and on top of each other, our parents never had to worry about us playing in the street. After all, we lived at the very end of a dead-end street.

One day, as Gigino and I were playing with the cart and cans, my upstairs neighbor Nepocchio Esposito, a skinny boy four years older than me, decided to take the cart away from us. As he was walking away pulling my cart, I jumped in front of him and demanded it back. He laughed at us and pushed me out of his way. Then, on second thought, he threw me onto the ground. Not stopping there, Nepocchio emptied the contents of the largest can of dirt on my head, and, yelling, banged the can all over me until a big gash opened on my forehead. After all these years that scar is still there. Alarmed and scared, I felt blood pouring over my eyes. Gigino was gone; he had run in to call his mother. I got up and ran in to my father. Gigino came behind me and behind *him* came his mother, from next door. She took one look at me and said to my father, "Ah, God, Don Salvatore! I have to take him to the emergency room immediately!" My father's sight was starting to fail him, so thank God that Gigino's mother was there. Otherwise, who knows what would have happened.

Leaving her two boys with my father, Mrs. Pelillo rushed me off to the emergency clinic, at least half an hour away by trolley, which was the fastest way for those of us without cars to get around back then. Once we got there, the nurses washed me of all my dirt and dust and stitched up my wound. When we got back home, it was already late. My mother, pregnant with my sister Sofia, had just come home from work.

When my mother saw me walk in with Gigino's mother, she could not believe her eyes—my head was wrapped up in a large bandage. She ran to me and, after looking me over from top to bottom, patting me for possible broken bones or damage, she thanked Mrs. Pelillo over and over. My brother Mario, who was older than Nepocchio, wanted to go upstairs and give him a beating right there, but my father stopped him. Instead, from downstairs, my father screamed abuse up at the Espositos through the stairwell, hurling accusations and angry pronouncements up through the building, which they of course returned in kind. This was the first bad argument between our two families, but it certainly wouldn't be the last.

Another day as I was running and playing on the dirt road in front of my building, a rusty nail penetrated the heel of my right foot. I pulled it out and only a small amount of blood came out. Not giving it another thought, I kept running and playing. Of course, I was barefoot. That night my foot swelled up pretty bad, and the throbbing was unbearable. It took me a long time to fall asleep that night.

The next morning, as my mother left for work, she asked Mrs. Pelillo to take a look at my foot for her. Mrs. Pelillo sent her two boys—Gigino and his younger brother Dino—out into the abandoned fields that bordered the projects to look for a particular type of wild leaf.

They came back carrying a small bunch of those miraculous leaves.

Gigino and I, c. 1960

Their mother soaked the leaves in olive oil, cut a slit in my swollen foot with scissors, and squeezed out a large amount of pus. After cleaning my foot with alcohol, she placed the soaked leaves on the wound, wrapped my foot with gauze bandage, and sent me on my way.

That evening, when my mother came home from work, I described for her the scissor procedure Mrs. Pelillo had performed on my foot. She took a quick look at the wound, then grabbed me by the hand and walked me next door to the Pelillos, where she straightaway pulled Gigino's mother into a hug. I heard her whisper, "Maria, I can't thank you enough. What would I have done if you weren't here?"

"Don't even mention it," Mrs. Pelillo said. "You would have done the same for my kids."

In reality, neighbors were always part of my life. My family shared our apartment with one family, shared half of our building with another three, while four *more* families occupied the other half of the same building, to say nothing of the eight families who lived directly across the street from us. These sixteen families were so intimately involved in each other's lives that if someone sneezed in one apartment, you'd hear "*Salute!*" coming from every other direction, across the street or through the walls.

The housing project where we all lived sat on what was once farmland, bordered on one side by the San Giovanni Cemetery and on the other by the wall of a soccer stadium. Ours was a large housing complex, made up of 24 two-story buildings arranged around four dead-end gravel roads, which we nevertheless called streets—one way in, same way out. Each building was divided into eight apartments, with three buildings on either side of each street. Our building and the one across from us were the last two on the last street. It was the end of the end of the end. The buildings were separated by backyards divided by barbed wire. Tenants didn't have to pay rent—one of the perks of emergency government housing.

The project was strictly residential and boasted no stores or any services on site. Back then, tenants would dispose of garbage down the street, as far away as possible from the buildings.

The children played most of the day and night in the street—soccer, race sprints, storytelling, singing under the streetlamp. We would mostly go home only to eat or to sleep.

"Savarese" was the second-to-last name on a long list of people left homeless by the war. The very last name on the list was "Esposito." These families were waiting for the local authorities to assign them a permanent place to live. There was only one problem for the final two names on the list: In this particular project, only one apartment remained.

According to a few of the more imaginative residents of the projects, there were two explanations for the problem: First, that someone higher up was poor in arithmetic, because if there were only 192 apartments why were there 193 families on the list? Second, another name must have been added to the list earlier on, either for money under the table or for a needy relative. Either way, there was nothing we could do. The only person who could make any changes was the district mayor, and he had more important things to worry about than one more damaged family who had lost everything in the war.

But more importantly, *we really needed that apartment.* So, the housing officer in charge decided that the Savarese and the Esposito families would share the last remaining available apartment in the last building on the street.

It was supposed to be a temporary arrangement, because the Espositos were scheduled to move out as soon as a new promised project complex was completed. Of course in reality it would be six years before my family finally had the place to ourselves. My parents stayed there many more years after the Espositos moved away. In fact, my parents did not move out until after I had already struck out on my own many years later. As a result, my entire childhood was spent in these projects.

Our building entrance gave access to four apartments, two on the lower level and two on the upper. My family was assigned the corner apartment on the lower level that was attached to the only bomb shelter on the whole street—the *ricovero*, as it was called. This concrete bunker was sunk partially in the ground, with access both from the street as well as directly from the hall of our apartment. The bunker had no lights and was always cold.

On a few occasions, the emergency sirens would go off up and down the street, causing panic in the neighborhood; suddenly, there would be dozens of people running and screaming towards our building to gather in the shelter. I found it funny, all these people dropping everything they were doing and bolting like scared horses towards the only safety nearby. Since *our* apartment had its own private door into the shelter only a few steps away, my parents, out of experience, would tell us to wait until we heard actual bombs dropping in the distance before getting up from the dinner table. In fact, on one occasion I remember my mother just standing there cooking a meal while everyone outside ran screaming past us into the bunker, her eyes distant, hiding something I couldn't see.

Since most of these were false alarms, I don't remember us spending much time in that shelter. Usually, the alarm would shut down after a minute or so, and from the window I would watch in amusement as all my irritated neighbors would spill out from the bunker and return home, complaining about the wasted half hour.

The apartments themselves were very plain and constructed of poor materials. Although ours had a separate bathroom with a toilet bowl and a cold-water only sink, there was no tub. Every time you had to use the toilet you had to remove the plywood cover kept in place with a rock, and then you'd better remember to put that rock back. On several occasions, rats had knocked off the cover and snuck into the apartment through the toilet bowl.

The apartment had no heaters and it was always cold and damp—all winter, all spring, and all fall. As a result we wore more clothes inside the apartment than we did outside. In the streets, we were always running, playing, staying active; but inside, you could really feel the cold. So at night, we had to wear flannel underwear and flannel pajamas to bed and cover ourselves with mountains of blankets. It didn't hurt that there were four of us—me, my parents, and Antonietta—sharing one bed. Even so, I remember falling asleep with my teeth chattering.

Winters in Naples were never extremely cold (thank you, God!), but sometimes, in the deep of winter, we would bring the brass brazier from the kitchen and place it directly on top of the bed, so we could warm up the blankets. (That dampness and cold must have been the reason why my father always suffered from bronchitis.) The Espositos would take their turn with the brazier before or after us, until both families' bedrooms were warm.

The kitchen was a large room. On one wall sat a big sink with a leaky faucet that dripped constantly, and a small ceramic wash tub by the window. We only had cold running water. On the wall opposite the sink was a tiled coal stove, and every time my mother cooked, it was my job to feed coal into the fire and fan it to keep it going. Every time I took up my place in front of the stove to fan the flame with my wooden paddle, the smoke inevitably blew into my eyes, bringing tears rolling down my cheeks. Although there *was* a vent at the top of the stove, the smoke always seemed to miss it and instead blew right into my face. What's worse, the only thing I had to wipe my tears with were my dirty, soot-covered hands, which just turned my face black and gave everyone an excuse to tease me. But once the food was in front of me, none of it mattered any longer. I was happy to eat with my dirty hands.

In the middle of the kitchen stood a big rectangular table with six plain wooden chairs with straw seats. We used that table for everything: to eat, to do the ironing, to stand on to clean the smoky walls, or to change the fuses, which always seemed to blow and leave us in the dark. Later on, Mama would even put Sofia in a basket on the table while she cooked, washed dishes, or did other kitchen chores—never letting her attention draw too far away from the basket and always tak-ing what seemed to me excessive care to make sure baby Sofia was safe at all times. I wondered whether she had shown the same overly pro-tective nature to me when I was a baby, and if so, how much of that was the result of her natural maternal instinct, and how much came about due to the tragedy of losing Pierino. How much of the mother I knew only existed because of grief?

From the hallway, each family had a private entrance to their bed-room. Even with such little privacy, we had a nice arrangement with the Espositos that made being together as a family easier. The two families took turns using the kitchen and spent the rest of the time either in our own bedroom or out in the street. Mr. and Mrs. Esposi-to had two children about my age who, like us, kept very much to themselves. They ran a kiosk selling an assortment of beverages in the middle of the municipal square in Barra. It was not only where they ran their business, but also where they spent most of their daytime hours. In reality, the Espositos would use their share of the apartment just to sleep.

Occasionally, our two families would mingle around the kitchen table, especially on cold winter nights when the coal stove kept the room comfortable. And because I was the youngest one who wasn't a baby, I had the job of doing everyone else's chores. God knows how many times I was told to fetch something from our bedroom. Outside the kitchen, the apartment was dark, cold, and empty, especially since the only electric light we could afford to turn on was the one in the kitchen, and even that one was dim.

Since my family's bedroom was furthest from the kitchen, I would have to pass the Esposito's bedroom on the way. In the far corner of their room, about six feet from the floor, they kept a picture of some dead relative with a small light in front of it, a disembodied face floating in the darkness. This picture, with its dim illumination and unchanging black-and-white expression, terrified me. If their door was open (which it always was, when they came out to the kitchen to mingle), I would run past it so fast that I covered those few meters in a split second—although to me it seemed like an eternity.

For all the warmth of the kitchen in winter, the bedroom was really where we did most of our living. It had a large window overlooking both our garden and the dead-end road on which our building was located. Inside we kept a large armoire, a cot, a wooden chair, and a large bed. On the wall at the head of the bed hung a crucifix and a small bowl for holy water, always empty. The bed itself was made of wood, with wooden planks laid across it to hold our two mattresses. These mattresses were stuffed with dried-up corn leaves, and each day my mother rolled and turned them so that at night we could sleep on the fresh side. Sometimes she would take them out to the building hallway to empty them out, fluff out the corn leaves, sprinkle them with a white powder (DDT), and re-stuff them. It was some job!

The only times we ever saw any type of vehicle in the projects was when either the garbage truck came to remove the garbage pile at the top of the street or when Mrs. Borriello's shiny Fiat Balilla drove by. Mrs. Borriello was the midwife who had delivered me and a multitude of other neighborhood children, and we would only see her car coming up the street if a baby was about to be born or, sadly, on the edge of death.

Most of the traffic, if you could call it that, came from the various vendors who came to our street to sell vegetables, fish, and housewares. There was also the eccentric knife sharpener, who came in riding on a bicycle that he had modified with a big grinding wheel mounted high over the handlebar, with the bike chain extended from the pedals to spin it as he rode. He would set up his bike on its stand, which lifted the rear wheel, so that he could keep pedaling to power the grinding wheel so he could do his work. For someone who specialized in sharpening knives, he certainly was a remarkably disheveled and unshaven fellow. One thing for sure, all us boys stood around fascinated by his operation, as our mothers came out one by one with ancient heirloom knives and dull scissors.

Another vendor who especially attracted the attention of the neighborhood kids was the milkman. He came early in the morning on a daily basis, pulling two cows behind with their bursting breasts. As our mothers came out holding empty containers, the farmer would fill it directly from the cows' udders. We children would gather around the cow to watch the milking process. Inevitably someone always ended up so close to the animal that he or she would get hit by the cow's tail as she swung it to shoo the flies that had landed on her rear end. If you were the new kid on the block, you might find yourself being pushed toward the cow's read end by the other kids. A cow tail to the face was just one way of welcoming you to the neighborhood.

Once a month Don Tommasino Pelillo would come home driving his boss's car. Along with his sons Gigino and Dino, I would help him wash the car inside and out and polish those chrome bumpers with paste and clean soft cloths. When the job was done, he would usually take us for a ride. What a pleasure showing off to the other kids on our block! This might have been where my fascination with cars began. We would wave to them from inside the car to make sure they saw us.

Our next door neighbors Mr. Pelillo, also called Don Tommasino, and his wife Mrs. Maria Pelillo had two kids around my age. The oldest, Gigino, would become my closest childhood friend. Don Tommasino, Gigino's father, was a good man and hard worker. He was the personal driver for the owner of a flour mill and a pasta factory. Gigino's family could afford some fancy things. In their apartment they had a record player, a radio, and an even an electric iron. Don Tommasino loved novelties and if he could afford to buy them, he did. He worked long hours, but when he got home at night, he never failed to bring out some of the products his boss had handed out to him that day. Occasionally he would even knock on our door and hand my mother bags of flour and pasta, out of the goodness of his heart.

Directly above them lived another family, the Cianos—Mr. Vincenzo Ciano (also called Don Vincenzino), who worked at the post office; his wife, Rita; and their son Pasquale, also my age. Though friendly and often complimentary of my father's cooking aromas, they were a bit cold and kept to themselves. As a result I spent little time playing with Pasquale, and—except for one particularly significant moment later in life with Mrs. Ciano—I have no strong memories of being in their home.

In the apartment directly *above* my family's, however, there lived a family who, for better or worse, overlapped their lives with ours almost as much as the family with whom we shared our actual living space. Like our roommate-family—the downstairs Espositos—this other family was *also* named Esposito, but there the similarities ended.

Curious to know why so many people we knew had the Esposito last name, one day I put that question to my father. He began by telling me what the word Esposito really means—*esposto* in Italian, or "exposed" in English. At the beginning of the second millennia and through the eighteenth century, Naples was constantly invaded by foreign powers. If a woman became pregnant and did not want her baby, in order to prevent that woman from ending her pregnancy or even worse for disposing of her baby in an unorthodox manner, an institution that was part of the Church of the Annunziata was formed, so that a mother could drop off her child without anyone knowing about it and no questions asked. The infant would be placed in a revolving vertical window, resembling a revolving door; the mother would turn the door jamb counterclockwise and the baby would disappear from her view. At this point, the mother was no longer responsible. The child would be cared by an order of nuns until he or she was healthy and ready to be exposed for adoption. Esposito.

These *upstairs* Espositos, as we called them, had three noisy children, a daughter and two sons, and they also ran a pottery shop inside their apartment. All the arguments between my father and the upstairs Espositos precipitated out of the noise that came into our apartment whenever they worked—*especially* when Don Ciro operated his big, creaky pottery wheel. Although we did eventually get somewhat accustomed to the noise, my father, whose eyesight was by now severely failing, would still become extremely irritated with the constant mouse-like *squeak-squeak-squeaking* of the pottery wheel, and would hurl curses at them from the bottom of the stairs.

Even with my father's and Don Ciro's bad relationship, I continued to visit their apartment and spend quality time watching Don Ciro and his family churn out pot after pot after pot. I loved to see Don Ciro working the big wheel, spinning up clay vases and plates. It took a lot of work to create those pieces; once they were shaped, they were left to dry, then burnished with glass rods to smooth out the nicks and fingerprints. About once a week, at night, when enough pieces were formed and ready to finish, Don Ciro would fire up the kiln that sat in their backyard like a tiny cathedral with an open top for loading and unloading. (After some time, I realized that the reason they baked at night was because running a factory, even a small one such as theirs, inside a residential apartment was illegal.) I spent many evenings by their kiln talking, eating, or listening to Don Ciro's many stories. I would stay often as long as I could, waiting until my mother called me in to bed. The last step was always hand glazing the pieces to sell at souvenir shops—as artifacts from "Pompeii."

The Accident

In truth, the rancor between our families wasn't all the fault of Don Ciro's squeaky pottery wheel. My father was by that time near the end of a prolonged medical decline that would soon turn even worse. It had begun in Barra five years earlier—a couple of months before I was born—in October '45. My father had run into one of his old Neapolitan neighbors, who told him that after being hit by bombs early on in the war, Salvatore's old building had completely collapsed, becoming a pile of debris. Once exposed, it had been thoroughly looted.

My father had to see the damage with his own eyes. Accompanied by my brother Mario, he hopped on the train for the half-hour ride to Naples. Upon stepping out of the train station, he noticed a great deal of confusion: American army trucks and army personnel, Italian soldiers and equipment were everywhere, with people scrambling to get out of their way safely. He was told that the Italian army was supervising the American troop withdrawal from Italy. Hearing those words, and seeing all that activity with his own eyes, he started to believe that the war really was finally over.

Holding Mario by the hand, my father managed to cross the wide avenue known as Corso Garibaldi. After a short walk, he reached what had once been his home and his shop. It was almost too much to bear. He took a few steps over the debris and recognized broken pieces of furniture, shards of dishes, half-familiar cooking appliances. He continued to pick through the debris for something that would remind him of the better times. But there was nothing. Everything of value was gone.

He told Mario that the war had been worse than he'd anticipated, but that he had a good strong pair of hands and technical skills with which to pick himself back up. Heading back to the train station, still holding Mario's hand, he attempted to cross Corso Garibaldi again. Suddenly, an Italian army truck roared up before him. To avoid getting hit, he jerked back and slipped on the ground. A second vehicle—an Italian army motorcycle traveling directly behind the truck—ran him over. Something hit his head so hard that he passed out.

When he regained consciousness, he heard Mario's voice crying out his name. He also noticed that he was bleeding profusely from the right side of his head, and he was unable to get up on his own.

By then, a mob of curious bystanders had gathered around him. The army captain who had been the rear passenger on the motorcycle immediately ordered one of the trucks to take him to the nearest functioning hospital. When they arrived, the hospital was filled wall-to-wall with patients and occupied beds everywhere.

Fortunately, he was given a bed in a hallway, albeit one flush with foot traffic, making it impossible for him to calm down. He spent the night with Mario lying next to him on the bed. The next morning, a doctor told him that he had suffered a serious head injury. There was a concern that he could possibly lose his eyesight and he would need to stay until they received the test results—which might be days.

Hearing that, Papá cried, "But who will tell my wife?" My mother was at that very moment pregnant with me. He right away attempted to leave, but the doctor advised him that it was too dangerous and that he would not discharge him until all the tests came back.

As soon as the doctor walked away, my father decided to leave anyway, and convinced a man who was standing nearby to go out and hire a coach to take him and Mario home. The man came back and said there was too much confusion outside, he was not able to get a coach, but he *had* hired a man with a cart pulled by a donkey. With the help of the Good Samaritan and the cart driver, my father slipped away from the hospital—at one point literally sliding down the hospital stairs on his rear end—and was loaded onto the donkey cart next to Mario.

When they finally got home, a day after leaving on the train, they were greeted by the usual nosy neighbors who crowded around him, helping him up the four steps to his apartment. My mother had been

26

My mother, Maria Levato Savarese (c. 1933)

thinking the worst. It was almost exactly a year to the day since the bomb that had killed Pierino. When she looked out of the door and saw my father in bandages and unable to walk on his own, she was aghast. Before asking any questions, she threw her arms around him and would not let go. In the meantime, Mario was telling everyone about the accident and about the hospital stay. My father was just happy to be back home in Barra.

From that point forward, however, things got harder and harder for him. Eventually he realized that the doctors' prediction was correct; his eyesight *was* getting worse and worse. This might have been why he suffered Don Ciro's squeaky wheel so much worse than the rest of us—his hearing was fast becoming his main sensing organ.

Adjusting

My father's worsening condition made it difficult for him to bring in as much money as he was used to making. To make up the difference, my mother took on various sewing jobs around town. She was in fact quite skilled with a needle and thread; as far back as the end of World War I, when she was in her early teens, she was an apprentice in a tailor shop, whose owner was a relative who'd taken particular attention to make sure Maria learned the profession well. Now more than thirty years later, those same skills were the only thing putting food on the table.

Being a skilled seamstress, my mother always found ways to make us new clothes out of used ones. I had to help her a little; my job was to thread the needle for her since she had trouble seeing the needle eye, even though she wore her funny gold-rimmed glasses. Those glasses looped around her ears like fish hooks, and I lovingly made fun of them, earning an occasional slap on my head. About once a month on Sunday mornings, my mother would travel to the nearby town of Resina to buy used garments that even organizations like the Salvation Army and the Red Cross couldn't give away. She would check each piece over and over until she was satisfied before buying it, but even still there were always pieces that no one would ever want to wear. In my mother's hands, however, garbage could turn into gold.

She would wash and dry every piece carefully, then remove all the buttons. She would completely take apart the collar, pockets and sleeves with a blade, then reverse the fabric to expose the inner surface and completely rebuild the garment. I don't think anyone could tell the difference between what she made and a brand-new piece of clothing. I remember one time, as she was removing the lining of a donated coat, she screamed out so loud she left me petrified. Inside one of the creases she had found three $20 bills all crinkled up. That was three times what my father's pension brought in every month. We were rich!

* * *

Later that year, my mother got a job as a seamstress in a factory that made army uniforms. After a couple of years, she became the foreman of over one hundred seamstresses. She went to work every morning except Sunday. My father, who had been a very hard worker himself up until his accident, felt awful that his wife had been forced to become the breadwinner for the family. However, I never would have grown as close to him as I did if it weren't for all those years he stayed at home with me.

In any case, when I say that my mother was the breadwinner of our family, I mean it literally.

Our meals were usually made from seasonal vegetables, potatoes, all kind of beans, pasta, rice, and—most of all—bread, bread, *bread*. Bread was the essence of our table: It filled you up and wasn't expensive. When cutting bread, we had to pay attention, slicing off the heels to set aside so that they would harden over the course of the next week into the perfect accompaniment to one of our favorite (affordable) meals: *Zuppa Di Pane Cotto*. With bread-heels sufficiently hardened, you achieve a wonderful effect of bread that can soak up the flavor of the soup without getting mushy. If my Mom had happened to work overtime that week, we could even afford to buy eggs to drop in the bread soup.

Meat was something I only learned about when I saw Gigino eat it at dinner with his family one night. He had offered me a piece to taste. It was good. Very good. When I went back to my apartment, I asked my parents, "How come we never eat meat? Gigino's family has meat all the time."

Instead of telling me that we couldn't afford to eat meat, my father said, "Too much meat, you know, is not really a good thing. Sometimes it can turn you into a cuckold, and you grow *horns* on your forehead."

I had no idea what he was talking about, but I accepted his answer anyway. Still, I couldn't deny that the bite of meat had been really tasty.

* * *

My father's eyes may have been going, but certainly not his libido. In February 1949 my mother gave birth to our new baby sister. Sofia was a tiny little thing, but when she was in bed with us she took up more room than the rest of us combined, so careful we were not to squish her. Even before Sofia's appearance, the bed was a tight fit, with myself, my parents, and my older sister Antonietta all squeezing into a single full size bed. Often I'd ask myself, "When did my parents find the *time* to conceive in that crowded bed?" In any event, to make more room I was unceremoniously bumped to Mario's cot, sleeping head to heel night after night. Imagine how many kicks in the teeth I got from that.

For Antonietta's part, rather than being upset about the lack of room, she was quite happy to have the baby close to her. She had always been a happy girl, strong-willed, and ready to help out around the house whenever needed. Whether she cooked or cleaned, you could always hear her singing the latest romantic songs from the Festival di Napoli, to the point that I would join in (and sometimes take over) from time to time. Her good disposition made it easy for her to have lots of friends. Everyone who knew her loved her. But the one that cared for her the most was our next door neighbor Mrs. Pelillo.

Antonietta loved Mrs. Pelillo just as much, and whenever possible she would go next door to visit while holding our new baby sister Sofia in her arms. Mrs. Pelillo, who was a stay-at-home mom to her two boys, also loved holding and playing with the new baby. Mrs. Pelillo was about ten years younger than our own mother, and many times Antonietta would come in from visiting her with rosy made-up cheeks and bright red lipstick on her lips. To both Antonietta and Sofia, Mrs. Pelillo became "Aunt Maria." (She was always Mrs. Pelillo to me.) Often when bouncing Sofia on her lap, she would muse that she would love to have a little daughter of her own. When she became pregnant for the third time, both my mother and Antonietta couldn't stop

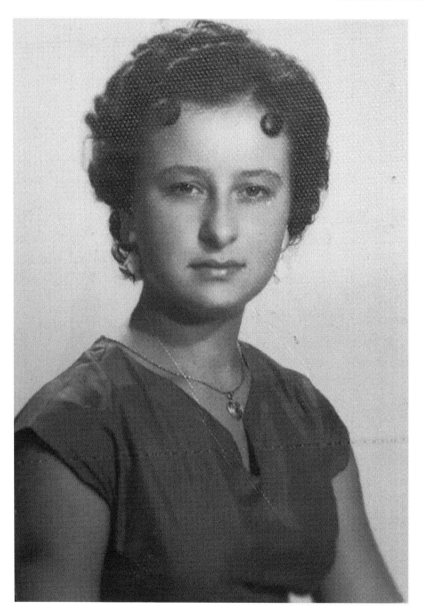

My sister Antonietta

whispering and laughing with her, saying how beautiful it would be if she had a girl of her own. Instead, fate gave her another boy—but this time the baby was stillborn. Antonietta couldn't stop crying about it for days. "What a shame," she kept repeating, "what a shame!" All the adults in our neighborhood came to express their sympathy, and to surround the Pelillos with love, attention, and food.

In the middle of the informal vigil, Gigino came looking for me.

"Miché, have you ever seen a dead baby? Come to my parents bedroom and I'll show him to you."

We snuck in without making any noise, opened the middle door of the dark wooden armoire, and looked in. Lying atop a neatly folded white blanket was a beautiful little baby, bearing no expression—like a doll with its eyes closed. Even though both Gigino and I were afraid of dead people, this one felt different. I turned to Gigino and told him what my mother had said to me just a short while earlier: "Gigino don't be sad, your little brother is going back home to God."

The next morning, the Pelillo apartment was full of people. The funeral procession that followed was slow and mournful. Even though the procession was all men—women traditionally stayed home to console the family during funerals—there were no dry eyes in the cortège. Two white horses pulled the all-white hearse, with Don Tommasino, my father, and Mrs. Pelillo's brothers right behind, followed by a sea of men. Everyone from the projects was there, and so were many people from our broader parish. My mother stayed at the Pelillo's along with my sisters to comfort her friend.

"Poor Aunt Maria," Antonietta kept on whispering while caressing Mrs. Pelillo's face. "Poor, poor Aunt Maria."

Like us, the Espositos were tired of sharing an apartment with another family. The new housing projects were still not ready, and as far we knew they never would be. Like us, their kids were now older, but still sleeping in the same bed with them. Blessedly, in 1951, after six years of living in the same space, they finally found an available apartment near the main square where they kept their beverage stand. As soon as they were gone, my family immersed ourselves in fixing up the place just how we liked it.

Things began to improve in our apartment right away. To start with, we began to expand our living quarters to a previously unknown opulence. My mother had grown quite tired of the plain white painted walls day in and day out. She was eager to pick a new wallpaper to cover the bedrooms, both ours and what had been the Espositos', and we converted the latter into a new dining room. This dining room doubled as Antonietta's sleeping quarters, too. It felt good to have all that space.

The dining room wasn't the only new additional space, either. Not long after Antonietta moved to her own cot in the dining room, Mario and I gained our own place as well. Peacetime had made the bomb shelter obsolete. Since it was attached to our apartment, we covertly took it over and converted what had been the *ricovero* into an additional bedroom. My father and brother together took up some spare wooden boards and nailed them across the street-side bunker door, restricting access to our private hallway alone. The only problem was that the bunker featured a huge rectangular opening onto the street, like an enormous window without glass. To fix this, my father, brother and myself installed a brand new window frame and pane to keep out the elements; we went on to install lights in the high-peaked ceiling and ceramic tiles on the floor. Mario and I each had a small bed, some shelves, and a chest of drawers for our clothes. Our new room was always damp, so we made heavy use of blankets. After school, Mario, who was then fourteen, worked at a café delivering coffee and pastries. It was so quiet in our room, however, that he would sometimes oversleep in the mornings, and my father would sometimes have to rip the blankets off of him and, once or twice, administer a couple of good strong smacks so that he would not be late for work.

If Mario wasn't home yet, I hated to be in that room by myself—especially when the electricity went out. On those occasions, I had to go to sleep in the dark. I would convince Sofia to come to my bed and we would light a candle because I was afraid of the dark. As we lay there, we would see Papá come slowly down the steps, guiding himself by the hand rail. Once he had stepped on the floor, he would walk slowly like Frankenstein's monster towards my bed, being careful not to hit anything that might have been in the way. As he would bend down to check on us, the weak light that came from the candle created a shadow of his face on the wall that made his nose look huge. Sofia and I would start laughing and Papá would chuckle as he took Sofia back to his bedroom, leaving me to deal with the cold dark room by myself.

Around this time, I began having a pair of dreams that would follow me all throughout my life in Naples. I'd try to stay awake as long as I could but those dreams would visit me again and again. In the first, I found myself standing at the edge of a deep ravine which, in order to cross, required me to step on a very thin plank that reminded me of a blade. With my arms held out, taking small, careful steps, I would glance ahead to see how much further I needed to go before reaching safety. I was really afraid to look down at the bottomless abyss all around me. At that point, the fear would become so great that I would startle myself and wake up.

In the second dream, I would be riding a beautiful, brand-new bicycle (even though I had never owned a bicycle before), one which I proudly kept clean and polished. Inevitably I would come upon a farm, where I had to cross a muddy irrigation canal in order to keep riding. I knew that if I got the wheels wet, the dirt from the road just a little further on would stick to them terribly and ruin my perfectly clean prize. To prevent this, my dream-self figured out that I could get off the bike and bend down to put my shoulder below the cross bar and thereby lift the bike up to walk it over the water.

However, every time I knelt on the ground, I would find an incredible pile of gold coins scattered in the water. Although I stuffed my pockets with them, the coins would just fall right through a large hole in my pocket and out my shorts, and I would wake up looking for the bike (which was never there).

My first real triumph in the renovation of the apartment was to fix the hook on the bathroom wall that held the towel. It was always loose, letting the towel fall to the floor every time you used it. Probably everyone in the family grew tired of it, but nobody did anything to fix it. At six years old, it was clear I had to take matters into my own hands to fix it.

One day, I begged my father for a few liras. I went to the store on Corso Bruno Buozzi and bought a small amount of Portland cement and *pozzolana* (volcanic sand) in a little cone made of paper that the cashier had given me. After mixing the substances together with water, I screwed the offending hook into a small block of wood and, using my fresh cement, plastered the block into the empty hole of the cinderblock that made up the wall. Then I left it to dry overnight. I must have done a good job, because the next morning, when my father realized that the hook had been fixed, he exclaimed, "Who fixed this hook?"

I proudly answered, "It was me, Papá!"

He smiled and gave me a friendly pat on my head "My son, you are going to go places in life."

Modern times were upon us, indeed. That year, the local municipality installed underground gas lines for the first time, and a shiny new gas valve suddenly appeared in our kitchen. I helped dismantle the antiquated coal stove, gleefully ripping the guts out of that old soot-filled beast. No more smoke on the walls! No more smoke in my eyes! In its place, we built a simple stone counter with a white marble top. A brand-new Fargas two-burner gas stove completed the scene. Mario and Antonietta would no longer have to trek across the borough of Barra just to buy coal. Overnight, cooking changed from a burden to a family pleasure.

Before going off to work, Mama would leave a shopping list for my sister Antonietta or me to pick up from Don Mariano's grocery store on the way home from school. Antonietta, at eleven, was already like a second mother to me and Sofia. She would go to school, shop for food, and clean the house. When she was done with the cleaning, she would prepare whatever ingredients were needed for that evening's meal, so that when Mama came home she could complete the cooking quickly.

Even with the addition of the new gas stove, our meals remained simple and hearty. Usually they were thick soups, sometimes thick enough to cut with a *knife* (just kidding), with pasta predominant as the main ingredient, since pasta was inexpensive. But the dual centerpiece of our dinner table was bread and conversation. I ate bread with *everything*—fruits, dry walnuts, oil—and also used it to wipe my dish clean of any sauce. (I still use my bread like that.) On Mondays we might have *Pasta e Lenticchie*, on Tuesdays it was *Pasta e Fagioli* and on Wednesdays, *Pasta e Ceci*. Pasta with red sauce was twice a week—on Thursdays by itself, and on Sundays accompanied by salad or other side dishes. After Mama became foreman at the military clothing factory, we added meatballs and spare ribs to the *ragu*. Fridays and Saturdays, especially in the summer, we might just have a robust salad, alternating beans and canned tuna as the main ingredient.

However, there was one dish that I could not stand: *Pasta e Patate*. This was a thick soup made mainly of potatoes and pasta. Whenever this dish was the meal of the day, I would carry on whining and complaining, "I don't want it! I'll just eat bread and oil!"

Patiently, my poor father would say, "Please, Michele, at least try it, and if you don't like it I'll ask your mother to give you something else."

The point wasn't really to get more food. Instead, I was more interested in provoking a reaction, something, *anything* to break up the boredom of the routine dinner table. By now, my father was having quite a lot of difficulty seeing, a fact which I shamelessly took advantage of by silently eating my meal anyway, even as I continued to whine. Sometimes the ploy worked: He would ask Mama to bring me something else to eat, as if she was a waitress at a restaurant. My mother, brother, and sisters went along with my tasteless skit, saying nothing but watching, probably because they were just as bored as I was.

One time, my father must have sensed something shady was going on, and decided to reach over and stick his spoon in my dish to check how much I had eaten. When he realized my dish was empty, he calmly put his spoon down, grabbed the back of my head, and with one shot pushed it right into my almost empty dish. When I finally cleaned the soup off my face, all I could hear was the sound of him laughing.

That laughter wouldn't last long. By now it was six years since his motorcycle accident. My father had had a few operations already to try to arrest his failing vision, one doctor even going so far as to briefly remove his eyeball entirely from its socket in order to manually tweak a nerve in the hopes that it would help. I remember that doctor holding my father's left eyeball in the palm of his hand.

"Doctor," my father begged at one point not long after, "Give me glasses as thick as dishes. I don't care how heavy they're going to be, I want to be able to *see* something."

However, there were no glasses thick enough to fix his eyesight, and nothing had worked so far to halt the progress of the vision loss. The next step was to try to repair some of the damaged nerves themselves, but the operation was risky, and failure could mean total blindness. He could have decided to let the injury run its course, but instead he opted for surgery.

I remember the day of the operation. Mario had to work that day, and Antonietta had to stay home to watch Sofia, so I accompanied my parents on the thirty minute trolley ride to Cardinale Ascalesi Hospital, in Naples. Both of my parents were visibly worried, while I was struggling to stay awake with the early morning trip. The doctor must have greeted my father and brought him in to the operating room, but all I remember was the long wait next to my mother in the waiting room afterwards, and the sound of her crochet needles clicking anxiously in her lap, hour after hour.

We had been sitting there for hours when I interrupted my mother, put my head on her lap, and asked if my Papá was ever going to see again. The sad, worried expression on my mother's face was not uncommon to me; in the few years I had been on this earth, I rarely saw her smile. She shook her head slowly now, as if she wasn't sure. And then she began telling me once again about the moment six years before when he was taken to that hospital bed with his head wound.

My mother had lately come to the realization that the chaotic conditions of war—no good means of transportation, lack of good telephone service—plus her advanced pregnancy with me had forced my father to choose between his family and his health. He had clearly sacrificed the latter for the former, and what we were living through now was just the consequence of that sacrifice.

I didn't know what to say to that. So I told her that the preceding night, before going to bed, I prayed to San Ciro to make my father see again.

She put her warm hand on my head stroking it. "Are you worried, Miché? I think he will be okay."

"Oh good. I can't wait to show him how good I can play soccer."

More time went by. Finally the doctor came looking for my mother.

"Signora," he said, and his voice was as low and heavy as a pallbearer. "Over the last several procedures, I have tried everything in my power to restore your husband's eyesight. I'm truly sorry to say that I have lost all hope of helping him. There is nothing more I can do."

She looked up at him without saying a word, and then she took me by the hand and we walked over to where my father was lying in the hospital bed. She put her head on his shoulder. Both of them started crying. Once again, loss had visited our family.

* * *

From that point on, we all had to up the sacrifices and contribute to compensate for my father's vision loss, for him and for the good of the family. He had already been adjusting to his failing eyesight, but now that nothing more could be done to restore his vision, he was determined to face forward and deal with his handicap as best he could. He was now totally blind.

Very quickly, his hands became his eyes. He used them to feel his way around our apartment—the walls, the shelves, the stairwell. We were told over and over to keep all our doors either totally closed or totally open so that he would not run into the corner of door edge-on and bang his forehead. He began to stroke our faces to engrave our features in his mind. This was his way of dealing with his limited world. After going to a new destination just once, he would remember the precise number of steps and landings, whether the doors opened to the right or left, and so on, so that he could navigate more easily the next time. Even years later, he would remember these exact details on repeating the trip.

Sundays in the Projects

Sundays were different from the rest of the week because my mother was off from work. However, her day began even earlier. For the better part of the early morning all she did was boil water, as each of us waited for his or her turn to bathe in the tub placed in the little foyer next to the bathroom. I always wanted to be the last one to bathe, because then I got to stay in the warm water a little longer. In the meantime, my father would sit at the kitchen table in front of a bowl of warm water to shave and once in a while would yell to me, "Michele, make sure you clean your ears well, inside and out." To watch a blind man shave is incredibly interesting. With his right hand holding the Gillette (the old style shaver that needed to be assembled before each use), he would follow the index and middle fingers of his left hand over his lathered face. Occasionally, he would ask whoever was in the room, "Did I cut myself?" and after taking a quick glance, one of us present would say, "No, Papá, keep going, you are doing good." However I must say that he made good use of his hemostatic pencil.

Like most Italians, my parents were Catholic. My mother was a believer, but not a full participant like my father. He had to go to church every Sunday, rain or shine. By 11:00 AM my father and I would leave to go to church. Many times, I would complain that it was always me who had to take him. Sometimes I wanted to go outside and play with my friends. That complaining didn't work all the time, even though once in a while my mother or Antonietta would go in my place. My father preferred the 11:30 mass at Saint Anthony's because it was shorter than the one at the S. Anna Parish where I was baptized. I always thought it was long and boring. Of course, if Salvatore had his way he would have chosen the church of Madonna del Carmine Maggiore, his native church and one of the most beautiful of all Neapolitan churches. Whenever we attended mass there, we always used the main entrance, because in the large atrium there was a huge Crucifix where he had to stop, say a few prayers and light a candle.

The church was as stunning then as it is now. We passed many separate chapels walking down the left corridor but the one my father visited often was the chapel of his favorite saint, St. Ciro, at the end of the corridor. Papá told me the story of St. Ciro so many times that I could recite it from memory word for word.

According to my father, St. Ciro lived in the fourth century. He was a medical doctor who had healed so many sick people that eventually he was made a saint. He granted many miracles. This was proven by the many silver and gold hearts, limbs and skulls that his believer's had pinned to the saint's gown, once they were cured. My father always told me to believe in him.

On the way to St. Ciro's chapel, we passed by many beautiful marble statues, one of which was the statue of St. Michael, holding a sword in his right hand while holding a snake (which represents the Devil) under his foot.

The statue that I admired the most was the one of Conradin of Swabia—it had so much history. In the thirteenth century, when Conradin was just sixteen years old (my age when I left Italy), his mother, Elizabeth of Bavaria, sent him to fight Manfred, the king of Sicily. After a number of battles in Sicily and Calabria, while heading north from Sicily to Rome, he was arrested and taken prisoner in Naples. He was brought to Castel dell'Ovo, where centuries later my father would stand guard at the end of WWI. Conradin was decapitated in Piazza Mercato when he was just seventeen. His mother sent four large vats full of gold coins that were to be used to build a church near the spot where her son had succumbed. Those four vats adorn the rear of the main altar of the church. One day I questioned the fact that if the church was so old, how come its' ceiling was new? That was when Papá told me that the original ceiling had been damaged badly in one of the many air raids in WWII.

By the time we returned from church, my mother, with Antonietta's help, had the meal ready. All she needed to do was to drop the ziti into the boiling water. Back then, pasta did not come pre-cut, it came in long lengths that had to be snapped by hand, so every single piece was different from the next. The times I was told to break the pasta, I was happy to do it because I made it a game to break each piece in equal lengths, wasting precious time. If the water was already boiling and I wasn't finished, my mother grew impatient and would urge me to hurry. Sometimes I ignored her until she gave my head a little slap. In the beginning I had trouble breaking rigatoni since they were too thick for my small hands. One thing I did love was stirring *Ragu*, while my mother and sisters finished the laundry or what ever chores they needed to do. The aroma that came out of that pot was impossible to resist, forcing me to dip in bits of bread and eat them. *Pasta e Ragu* was by far our most common Sunday dinner and in addition to the sauce there were baby back ribs and meatballs. Once the pasta was cooking, I grated Parmigiano cheese on a very old grater that probably had been around for many generations. As the piece of cheese became smaller and smaller it would be more difficult to hold, and unfortunately parts of my knuckles wound up mixed in with the grated cheese.

In the summer, when fish was in abundance and therefore inexpensive, another Sunday meal was *Zuppa di Pesce* over *friselle*, (dried out slices of bread) which picked up the delicious flavor and character of the dish.

In nice weather, after Sunday dinner, my parents would take all of us kids, along with Gigino, for a trolley ride. After enjoying the ride, they would take us to an ice cream store to buy gelato. What a treat! It was one of my mother's favorite things to do, to have us kids dressed nicely and to make that short trip, no matter how bad things were. It meant a lot to her.

One Sunday was particularly interesting. While waiting for dinner, I went next door to the Pelillos. Don Tommasino was arguing with his wife who had forgotten to pick up wine. "What do you mean we don't have wine? How do you expect me to enjoy my Sunday dinner?" he yelled. Mrs. Pelillo calmly said, "Come on Tommasino, don't be such a baby! Get in the car with the boys and go get the wine!" He stubbornly answered, "Eh, Maria, I drive all week long for my boss and I refuse to drive on my day off!"

Mrs. Pelillo, without missing a beat, asked Gigino and me to go to the wine store. Armed with an empty bottle and a bag that looked like a fishing net, we got on Gigino's bike, and off we went. This winery sold cask wine from the barrels. Don Ciccio, the host, recognized Gigino and took the bottle, filled and capped it and handed it back to us. After sending regards to Don Tommasino, he waved us on our way. We got on the bike and headed for home.

Gigino had an idea and asked me to stop the bike. "I think we should try this wine out to make sure it is good. My father can be very picky." I agreed and we both took a small gulp of wine. I said, "I normally don't like wine, but this one is good." Gigino, who was accustomed to drinking wine with his parents at dinner, took the bottle from my hand and began to take more swallows. He said, "You know, Michele, I believe this wine is even better than I remember! Maybe Don Ciccio gave us something else? Do you think he recognized me? Is he going to charge somebody else for this?" Laughing, I said, "Gigino, I don't think it's our problem. Let's go!"

We made another stop along the way to make sure the wine had not turned. Actually, we started taking more little swallows until the bottle was half empty. We arrived home and were greeted by Don Tommasino, who looked at the bottle.

"What happened to the rest of the wine?" Gigino immediately answered, "Papá, we didn't realize that the shopping bag had a hole in it and we dropped the bottle, spilling some of the wine."

"You two scoundrels; I should kill both of you! You are both drunk, you little bastards! When the time comes, I'm gonna fix you up!"

They sat at their table to eat, and I went into my apartment for my dinner. My mother gave me a funny look, as I walked in and sat at the table in her chair instead of my usual seat. When she realized that I was drunk, my mother took a towel, soaked it in cold water and wrapped it around my head. Later that evening, when Mrs. Pelillo told her about our 'mishap,' they both started to laugh so loud you could hear them a block away, while Don Tommasino was still so upset that he was still red in his face, plotting his revenge.

Television was introduced in Southern Italy around 1953 or 1954 and it was so expensive that only a few people could afford it. Well, Don Tommasino got one—a 'Telefunken,' made in Germany—only the best for the Pelillo's! Gigino and Dino were considered rich kids, but I knew better. Don Tommasino just liked to keep up with the times. He worked harder and longer hours when he wanted something new, and television was definitely new. It was so new that the only programs being shown were between 6:00 PM and 10:00 PM—mostly news, game shows copied from American television, and an occasional movie.

Advertisements were at the beginning of every program and lasted about 10 minutes. Many times the advertising skits were the highlights of the evening and I still remember them. We may not have known what the product was, but we memorized all the commercials.

As soon as the television was placed on the stand, the technician went on the roof to install a big antenna. The show was on - how exciting! Gigino, Dino and I were in all our glory. As with everything else between our families, Mrs. Pelillo came in and invited my parents to see it. My mother's first words were, "Jesus, Joseph, Santa Anna and Maria, I cannot believe my eyes!"

My father inquired suspiciously, "Maria, what is it? I've never heard you so stupefied!"

My mother said, "Oh, Salvatore, too bad you can't see, but this is like being at the movies." And Don Tommasino in his mild and humble manner took my father by his arm and told him that Salvatore's family was welcome any time—"Just bring the chairs."

There was only one channel on television. A popular magazine "Sorrisi e Canzoni," regularly carried the weekly programming, so when something nice was about to be shown, Antonietta would promptly alert Mrs. Pelillo and together plan for the evening show. Most of us spectators enjoyed whatever was shown on television. Don Tommasino preferred to watch dramas though, and if something even a little bit sad came on, you would hear quiet sobs coming from him, followed by tears that came rolling down his cheeks. My father would lean toward me and ask what was happening in the show. I would struggle to hold back my laughter while giving him an explanation, until I would burst out laughing while explaining it to my father, who could not follow what was coming out of my mouth. My laughter kept me from speaking clearly, making all those present laugh very loudly with the exception of the host, who would warn everyone to keep quiet or have the television taken away. One evening, a tear-jerker was on the program, and Mrs. Pelillo told me about it and asked me to come up with something funny to play at the expense of poor Don Tommasino. I let everybody go ahead of me, once the lights were out, I snuck in hiding an empty bucket and a towel, and sat on the stool next to Don Tommasino. To be honest, I was not paying attention to the television but was waiting for the appropriate moment to strike. Poor Don Tommasino had taken his usual seat next to the bureau, resting his elbow, head in hand. When the tragic moment came, we could hear his sobs, and as he reached for his handkerchief to wipe his tears I jumped up and handed him the towel and the empty bucket. The laughter was so intense that even Don Tommasino started to laugh, and my father, with a smile on his face, kept on asking what was going on and for somebody to fill him in.

Bonding

Before I started to attend school, in the morning when I got up, I would go in the kitchen to eat my soup made of hot milk, orzo (postum) and stale bread. Wash my face, wear my usual shorts and T shirt so I could tackle my favorite activity: to take my father for a walk, along with a bit of grocery shopping thrown in. We'd stop at Don Mariano's salumeria and get bread, pasta and groceries for whatever meal we had to prepare that night. Don Mariano would keep track of what we owed. When we left Don Mariano's shop, the next stop was for fruits and vegetables. There was always an abundance of seasonal produce, and I had developed a knack for picking the freshest and the best. Many times Don Alfonso would reprimand me for touching the produce, but my father would interject and tell him, "Don Alfonso, I beg of you. I try to teach him to pick the best so that when my wife gets home from work, she will be happy with our food shopping and won't yell at us. You know how picky my wife can be." On Saturdays, when my mother got paid, Don Mariano's was the first stop she made once she got off the trolley. She would pay him for the weeks' worth of shopping and then come home.

Papá had always been involved with food because of his own mother's business. My paternal grandmother was a woman ahead of her time. Maria Sofia Vollaro might have been the name on her birth certificate, but everyone in her neighborhood knew her as *Sofia la Sensale*, or Sofia the Broker. She became a true entrepreneur after the sudden death of her husband, Mariano. He died of a heart attack on Christmas Eve day in 1903 while working at his job installing railroad tracks. My grandmother was pregnant and my father, her youngest son, was just three years old. She was a strong and driven woman, and constitutionally incapable of giving in. This served her well in her first career as a real estate agent, but her true passion was food. She owned a small building on via Giacomo Savarese (family relation? Maybe hundreds of years earlier…), so when her street-level tenants moved out, she converted their *basso* into a beautiful bakery, which became my father's playground, an extension of the home environment in which he was raised.

Once, when my father was in his early twenties, his mother fell ill and he had to step in and run the store. This knowledge of and familiarity with food carried on to my own childhood, where it took on a new meaning after his blindness. The both of us were stuck at home most days—him because of his blindness and me because of my age (I was not even six years old at this time). To fill the hours, he began to teach me how to prepare the family meals: How to chop celery, how to slice onions, how to peel garlic cloves, and most fun of all, how to beat a piece of lard with a dull knife while mashing garlic and parsley into it.

I felt like a musician following an opera conductor. Under his direction, I would place the pot over the stove, turn on the gas, and add the olive oil, all while balancing on my wooden stool. I was always ready for the next instruction: "Make sure you place the lard on the fatty side and not on the skin side." "Chop that parsley very finely!" "Make sure the flame is nice and low." Once our concoction was simmering, and the aroma filling the kitchen, my father would get a little taste to check for flavor. If he was satisfied, I would turn off the heat and cover the pot.

No matter what we cooked, our neighbors always had praises for us, as our door and windows were usually open. Whenever Mrs. Ciano happened to pass by our door, she would praise the cook, saying loudly, "What a delicious smell! Don Salvatore must be cooking today."

When my mother got home from work, we would sit at the table at our usual seats. (Mine was next to my father, facing the window.) To my left sat baby Sofia, who already at three years of age would drain her tiny glass of wine and then reach for the one in front of me.

Wine was never my favorite beverage, so I didn't mind it too much.

I would trade her for most of her food, especially when dinner was *Fagioli e Scarola* and *Zuppa Di Zucchini Cacio e Uova*, which she detested. Sofia was a poor eater to begin with, which must have been the reason why she remained skinny throughout life.

Despite all our good times in the kitchen, my father still hated to be stuck inside the apartment—if it were up to him, he would have stayed out as long as possible. On many occasions, when we were done with

My father, Salvatore Savarese

the food preparation, he would ask me to take him to the army uniform factory to pick up my mother from work, so she wouldn't have to ride the crowded trolley by herself. Until the day he died, my father remained protective of her. There were times I just wanted to go out and play with my friends, but he would insist that I accompany him, and I had to obey, grumpy as I was. And yet, when I finally saw her walking out of the building in the company of other women, I always ran up to her and grabbed her hand, and we'd walk towards my father, who would be leaning against a lamp post while he waited for us. The trolley ride home was even better because I could sit in her lap and tell her about our day and the meal my father and I had prepared.

Late one afternoon, my mother arrived home from work and found my father lying on the bed, and me sitting next to him. This was very unusual for him, and she became alarmed as he looked extremely lethargic. She called Mrs. Pelillo, who rushed into the bedroom. Aghast, she put her right hand over her mouth and said to go and get a doctor. I don't know how much time passed then. All I remember is that three or four men came in and crowded around my father. One of them was Doctor Sasso. Another was the barber, who would bring these ugly-looking wormlike creatures and stick them one by one to the back of my father's ears. When he was done and wiping his hands, he said, "Okay, this should do the trick."

The doctor called my mother and Mrs. Pelillo off to the side and, looking at my mother, said, "He's had a thrombosis attack, but he should recover nicely. The leeches will suck all that bad blood from his head. When they get full, the barber will decide if he needs to repeat the application. Your husband is going to be fine."

Over the next few years, I would see that scene played over and over again.

During the 1950s, my father was constantly sick, and very often I had to accompany him to the doctor for various reasons, mainly for his thrombosis. He was prescribed a medication that required administration by syringe. Every day a handsome middle-aged woman by the name of Donna Concetta would come over to the house to give him his shot. I would watch her intently. She started by filling a small rectangular pan with tap water, then placed the syringe in it, set it over the stove, and waited until it boiled. She would then remove the pan from the stove and place it on the table, take out the syringe parts and shake the water from them. Then with a very small saw that came with vials, she would saw off the top of a vial, insert the needle into the vial, transfer the liquid into the syringe, bring it up to the light, and squirt out a few drops to remove the bubbles.

Only then would she speak: "Don Salvatore, which side you want me to stick you today?"

Without answering at first, my father would drop his pants to expose his rear and say, "Today you get to do my right side."

She would then take a bit of fluffy cotton, soak it in alcohol, rub the part that she was going to inject, and with one stroke penetrate his flesh with the needle. She would always ask, "Did you feel any pain?" and he would always respond the same, "No, Donna Concetta. You have magic hands." After washing everything up as he pulled his pants up and tightened his belt, she would leave by saying, "I'll see you tomorrow."

One day my father asked her to find a spot on his rear that was not too pierced. She bent down on her knees behind him, as was her custom, and with her index finger, felt various areas of the cheek. While holding the syringe between the middle finger and her thumb, looking for a spot, she said "Don Salvatore, your ass has more holes than a pasta strainer."

The medical saga continued: My father had a hole on the top of his right foot that required medication. This hole was about one inch in diameter and about half an inch deep. I thought it looked like the crater of Mount Vesuvius. Once a day I had to clean it, spread a bit of cream over it, cover it with gauze, then slip his sock over his foot. He told me the story of how he got that hole so many times, that I could tell *him* how it happened!

The year was 1918, and he was seventeen years old. It was World War I, and Italy was losing the war against the Austro-Hungarian Empire. General Armando Diaz, a Neapolitan, had sent for more soldiers to be inducted in the service. A new batch of young men barely seventeen years old were sent to fight in the northeastern region of Italy. The famous Piave battle was fought over the Piave and Isonzo rivers. My father and thousands of other young men his age were called to the front, with none of them having any knowledge of or preparation for it. They put uniforms on these young recruits and, with no instruction whatsoever, sent them to fight for their country.

My father knew that they had been sent there to show off Italy's army force, but against such a powerful enemy, more experienced soldiers were needed. After Papá had spent a few days on the front without shooting a single bullet, an angel in the form of an older soldier intervened. He must have been able to see that my father was the furthest thing from a natural soldier. He told him in pure Neapolitan dialect that he was going to get himself killed. He convinced my father to get an injection of sulfur in his right foot. The older soldier told him that the shot would make his foot swell up incredibly fast, preventing him from walking on it. Papá never told me how or where he got the sulfur, but in the end he agreed to do it.

The pain was excruciating. But in suffering that pain now, he avoided being sent to the front. Italy ended up winning that battle and capturing the town of Vittorio Veneto without my father. By the time his foot healed the war was over and he was sent back to Naples to serve the remainder of his years in the military, where he served in the Castel dell'Ovo, under the command of one Captain Tuccillo. The captain was a gentleman from Northern Italy who loved Neapolitan food, and so he *really* liked my father, who was that rare soldier actually stationed in his hometown. Castel dell'Ovo wasn't too far from my grandmother's bakery, which meant that Captain Tuccillo wasn't too far from authentic Neapolitan cooking, courtesy of Sofia *la Sensale*.

The Captain let Salvatore go home for dinner a few nights a week, and in exchange for such a privilege, my father would bring him dinner prepared by his mother, who was so grateful to the Captain that she went out of her way to keep him well fed. She even sent *Salsicce alla Pizzaiola*; other times she sent him *Spigola Marechiaro, Zuppa di Fagioli*, fresh eggs collected the same morning, and all the bread his heart desired.

For all my father's medical issues, I never viewed him as a sick man. Through him, I learned of the streets of old Naples: the famous buildings and churches, the best stores, the most delicious pastry shops and the tastiest pizzerias. My father had gone to the local public school up until fifth grade. When I was of school age myself, I accompanied him on more than one occasion walking along Piazza Guglielmo Pepe. Even without sight, he delighted in pointing out the building that housed his school and tell me stories about his time there. I learned about the main train station built by Benito Mussolini on Piazza Garibaldi before it was demolished and the new, more efficient (but uglier) station was built in its place. I knew about the size of Giuseppe Garibaldi's shoes, and the pen in the hand of Ruggiero Bonghi's statue across from the University of Naples. I knew the meaning of the bas relief depicting the peak of the University building: *Ad Scientiarum Haustum et Seminarium Doctrinarum* ("For the inculcation of sciences and the dissemination of knowledge"). Often I'd ask him, "Papá, how do you know that?" and his answer was always the same: "As a child, I was very curious. As an adult, I read a lot. And now that I am blind, I learn by listening to the radio."

The older I got, the more time I wanted to spend with him. We became one person with two souls, four hands, and four legs. I started to think like him. I understood him immediately every time he spoke.

I was an adult in the body of a boy, six or eight or ten years old. Many times, as the two of us sat by ourselves at the outdoor café in front of the Bar dei Fiori (a coffee bar and pastry shop in his old neighborhood), he might hear a woman go by and say to me, "As you know, I can't see with my eyes, but even though I've lost one sense, I have developed another. I say that the lady that just went by is under twenty-five years of age and is very pretty."

I would blush and tell him, "Yes, Papá, you are right, but how can you tell?"

Without giving anything away, he would just answer, "I told you, I have developed another sense."

I was a curious boy myself and I had picked up a little here and there about women and sex. Whenever I stood by my father in the company of his friends, if the conversation turned to sex, he would ask me to leave, but his friends would hold me there by force as a joke. They would squeeze a hand over my mouth to prevent me from making any sound that my father could hear, and I would be forced to hear the conversation. I put on a show to those adults and let them believe that I was not enjoying the situation, but in reality, I was very much paying attention to what everybody was saying.

My father had a good sense of humor, it was not unusual for him to make clever quips just for a laugh. He was also a teaser. One day as he was sitting at one of Bar dei Fiori's table with his friends, he sat up and asked them if I was present. They said no, and I said nothing; I was curious, what was he going to say? One of his friends was a fellow named Don Ciccillo, a man at least thirty years older than the rest of them and very skinny, without a tooth in his mouth. In fact his mouth was caved in, and when he spoke every one of his words came out with a lisp. Once my father was assured that I was not nearby, he blurted out, "Don Ciccillo, did you notice that woman who passed by a few minutes ago?"

Don Ciccillo gave a snort of laughter and answered, "Of course I did! I'm not blind like you."

My father asked him, "Tell us, what would you do to her if she'd let you?"

Don Ciccillo shot back, "You know, Salvatore, that some things still work in my body—specially my toothless mouth!"

Everyone roared with laughter but me. Even though I was already in school, I still had so much to learn, because I had no idea what Don Ciccillo was talking about.

I loved being around my Papá. Not just for the fact that he was my father, but also because he was blind, which made me love him even more. His blindness was an aspect that deepened our relationship. I truly believe that my father could never have overcome the handicap by himself; he needed and depended on me. When we went somewhere, anywhere, he would have his left hand on my right upper arm and I developed the skill of giving him the sensation that he was on his own, independent. I would touch him in different ways, like an accordion keyboard, and I rarely had to verbalize with him.

Papá would talk to me and tell me everything about his life as a little boy but also about his life as a man. He told me about his experiences and also about the tragedies. He often talked to me about of his mother, Maria Sofia Vollaro, of his sister Maria, the youngest of the siblings, who died of an obscure sickness when she was just 27 years old. He was fond of his two brothers: The older was Michele, who owned his own shoe factory and eventually emigrated to the United States with his family, while the younger was Vincenzo, a leather craftsman.

My father usually made conversation with me on our walks, but if he was deep in thought I would try to get his attention by describing where we were, what the people around us were doing, and especially if something out of the ordinary was happening, like an argument that might end up in a fight or a friend or relative coming towards us (or a pretty woman passing by). I became his eyes, and he experienced life through me.

School Experiences

Antonietta took me to school for the first day of my first-grade. My parents had opted not to send me to kindergarten, deciding that I was of better use at home helping my father with his needs. That day is very vivid in my mind. It was a long walk from our housing complex to the public school. On the way there, Antonietta was telling me all about school and how important it was. She did not want me to be like my brother Mario, who hated school and would skip all the time. Mario was very clever (or so he thought). Most mornings he would get dressed, get his school books, and leave as if he were going to school. Instead he would join a group of his friends who also liked skipping. At school closing time, he would come home, do his make-believe homework and act as if everything was normal. This led to him getting tremendous beatings from my father every time a note came home advising my parents of the problem.

For my part, I had never been away from my family before. I was scared. As we started up the stairs to the second floor, I began to cry. Patiently, Antonietta took me to my classroom and talked to my teacher, who had also been *her* first-grade teacher. I was crying and sobbing, and seeing that her good manners did not work, Antonietta pulled me to the side and sternly whispered in my ear.

"Michele, you better stop crying! Take a seat and pay attention, otherwise I'll give you such a smack that your head will spin!" Obviously that warning did it, and my tears stopped rolling down my face. She wiped my face off and left the classroom abruptly.

I turned out to be a good student. At the end of second grade I was chosen along with another boy in my class to spend two weeks at a beach camp in the town of Castellammare di Stabia. Only a handful of students were picked from each school, and my parents were very proud of me. After all, neither Mario nor Antonietta were ever awarded such a treat. In the days before my departure, my Mom washed all my underwear and pressed my shirts, shorts, and small clothes. She made me a little cloth pocket from religious scapulars that she had sewn together. It had the faces of saints on them and ribbons on each side. In that pocket she put a few coins and hung it around my neck.

It was a Thursday in July when they took me to join the group of the chosen children to embark on the 45-minute train ride to Castellammare di Stabia. The train ride was fantastic, my first-ever train ride. I loved the speed, the few stops it made along the way, and the beautiful views—Mount Vesuvius, the glittering gulf of Naples. It was only after we got off the train at Castellammare that I realized I was part of a large number of boys between the ages of seven and ten. We were escorted to a convent where we were greeted, then separated into small clusters and introduced to the nuns in charge of each group. Next we were shown to a huge room filled with bunk beds. I was assigned a top bunk.

Supper that night was served in the large dining room that had been part of a castle. What else? *Penne al Sugo Di Carne,* accompanied by *Scarola in Padella* and *Gatto' di Patate,* made with pieces of cured meats. We sat at long rectangular tables. It was noisy. At the end of the dinner, a few nuns took turns explaining to us about the two weeks we were going to have with them. Bad behavior was not accepted, and if you stepped out of line your parents were to be notified and the vacation was over for you. As soon as we finished dinner, we all went for a walk accompanied by the nuns. As we got to know one other, we realized that we all had one thing in common: our poverty. These two weeks were going to be happy weeks, filled with food and fun.

In the morning, I noticed that my pocket necklace that my mother had made me was missing. I went back to my bunk bed to check in case I had lost it in the bed. I did not find it, so I went to one of the nuns and reported it missing. The nun said she was sorry, and that rather than being lost, it had most likely been stolen from me while I was sleeping. She was probably right. Even though I was only seven, I had already seen quite a few bad things accompanying my father through the streets of Naples.

Normally I was an easy going type, and took things as they came. But after that, I didn't feel safe in that place. I couldn't relax.

That Sunday for lunch, the nuns served us *Spaghetti con salsa Marinara*, *Polpette di Manzo* and *Friarielli in Padella*. When lunch was over, they took us to the beach.

I could see that most of the children were having fun playing in and out of the water. I was not one of them. My father had a niece who lived in Castellammare, Nunziatina. She was married to Catiello whose family had been living there for generations. They had a couple of children my age, and I knew them well since Nunziatina had always been close to my father. I kept looking toward the boardwalk, hoping to see somebody that I recognized.

Suddenly, I could not believe my eyes. I started to jump as high as I could, yelling at the top of my lungs, "Papá, Papá, Papá!" Up on the boardwalk, in the distance, I had spotted my father's white Panama hat. It was my parents! I ran up to them, followed by a number of other boys. Gasping as I tried to catch my breath, I blurted out, "Papá, I want to come home with you!" Those were my first words to my parents.

The other boys, grabbing and pulling on my parents, begged them to take their addresses to notify their parents to come and get them. They did not want to be there either. One kid begged, "Mister, please, my mother does not live too far from you! I will give you her address, please go there and tell her to come and pick me up. I don't want to be here! I want to go home!" Another kid, crying hysterically, grabbed my mother's hand and yelling at the top of his lungs begged her, "Please, Signora, go to my house too and tell them it stinks here and I don't want to stay!" Knowing my father so well, I am sure that he wished that he could have taken all those crying kids back to Naples to their parents right then and there.

Hearing the commotion, few nuns ran up to my parents and, after realizing what was happening, pulled the children away—including me. Later that day, my parents met with the Mother Superior and insisted that I go back with them. They were told that this was a new charity program that city officials had started a couple of years before, but that this was the first time the nuns had ever seen children behave the way we were behaving.

After a long conversation, I was given special permission to leave. I collected my things and we were on our way back home. On the train ride back to Barra, my parents explained to me the reason they had decided to come. Apparently that afternoon, when my parents, my brother, and my sisters Antonietta and Sofia were sitting down for the Sunday dinner, they found that nobody wanted to eat. Everybody was in a bad mood, and no one was saying a word.

It was my brother Mario who finally looked up from his plate, where he had been pushing his food around and around, and said, "Is it possible that without that little piece of shit here to bother me, I've lost my appetite?"

My father said, "Mario, you are right," and, looking at my mother, said, "Maria, leave everything on the table as it is. You and I will go to Castellammare Di Stabia and bring Michele home."

When we finally arrived home, it was very late, but still in time to start dinner. That was the first time that I remember my brother hugging me. As my mother heated up the food, she kept telling me that the next day I had to accompany my Papá to the addresses given by those unhappy kids and notify their parents. Hopefully, they would all be picked up quickly!

Third grade was at a different school located at the opposite end of Barra, near the train station. This was the farthest point away from where we lived, at least a two mile walk. I had to wear a black smock with buttons in the back and a red ribbon around the collar. The color of the ribbon signified the grade. A yellow ribbon meant fourth grade and a red, white and green with horizontal lines (the colors of the Italian flag) was for the fifth grade. As a boy, I was short for my age, so I was assigned one of the front desks, while taller boys sat towards the rear. (Not just a few of them were taller because many were repeating these grades for the second or third time.)

Every morning before leaving for school, we had to make sure that we carried a pen with a good point and the inkwell to place in the appropriate hole at the top of the desk. One day our teacher gave us an assignment to do while he was out of the classroom. A kid who sat towards the rear of the room came over to my desk, took my inkwell, and went back to his seat. Without getting excited, I went to his desk and took back my inkwell. I had almost reached my own desk when another bully ran up to me and snatched the inkwell back out of my hand, spilling the ink all over the floor and on my clothes as he did that.

At that point I reached for my pen and, using it as an arrow, threw it at him, aiming at his face. I hit him right below his left eye. A fight erupted, and we were punching and slapping each other, wrestling for the ink pot. Ink was everywhere, and everybody in the class stood up yelling encouragement at one kid or the other.

When the teacher came in and saw all that mess, he called the class president to the front, and asked him what had happened. Pointing his finger at me, he said, "Professore, it was Savarese who started this."

I couldn't believe what I was hearing. Why was this kid lying? Was he friends with those bullies, or was he afraid of them? Before I could figure it out, I was called to stand in front of the teacher myself. Mr. Fornari was a tall man who put fear into us kids every time he raised his voice or singled you out, and Lord help you if he ever got out his whacking stick. He looked at me now for a long minute, then ordered me to hold up my hands. Looking straight up at him, I started to say, "Professor, can I tell you what happened, please?" I brought up my open hand and started to tell my side of the incident.

I had just started talking when he raised his stick and struck the palm of my left hand with so much force that I lost my breath and almost started to cry from the pain. He started for my right hand, but

I reached out and grabbed the stick first, pulling it from his hand. In a rage, I hit the front of his desk, denting the wood.

That was it. He grabbed me by my neck and slapped me across my face and head. The more I complained, the more he hit me, and not just with his hands but with his feet as well, kicking my back so hard that I fell down. It was only then that I began to cry, not just from the pain but from the embarrassment. The whole class was very quiet.

He dragged me to the principal's office by the collar. After listening to the teacher, the principal sent me home with a note for my parents to come up to his office the next day. Antonietta immediately read the note to my father, who told her to drop everything and go to my school to find out what had happened. In the meantime, I told my father all about the incident, without omitting anything.

My father knew me well enough to know that I was not lying, but still his reaction was even worse than my teacher's. He screamed, "What's the matter with you, Michele? Do you know that if you had thrown that pen a little higher, you could have made that kid blind? Do you want to make somebody else like me?" He pulled me towards him and gave me a beating that I still remember. It was my first and last beating I got from my father.

When my mother came home that night, I was still sobbing in my room, so she came in there and took a look at me. She noticed that I had a big bump on the back of my head and became furious. The next day, my parents took me up to school to talk to the principal about the treatment I had received. My father told him that the teacher should watch his temper and refrain from using such brute force on the students. He demanded that my suspension be removed and that the teacher himself be suspended right then and there, otherwise he was going to report him to the police.

The principal was not willing to make a decision until he knew all the facts. He wanted to talk with my teacher, so he called him in. When Mr. Fornari came in, the principal pulled him to the side, and they spoke in low voices for several minutes. They turned back towards us, and Mr. Fornari started to explain what had happened, and why he thought that I had deserved my punishment.

My father interrupted him and said, "My son has been punished enough." He told them about the even worse beating I had gotten from him for throwing the pen. But he also added that my teacher had been totally out of line to have used that much brute force on a child. My mother was ready to hit the teacher, but instead she bent my head down and moved my hair out of the way to expose the bump on my head and asked him, "So, is this the way you teach a child? What is wrong with you." With each word, her voice rose higher and higher.

The teacher who had been standing in front of her started to back away and slowly walked behind the principal's desk. My suspension was removed, but I stayed home a few days so that my bruises and scratches could heal.

Every evening for the next few weeks I would sit at the table at home and complain of headaches. As a matter of fact, my head hurt so bad that I would eat with my head resting on my left hand. A lot of times I would fall asleep at the table with my head resting on my crossed arms. Eventually I was back to normal, but it did take a while.

As I got older, my father allowed me more time to spend with the kids in Barra, especially in the summer. I would get to go to the beach with a number of kids. The evening before, I had to prepare my own sandwiches, which were very simple—just whole wheat bread, a few drops of olive oil and Gaeta olives. No cheese, no cold cuts; they had to be able to last the day without spoiling. I would pit the olives myself in order to extract all the juice, and smear the olives on the bread. (Another treat was the *Frittata di Spaghetti*, a satisfying concoction made of cooked spaghetti, eggs and cheese.)

There was no public transportation to the beach, so at around 11 the next morning we would head out on foot, walking through a few neighboring farms and fields, waving at the farm hands with our beach umbrellas bouncing on our shoulders. At one point, just before the beach, we had to duck under a rail overpass, where trains traveled south to Calabria and Sicily, or north to Naples and beyond.

Once settled at the beach, all the kids would dive into the water to play and cool off. But whenever a freight train would rumble by on the overpass bordering the shore, we would pop up out of the water and stare at it, amazed by its length. We made a game of guessing the number of freight cars, which often reached one hundred or more. But it was the passenger trains that made me stop and stare. I would imagine riding in one, traveling to so many places, dreaming of exploring life outside of my small world.

From sixth grade on, every school I attended was in the historic district. Old Naples offered all kinds of experiences, while Barra was just a cheap, run down extension of it. I was familiar with the streets of Naples, as I had walked many of them while accompanying my father.

This knowledge became my first roadmap to love. On the bus from Barra to school in the mornings, I had figured out that I could hop off many stops before reaching the school in historical Naples, which allowed me to take a detour and pass by Lucia's house.

Lucia Esposito was a girl I had met when we were fourteen, she was working at Scaturchio pastry shop near Bar dei Fiori, not far from my usual trolley stop. She was a pretty, round faced brunette from the center of town, but what really separated her from all the other girls was the beauty mark that sat on her left cheek. I was struck by her beauty. I memorized her work schedule and would visit the shop with the excuse to buy me a pastry—so I could look at her. However I didn't have the guts to ask her out on a date. The reason was my shorts.

According to my mother, I was not old enough to wear long pants yet. In her mind, pants were reserved for truly mature individuals, men and older boys on the cusp of manhood. *Not* fourteen year old boys like me. Until I met Lucia, the problem of the length of my pants had never once crossed my mind. But suddenly, I became obsessed with proving that I was a man—a man worthy of asking a beautiful girl out on a date.

A few days after first laying eyes on her, I realized I had to do something. I approached my sister Antonietta and asked *her* to convince our mother to let me wear long pants. I knew she would listen to me, and I knew our mother would listen to *her*. Antonietta got a kick out of that, and after working her secret magic, convinced our mother to buy me some long pants.

The following week, dressed in my new pants, gleaming shoes, and with my black hair greased back, I walked into Scaturchio's shop and fixed Lucia with an intense stare.

She noticed me. "What would you like today?"

"To go out with you."

She blushed, and smirked. "Can I think about it?"

"It's okay, I'll wait for you outside until you finish work."

Shyly, she answered yes.

Three long hours later, she came right up to me outside the store, smiled, and simply asked, "What is your name?"

Together we walked to Piazza Garibaldi side by side in silence, until we parted ways.

I couldn't wait to go to school the next morning, and every morning after that. I began to take the bus instead of the trolley. It had a stop not far from where Lucia lived so I could walk past her apartment building to get a glimpse of her standing on her balcony waiting for me. I always carried a few small pebbles in my pocket just in case she wasn't out there. I would throw the pebbles at her window, and if I was lucky the window would open and she would lean out and exchange a few words. Every glimpse I got of her was stolen time, since I had been warned by her father and her older brother to stay away from her. But I had to take my chances.

Riding The Trolley

I made that anxious trolley trip to Scaturchio's as many times as possible, hoping to catch a glance of Lucia, because that was really about all I could get out of that relationship for the time being, given our young age. Riding the trolley taught me more about people and their behavior than nearly any other experience of my life. From the age of five on, I had accompanied my father every time he left the house. In my early school years, I was lucky enough to attend only the morning sessions of class, in order to make room for the separate afternoon group of students who couldn't all fit into the building at once. (Naples was and still is one of the densest metro areas in the world.) This had the happy side effect of letting me out early enough to spend the afternoon with my father. Throughout my youth, we frequently made the ten minute walk to the Municipal Square in Barra, his hand on my sleeve or shoulder for reassurance, so we could catch the trolley to Porta Nolana in downtown Naples. Even as a teenager, I had no problem showing my closeness to my father, being his guide and protector throughout the city.

Because of his blindness, my father did not have to pay for the trolley, and he was legally guaranteed one of the two front seats. However, my father never took advantage of that rule; as a matter of fact, if I murmured to him that there was an older or pregnant woman standing on the trolley, he never failed to offer his seat no matter where he happened to be sitting.

During rush hour the trolley was always full. You were lucky if you could find a spot on the steps while hanging onto another passenger, who might only be halfway in holding onto a pole or the open door. Eventually you'd find your way in. For the morning rush, the rear doors of the trolley were rarely closed as it moved from stop to stop. When the trolley was overcrowded, the conductor would yell out, "Is anyone getting off at the next stop?" and if no one answered he would blow right past the stop. If anyone happened not to be paying attention or was unable to hear the conductor, you could be sure to hear a panicked shout from somewhere in the crush for the trolley to stop. The rest of us riders, would have to wait impatiently for the offending passenger to make their way off.

A crowded trolley was heaven for pickpockets. Wallets, handbags, bracelets, even *socks* were all up for grabs. (There was a local saying that the thieves of Naples were so clever they could rob your socks without removing your shoes.) After riding for a while, I learned to recognize when a pickpocket was in our midst. If I was with my father, I would tug at his sleeve as a signal, and he would say out loud with his deep voice: "Pickpockets onboard, everybody. Be on guard!" These were usually boys a bit older than me (ten, twelve years old) who would not even flinch! They would keep a blank look on their faces as if it was not them that Papá was warning against. After a couple of stops, they would get off, probably going to look for other prey; like most of us, they had to bring home the bacon somehow.

I remember one particular afternoon, we were on our way home from the pawn shop. In the years after the war, pawn shops were quite popular, especially for things like jewelry, which we had pawned off that day. We were both standing, and while holding on to a seat grip my father kicked my shoe and motioned with his head to look behind him. I did, and saw a boy with his fingers in Papá's pocket. I tapped my father's foot; he got my message and immediately grabbed the boy's arm and twisted it.

"Conductor, don't open the doors. We have a thief on board!"

Looking at the pickpocket, my father said, "You little punk, what were you trying to steal from my pocket, the receipt I got from the pawn shop? A piece of paper?"

At that, from his back pocket where the thief had been fidgeting, my father pulled out the receipt and stuck it under the boy's nose. Some of the passengers began to grab at the thief to give him a beating, but my father took pity on him.

"Let him go. Good for me he has no experience, if he can't tell the difference between money and a piece of paper!" The conductor opened the door, and a lady gave him a kick in the butt as a couple of passengers pushed him off.

Besides that, the only regular excitement came from the occasional dirty old man inching himself up next to a woman on a crowded car. Soon after you were sure to hear a brave, usually older, woman call out, "Hey, mister! I hope you're having fun, you dirty bastard! Why don't you go home and bother your sister!"

Whenever I had the opportunity to, especially while younger, I would go all the way to the front of the car to stand next to the conductor. I knew every corner of that trolley route, and I loved to see the conductor operating his Westinghouse brake and accelerator to keep the trolley running smoothly down its tracks. Once in a while, I would hear him complain under his mustache about the traffic, usually horse-drawn carts whose wheels would slip into the rail grooves and get stuck. More often than not, the conductor and even some passengers would have to get down off the trolley and help the horse-cart owner dislodge his wheels and get out of the way. *Sometimes* the horse itself would slip on the shiny tracks, its front legs buckling under its weight. It was a struggle for everyone—especially for the horse—to get the poor creature back on its feet The owner would curse the animal while all the rest of us screamed at *him* to stop.

The other major hazard: motorists. They tended to leave their cars "temporarily" parked on the tracks while they made quick drop-offs or pick-ups from the shops. Then you heard the trolley conductor banging his foot on the floor bell—*ding! ding! ding!* The motorist would come running, gesturing in apology, while the conductor mumbled under his breath, "Yeah, yeah, you son of a.....what do I care? I'm getting paid either way. Heh. *I'm* not the one in a hurry. It's everyone else!"

* * *

I enjoyed riding the trolley, even though most riders were disgruntled about the service; something was always wrong—a malfunction, an electrical system failure, delays due to horrendous traffic conditions, or even an unexpected strike. But I didn't care. For me, the trolley was just one place for me to learn about life.

The ride home on Saturdays was always especially nice. Saturday was when everyone got paid. It was a treat watching all those people carrying their bags of food home at the end of the long week. You could see the satisfaction on their faces. It was never easy making an honest living in that city, but now at least they had money in their pocket to take care of (some of) life's demands.

From time to time, the electricity would go out for a whole swath of neighborhoods and everything ground to a halt—including the trolley. Horns blared, cart drivers yelled, and people would have to push the trolley from behind to move it out of the intersection. Other times, the transit system would go on strike. Strikes that were unannounced came to be known as "hiccup strikes," affecting regular buses, electric buses, trolleys, and trains. These strikes usually only lasted about four or five hours, but because they came out of nowhere, they created chaos for everybody on the road. The notorious heavy traffic turned into a frantic nightmare with angry horns blaring from every direction. If the strike went into effect in the late afternoon, my father and I would have to walk the seven mile stretch back home from Bar dei Fiori. With my father in tow, leaning on my right arm, we would head home along with some of the other stranded riders, complaining and cursing the whole way.

As darkness fell and the shadows stretched long, my father would start telling stories to reassure me—stories about anything, about family, history, or just the things that had happened on that day. At one point in the seven miles we had to walk through a bad neighborhood, and Papá's talk got louder. At the same time, he would prick up his ears in order to listen for any danger. It must have been his sixth sense;

somehow he made me feel safe and relaxed.

Once we reached San Giovanni a Teduccio, instead of following the trolley tracks we would take a shortcut through the cemetery. The first time we took that route, Papá could hear fear in my voice. Stopping for a minute, he took my shoulder and faced me to him.

"Tell me, my boy, why are you trembling? Are you cold?"

"No, Papá, I am not cold. I am afraid!"

He shot back, "Afraid of what?"

"You know, Papá. All these *dead* people."

Bending his head down to me he said, "Remember this, Michele: You must never be afraid of dead people because they can do no harm to you. It is the live people—they are the ones that can hurt you!"

Still, it took a while before I completely lost my fear of walking through the cemetery.

When I got out of school early and took Papá to Bar dei Fiori, the trolley was always empty. We could sit anywhere, but I still chose the spot by the window next to the conductor, so I could watch him operate.

Occasionally he and I would chat, despite the sign over his head reminding riders, for safety, not to talk to the conductor while the vehicle was in motion. One particularly lazy afternoon, the conductor was in no particular hurry to go anywhere. At one point, he stopped to pick up a bag from a woman—his wife?—at the side of the road, then sat back in the driver's seat with the bag in his lap and took out a sandwich. The trolley resumed its course, the conductor driving with one hand while holding his sandwich with the other. A few stops later, when we came to a public drinking fountain, he got off and took a nice long swig from the spigot. On his way back into the trolley, I could hear the dry sound of his hand absently rubbing his unshaven face.

An older gentleman had been sitting by the front door, watching the conductor's every move. At our next stop, the conductor paused to exchange a few words with a pedestrian he knew, then closed the door and picked up speed. The older gentleman rose and stepped over to the conductor and, holding on precariously to the overhead strap, jokingly said, "Young man, at the next stop there is a barber shop. Why don't you go in for a shave while you're at it?"

With time, many trolley riders came to recognize my father, since he was always cordial and well dressed. For him, a tie and jacket were imperative in public. He would say, "A well-dressed person behaves well. It does not matter if you have stitches in the clothes as long as they are neat and pressed." Whenever he went anywhere, even if it was just going for a walk (something that he loved to do), he never failed to ask if his shirt was clean and if the tie matched the jacket he was wearing. Another thing he drilled into me and Mario was, "Shoes are the reflection of your soul. They must always be shiny." Many Sundays, Mario would come home from work and hand me his shoes to shine. When I handed them back with a shine like glass, he would tip me ten *lira* from the pay he had just brought home. Enough to buy a candy.

The trolley ride I enjoyed most was the water trolley. This was a cleaning car equipped with huge tanks used to wash the streets. The filling station where these tanks filled up was right by Piazza Nolana, between the rear door of the Bar dei Fiori and the barber shop where I got my first crew-cut at age seven. I loved watching the refilling operation, the hiss and rush of water running through hoses from the fire hydrants into the big tanks. Once in a while, when the conductor was in a good mood, he would take me along for the ride. Many times he would even let me operate the water-release lever that sent gallons and gallons streaming to the curb. Once I over-pushed the lever and squirted water all the way up to the building line, soaking all the street vendors and their merchandise completely. I had so much fun watching those people running after the trolley, waving their fists in the air and cursing all of us on board.

That was the Naples of my youth; poor but entertaining, always mysterious and never boring.

Getting By

One of the ways I learned was listening to my father talk. He told especially vivid stories about the war. Often, I would come to him with bits and scraps of history from my school books, wondering whether it could all be true. Indeed, he told me that during World War II, Naples suffered heavy aerial bombings by the Allied Forces against German troops, who took to hiding in various landmarks around the city in the hopes that those landmarks were too valuable to destroy. They were wrong. The result was entire neighborhoods turned to battlefields. Meanwhile, the city's residents had to run and hide in order to avoid the bullets and bombs that nevertheless killed thousands of them during those horrific days.

Eventually, the people had enough. One day in late September 1943, thousands of armed Neapolitan civilians rose up and started fighting back. For four days, they chased the Nazis out of their city, root and stem. In so doing, hundreds more Neapolitans lost their lives, but their determination helped defeat the Germans and paved the way for the American army and other Allied forces to enter the ravaged city. Just like the Masaniello Revolt of 1647 when Tommaso Aniello, a twenty seven year old fisherman led the revolt against the Habsburg of Spain for overtaxing the population, these Four Days of Naples became part of the city's identity forever.

After the war, the people had to deal with an economy in shambles. Food was in short supply and unemployment was high. The streets of Naples, which had so recently seen such heroic acts, soon were taken over by organized crime cells and petty thieves. "Getting by" became the new way of life for law-abiding Neapolitans, while loosely organized groups of criminals put pressure on every honest businessman to pay protection money or suffer unsavory consequences.

People did all kind of jobs in order to put food on the table during these hard times. Occasionally, before he lost his sight completely, my father could still get some work doing minor electrical repairs, especially for jobs he had worked on years before. At first, Mario would escort him to the site, and then it became my job to take him. My father impressed me with the use of his hands, and he worked swiftly. Sometimes I had to point out the different colors of the wires he had to reconnect, but he always got the job done. Eventually, though, it became too dangerous for him to work directly with electricity, so he had to stop.

Around this same time, in the early '50s, my mother (or 'Mammina' as we kids called her) fell at work and seriously hurt her back. This took her out of work for months. The factory where she worked was not unionized, so the policy was: "If you work, you get paid. If not, you best think about getting better." Our precarious situation became even worse. She continued doing the occasional minor sewing job, but it wasn't nearly enough to keep us going. The good thing is that we didn't pay rent, but we needed money to buy food and other necessities. The little bit of pasta and flour that Don Tommasino occasionally gave us was hardly enough to feed the family. The tip money my brother and I earned from delivering coffees or doing neighborhood errands was just a drop in the bucket. What were we to do?

Mammina started selling loaves of bread and loose candy from our apartment. This was something she already had experience doing during the years our family were refugees in the town of Sarno. At that time, before I was born, my father would take train trips into Naples to sell bread and coffee, foodstuffs that were in high demand because of the war. Back then it was a decent business; but now in Barra, peacetime conditions made it easy for anyone to buy bread anywhere, so our business didn't do so well. After a while, my mother gave up. A lot of hauling bread to the house and waiting around for nothing. Oh my, did we eat a lot of bread then.

Papá had applied for disability, but before it was approved he had to take several trips to doctors and the blind people's association, on Via Costantinopoli. Since I was in school in the mornings, my mother would accompany him to his morning appointments, which she was available to do because *she* was home with her back injury. Later on, my father would sarcastically say, "What a pair we were: The blind man and his crippled wife. No wonder they approved my disability pension", (He briefly considered getting a seeing-eye dog, but I guess he was happy with his seeing-eye son).

In Naples, everyone could find *some* way to earn money honestly, but there were always those who would rather take shortcuts and do things illegally. On the black market, American goods dominated: whiskey, candy, food, cigarettes. Thieves and pickpockets were a constant threat. You had to be on your toes at all times on those streets. You couldn't trust anyone; scam artists were everywhere.

The Black Hand—or Camorra—was as powerful and ruthless then as it is now. The moment a business or a peddler did well, someone would show up and demand a *pizzo*, or protection money, fees that were in most cases small and based on the size of the business. Because it was such a small amount, most shopkeepers quietly paid it. Paying the *pizzo* helped to prevent local criminal organizations from setting fire to businesses or sending groups of thugs to scare away potential customers. In some extreme cases, if a businessman kept refusing to pay, he might get a major beating or—for the real complainers among them—shot. (Even so, it was usually just a shot in the leg, to make an example. After all, dead men don't pay *pizzo*.) It was easier just to pay up.

So many times I say to myself, "Where are all the heroes who aren't afraid to stand up and fight? Where are the Masaniellos, the next Four Days of Naples, to clean up the scourge that is ruining this city?"

My father's old neighborhood was no different. Corso Garibaldi—the very same street where he had suffered his accident, years before—was lined on both sides with merchants' stands and peddlers' kiosks. According to Papá, money earned the right way went far and let you sleep at night. With his expertise and my labor, we succeeded in setting up shop on the sidewalk between Bar dei Fiori and the lotto store. Though business was less than brisk at first, it did improve over time. We repaired flashlights—very hot items since electric blackouts were so common—and cigarette lighters. The operation was simple: All you needed were a few tools and supplies, some pliers, a screwdriver or two, light bulbs, batteries, flints, cotton balls, lighter fluid. My father kept a nine-inch metal file in his back pocket in case I needed it for more complicated repairs. Occasionally, I would play the young d'Artagnan, and the file became my rapier, poking and slashing in the air at imaginary foes. We kept everything in a small wooden case with a hinged top, a former gift package originally containing six bottles of Italian sparkling wine, now balanced on a stool.

Eight year old businessman that I was, I built my own clientele. Smoking cigarettes was very popular, especially among men—but unlike in America, matches didn't come free. That's why most smokers carried lighters. They would come up to me and say, "Little boy, I need to replace the flint." Someone else might come for a charge of benzene, easy enough. Others might need me to do a full clean of the lighter's chamber, which entailed replacing its cotton and filling it back up again with benzene. Many times I had to replace the strike wheel that caused the spark, test the lighter, wipe it clean, and hand it over to the customer. When asked, "How much is that?" my answer was always the same with every customer:

"Whatever you want to give me."

Neapolitan people have always been known for their generosity. No one ever disappointed me.

One day, a thug came by and asked my father to pay protection money. In a humble way my father told him that our operation was not a money maker, and that we were barely making a living as it was. The lowlife looked down at our set-up, turned to my father, and said, "In that case, move your little stand somewhere else far from here, because we need to collect for this spot," and with that, he took the stick he was carrying and tapped my wobbly stand, knocking everything to the ground.

Right away my father changed his attitude. In his deepest voice, he said, "Look mister, I don't know who you are or who sent you here, but I don't care one way or another. I am in this spot, and no one will make me move."

"Yeah, well we'll see about that." The thug turned and as he walked away, he yelled back over his shoulder, "This is our neighborhood. We are in control here. Next time I come by, if you're still here, I'm kicking you *and* your son to the curb."

A few days later, we learned that the thug had come at the request of another peddler whom we had known for years, a man by the name of Don Vittorio. He operated a much larger stand than ours, but he offered the same services, and apparently he didn't appreciate the competition. He'd sent his thug to scare us.

When my father heard that, he went ballistic. He ordered me to bring him directly to that peddler, a block or two down Corso Garibaldi, so he could give him a piece of his mind. As we walked, he told me not to be afraid, because he was in control. He needed to set the facts straight.

"Just make sure Don Vittorio is facing me when we get there, okay Miché?"

I assured him that I would. We reached the end of the block and crossed the street.

Don Vittorio's stand was much bigger than ours; as a matter of fact he operated out of a booth with a table loaded up with various repair tools, as well as cigarette lighters of all types that he sold new and used. He was sitting behind his table when we arrived. I brought my father directly around the table so that he could confront him face to face. Surprised, Don Vittorio stood up. My father was already berating him at the top of his voice.

"What's the matter with you? Don't you have enough business already? Do you need mine too, you greedy bastard?"

Don Vittorio, taken by surprise, stumbled over his response. Whatever he managed to mumble was irrelevant; as soon as my father heard the sound come out of his mouth, he calculated the distance that separated them. He moved one step closer to him and grabbed Don Vittorio's neck with his left hand, and with the other he brought out the nine-inch metal file and stuck it against Don Vittorio's belly.

"I have been in that spot for a long time. I don't intend to move *anywhere*. Let me tell you something: I don't have much to lose. So the next time you try to pull some shit like this, my hand is not going to stop until this sticks out your back."

When the other peddlers on the street realized a fight was breaking out in Don Vittorio's booth, several jumped in between the two men to separate them.

Abruptly, my father pulled me by my arm out of there. We walked back toward our own spot. As we walked, leaving several shouting voices behind, my father said to me, Miché, let this be a lesson to you. *Always* protect your rights. Don't be afraid of bullies. Otherwise, imbeciles like that will take advantage of you, and you'll never get rid of them. If you show weakness, you're finished."

Across from my stand on the same sidewalk was Vincenzo, the shoe shine man. Vincenzo was a short goofy little guy who was quite fond of my father. He shined and repaired shoes. One day he became famous because he was taken to be the shoe shiner on a movie set. His business doubled overnight; many people came to Vincenzo for their shoe-related needs. Several times while waiting for my own business, I would sit on Vincenzo's shoe shine high chair, and my father would stand next to me holding on the chair as we talked to the cobbler.

In my down time, I loved to watch Vincenzo make good use of his skills, repairing shoes with his crafty hands. He only used a few tools—a very sharp curved knife, a hammer, two needles, and a metal shoe anvil. Something I'll never forget is how he would throw small nails in his mouth the same way I threw bread crumbs in mine, the reason was that his mouth helped him handle the nails faster. One afternoon, as I was sitting on the shoe shine chair watching him work, we heard a loud *pop*. Immediately my father threw himself onto me. There was a rush of people scrambling in every direction. We all made a living in the streets, and we all looked out for one another, but any loud noise would bring back bad memories in anyone older than me. Everybody would immediately run for shelter. It turned out that this particular noise—which had resembled a gunshot—was nothing more than a truck backfiring. After a sigh of relief, we all went back to whatever we were doing.

Papá and I went to Naples whenever possible for a number of reasons. He hadn't made many friends in Barra, and the ones he *had* were too busy earning a living to socialize with an unemployed electrician. Because of his condition, he felt more comfortable in his old neighborhood, too. In Barra, people referred to him as *the blind man*, and I was *the blind man's son*. In Naples, he was Don Salvatore, and everybody there knew and admired him.

Barra was the farthest district to the southeast of Naples. Once you left Barra, you were in the province. The place was mostly farms, so if you had any important shopping to do—clothes, furniture, a good pair of shoes—or if you needed government paperwork for a school transfer or marriage license, for example, you would have to go to Naples.

Another reason people commuted from Barra to Naples was to learn a trade beyond what their parents could teach them. Generally speaking, children followed in their parents' footsteps, so that the son of a carpenter became a carpenter, the daughter of a seamstress became a seamstress and so on, but if a young person wanted to learn a different trade, Naples was the place for that. *My* parents, however, wanted me to continue with school and graduate with a degree that would make me a better living than my father's electrician skills ever could. They must have seen some potential in me that they didn't want to waste on a menial career. For my part, I wanted to follow in my dad's footsteps, but go *further* and become an electrical engineer. While most other boys my age were itching to dump school and start earning money by learning trades, I was happy to stay in school because I had something more I wanted to achieve.

During the summer when I was *off* from school, however, my father and I stumbled on a way to turn our down time into money. Illiteracy was prominent in Barra at that time, especially in the older population, and a lot of folks had difficulty filling out and submitting the many government forms that were required in every aspect of life. In particular, the people in our housing complex often needed birth certificates, certificates of residency, family status certificates, and so on. They also knew that my father and I went to Naples on regular basis. One evening, our neighbor Don Giovanni came in and asked my Papá if we could do him the favor of applying for his birth certificate at the Bureau of Births, located in the historical part of the city. I took all his information down and promised to keep it confidential. The next day, my father and I took the trolley and the bus to the appropriate office.

Upon arrival, I saw that the lines were *extremely* long, and realized that we probably needed half a day to get that piece of paper for our neighbor. If you didn't know about my father's disability, you would never guess that he was blind, particularly when he was with me. In order to try to get a little advantage and maybe get to the front quicker, my father stopped, put on his dark sunglasses, and then took out his certificate of blindness. "Miché!" he said to me, in his most business-like voice. "Take me to the front of the line!"

A little embarrassed, I whispered, "But Papá, there's going to be a revolution in here if we do that. There must be a thousand people waiting here!"

He answered, "Listen, Miché—Keep your mouth shut and do what I tell you."

We were out of there in *no* time. After a follow-up visit three days later, we presented the certificate to our neighbor. And he paid us for a job well done.

In the projects news spread fast that we could assist people with acquiring certain documents. This included filling out forms for them and standing in line at the administrative offices so they wouldn't lose a full day's pay. Business was so successful that we even expanded our services to pawning people's precious belongings at the Bank of Naples, which by then was running a cash-for-goods program to help the poor. Jewelry, blankets, crystal vases—all these things we carried on the trolley, in one direction or the other. The formula worked over and over, and we finally made a little money at a time when we needed it the most.

During my early teens, I continued to be my father's eyes, bringing him to Bar dei Fiori and running errands there to earn tip money and—more often than not—passing by Scaturchio's to catch a glance at Lucia through the glass showcases.

Every Saturday, my father would try his luck with the lotto. Back then, lotto was a serious business, almost a science: You picked up to five numbers out of a total of ninety, and five were drawn across ten different Italian cities, from the north all the way to Sicily. Most players picked two or three numbers, max. If you played five numbers, and they all came out, you wouldn't have to work for the rest of your life. Guaranteed!

One Saturday morning, as I went into Papá's bedroom to bring him his espresso, I noticed that the crucifix on the wall above the bed had broken in two pieces, split right at the waist, so that Jesus' legs dangled free and upside down.

In a voice full of disappointment, I said, "Papá, the crucifix broke!" He asked me, "How is it broken?"

Thinking he might suspect me of having fooled around with it, I said, "I don't know, but it was not me who broke it."

"It's OK, Miché, just describe to me how it is broken—in the legs, in the arms, where?"

Nervously, and keeping far from his reach lest he think to punish me for the suffering of our Lord, I said, "It's broken in two pieces at the waist and now from the belly down, Jesus is hanging upside down."

"Son!" he said. "Do you realize what this means? We are going to win today! I have saved five hundred lira, and I am going to play it all on 2 and 33 on the Naples draw." (In Italy, you not only have to match the numbers but also correctly pick which of the ten participating cities those numbers will be drawn in.) Five hundred lira, about ten U.S. dollars today, may not have been much money for most people, but for us, it meant food for our family for a day. Yet if those numbers came out, my father would win a sum that would feed us for three months or more. No longer afraid, I went closer to him and asked how he had come up with those numbers.

Smiling down at me, he explained: "It is very simple. Christ died at 33, and the crucifix broke in how many pieces?"

"Two" I said.

"Well," he said, matter-of-factly, "Do I have to say any more?"

Five o'clock came, and the family crowded around the radio, like we did every Saturday waiting for the winning numbers to be called out in the flat, deep monotone of the radio announcer's voice. Mammina was in the kitchen cooking but still listening close. The rest of us were on pins and needles. The winning numbers were called out in order of their anchor city alphabetically—Bari was first, then Bologna, and finally Naples. I could hardly breathe, but my father seemed relaxed, as if he was already ready to rip the tickets up and move on, as he'd had to do so often before. But the fever was in me. Antonietta, too, sat hunched in front of the radio, head in her hands, eyes wide open.

The first number for Naples was called out: "Thirty-three."

Everybody jumped.

I looked at my father; but he was cool as a cucumber, too busy lighting a cigarette butt to care, it seemed. But I was quivering with the electricity of the moment. Please, Jesus, come through!

Four more numbers remained. All we needed was one of them to match. There was a pause, then the announcer's voice read the second number: "Seventeen." I felt my shoulders drop. Three left. My father took another puff, looking off in a random direction. The announcer's voice came on again. The third number was called. "Eighty-four." I felt my spirits crushing.

C'mon, Jesus, I thought. *How about a miracle now?*

The announcer's voice came on the fourth time. I was ready to give up right then. Dinner was around the corner, at least that would make me feel better. But then I heard the voice say: "Two."

Everybody screamed. Mammina came running from the stove with a spoon in either hand, waving them around in the air. And nobody yelled louder than Papá: "Miché! Take the ticket from my coat pocket! Read it back to me!"

I took the piece of paper, unfolded it, and read the numbers out loud: "Two, and thirty-three."

"Thank you Jesus!" he cried, and picked me up in a hug. I'll never forget it.

We still had to wait until Monday to collect, but we were in no hurry, because it was money in the bank, guaranteed! The next day was Sunday, and we celebrated with *Sfogliatelle* and *Baba au Rhum* from Bar dei Fiori Pasticceria e Caffetteria. Even though there were pastry shops in Barra, if we wanted a piece of cake to celebrate a special occasion there was nothing for it but to take the thirty minute trolley ride to Bar dei Fiori. Of course, we invited Don Tommasino and his family to join us. What a feeling that was. The good luck was wonderful, but even better was the ability to sit at a table enjoying a good meal with Don Tommasino, with *our* family treating *his* for once.

Bar dei Fiori

I took that trolley ride more times than I could count. I can still envision every corner of every block from our house all the way to Bar dei Fiori, or as we simply called it, the Café. Once the trolley made the stop at Spigolo al Muro, the tracks would separate from the main road and run on their own gravel ground. Then the trolley enjoyed a long run without any stops, running over Ponte della Maddalena and Ponte dei Granili, picking up speed until it reached my mother's work stop, in the neighborhood of Gianturco. I loved the wind hitting my face through the open windows. I'd go over to my father and narrate for him where we were, as if he didn't already know.

The Café was his favorite pastry shop and coffee bar in his old neighborhood of Porta Nolana. I looked forward to every visit to the Café. I felt connected to the world there. There was always something interesting going on, whether amongst the staff, the patrons, or just the neighborhood in general. Much of who I am took its first shape on that corner of Piazza Nolana, between the trolley tracks and the towers of the ancient door.

The owner of the Café, Don Gaetano Esposito (yet another one), was a childhood friend of my father. When he built the place in 1932, he gave my father the electrical contract, and my father paid him back by doing an exceptional job, working day and night with his three man crew to make sure that every wire and socket was installed according to the latest standards. This job ended up propelling my father's reputation as an electrician to new heights.

Over the years Bar dei Fiori became a popular pastry shop and coffee bar known throughout Naples. Its large sidewalk fit twelve comfortable tables of four, and they were full more often than not.

My father wasn't the only one to receive a career boost there. While he spent his leisure time at the outdoor tables with friends, I would gravitate into the kitchen area in the back, where the bakers were happy to see me and to teach me their skills. I spent much quality time there, observing all ten kitchen workers creating beautiful cakes, tasty pastries, and cookies that crumbled in your mouth. Other times I helped the manager and showcase decorator, a man named Don Salvatore Gargiulo, to clean and prepare the Café's attractive displays. These glass cases could include everything from intricately frosted cakes to stacks of cookies of every flavor and shape. Outside we would arrange bags of candies, bottles of Italian liquor, and crates of sparkling wine with their lids up and the bottles within angled handsomely to catch the eyes of passersby.

However, my favorite pastimes would have to be when the teenaged girls who worked there would bring me behind the counter, so I could keep them company. At the same time, they would teach me, among other things, the proper way to address the customers, how to wrap packages with fresh pastries and cakes, and how to sell loose coffee, sugar, and candy. Sometimes I sold loose cigarettes behind the tobacco counter, where customers also came to buy matches, postage stamps, and other things regular stores weren't allowed to sell. Other times, I would stand next to Signora Esposito when she worked the register. As I got older, I began to spend time behind the wet counter making espresso and cappuccino, and even selling a glass or two of aperitif wine.

All these chores kept me busy and at the same time, away from the dangerous streets that crawled with petty crimes and *not* because my father wanted me to learn to be a pastry baker. In fact, to reinforce his views, every once in a while he would remind me of his personal feelings on the matter.

"Remember—if you become a pastry chef, although it is a noble trade, you will have to work during the holidays when everyone *else* is celebrating."

Go figure—who knew that years later, I would indeed find myself in the restaurant business, a business that demands dedication and long work days, and just like my father said, the busiest times are during the holidays, when most people are off work. Somehow, I still managed to celebrate holidays with my family, though. It wasn't always easy, but my wife and kids could at least come in and sit at one of the less popular tables. I wonder sometimes if my father, back then, even contemplated the possibility that one day I might end up in the restaurant business. In his view, I was destined to be a white-collar professional working behind a desk, creating charts and architectural designs. Even though that destiny never arrived, I like to think that he would still be proud of everything that I *have* achieved.

Don Gaetano was very involved in his business, and even if you rarely saw him perform any tasks, he was there most of the time. My father had nicknamed him The Ghost as he would appear and disappear at any given moment or place. His three sons were in charge of the different aspects of the operation, and Signora, whenever she was in, always sat at the cash register. It was a good arrangement.

The Espositos also had a daughter, Carmelina, a beautiful twenty year old, the youngest member of the family. She rarely came into the cafe. Instead, she spent most of her time upstairs where the family lived, in a beautiful large apartment in an elevator building, on the third floor directly over the bar. On many occasions, Signora Esposito would hand me a package to bring upstairs to Carmelina. At first it was just an errand, but as those trips upstairs became more frequent, I started to look forward to going up there and look at her beautiful face. Carmelina always seemed happy to see me, her face glowing as she greeted me. I'd hand her the package and most of the time she would place it on the table, but at times, in front of me, she would open the package take out the money and store it in the safe. Wow, they trusted me with the money.

When I told Papá about that trust, he said to me, "My boy, trust is what makes you a man. Never do anything to jeopardize that."

However that advice didn't last long. Soon after that counsel, I was part of two incidents that made me grasp even further my father's teachings.

The first one was when her brother Alfredo had to give my father change back from a purchase we had made at a supermarket they owned just few doors down from Bar dei Fiori. He told my father that he rolled the 500 lire bill and placed it in Papá's vest pocket. When we got home, my father took the bill from his pocket, unrolled it and exclaimed, "This money feels phony to me, Michele. Here, take a look."

I couldn't believe it. "Papá, it's a piece of newspaper."

A disappointed expression came over his face as he said, "what a rat! I can't believe he did this to me." I couldn't believe it either; I liked Alfredo, he was my favorite of the three brothers. My father decided not to do anything about it, but said that we needed to be careful. A few days later I confronted Alfredo about that incident. With a faint smile, he took 500 liras from the drawer and handed it to me, saying, "I just wanted to see if your father could tell the difference between real money and a piece of paper." I didn't buy that explanation, even though I wanted to believe him.

The second incident occurred not long after. I hid a small bar of Perugina chocolate inside my shirt right above the belt, to bring to my sister Sofia.

A little while later, Signora Esposito stopped me on my way out of the Café.

"Michele, I didn't know you liked chocolate?"

I was confused. "Not really, Signora Esposito. I like it okay..."

She pointed at my shirt. I looked down in horror to realize that there was a giant brown spot, right where I had hidden the candy bar. I blushed so red that I could feel my blood suffocating me, and I wanted to disappear.

Why had I done that? Signora Esposito was the most generous person in the world. She used to give me extra bags of food to take home. Sometimes she even put money in my pocket and said, "Bring it to your mother." How could I make such a mistake? And for what? How was I going to tell my father that I had stolen? Could I possibly keep it a secret from him?

Signora took the melted bar from under my shirt, cleaned the spot as best as she could, and in a firm but friendly way told me, "The next time you want something, you ask me. Okay?" She had already forgiven me, but I was not yet ready to forgive myself.

On the way to the trolley, my father asked me, "Michele, what took you so long coming out?"

What could I say? "Signora was cleaning me. My shirt was dirty."

"Dirty with what? Did one of the boys throw a barrel of *baba* on you again?"

"No."

"Well, did you spill some coffee on yourself?"

"No…"

He stopped walking, and I regretfully stopped with him.

"Michele, what is it? What aren't you telling me?"

I had no other option. I had to tell him the truth. "Papá, Signora was cleaning me because I took a bar of Perugina to bring to Sofia, and I hid it under my shirt, but it melted."

"Well who gave it to you?"

"No one." I looked at the ground. "I just took it."

"You *stole* it?"

"I just wanted to—to see if Sofia would like it!" But as soon as the words came out of my mouth, they tasted dirty. And I knew why.

"Would Sofia like a bar of chocolate that was stolen? Would *anyone* in our family like that?"

"No, Papá, I don't think so."

"Did Signora Esposito forgive you already?"

"I think so, Papá. She cleaned me up."

"Well then I'll have a conversation with her tomorrow. But you promise me this will never happen again?"

"Yes, Papá."

"Not just chocolate. *Anything*. Understood?"

"Yes, Papá."

"Okay, good." He took my shoulder, kissed my hair, and we walked on. I felt better because he had forgiven me, but I couldn't shake the taste of Alfredo's words out of my mouth: *I just wanted to*. What was the difference between *just wanting to* take a bar of chocolate and tricking a blind man out of his money? At the moment, I couldn't see one. That was an unforgettable life lesson, and years later honesty became my way of operating my business.

"Papá?" I said as we got on the trolley home. "Are you gonna tell Mama what I did?"

"Is that what you want?"

"No, Papá. No."

"Don't worry. This is just between me, you, and Signora Esposito." And with that, the doors of the trolley closed behind us.

Over the span of ten years, ever since becoming my father's guide, I had become an integral member of the Bar dei Fiori extended family. Not only did they welcome me into their community, but eventually they came to rely on me to handle small chores for them throughout the day, and in return they gave me tips that I would give to my father. But sometimes I caused more problems than I solved.

For instance, one day Don Gaetano was roasting coffee beans, and as usual I hovered observing him without saying a word. Being a friendly person, he would talk to me as he worked and narrate each step of the process to achieve the perfect roast. Naples was (and still is) the espresso capital of Italy, and the pride of every coffee bar in the city was its blend. Like masters in every discipline, the best Neapolitan coffee bars kept their recipes as secret as the alchemist's formulas of old. None of Don Gaetano's many employees were allowed near him when he prepared his raw blend. But he must have known that my future pointed in different directions than the coffee business, because he had no problem with *me* watching his every move.

I watched him do it so many times that I thought I memorized the formula. In fact, I picked it up so fast that he even let me try my hand at the most important part of process: testing the beans while they were still roasting. I would climb up onto the big heavy jute sacks of imported beans in order to reach the testing scoop, where you checked random samples of beans for roastedness. After a few repetitions, I had the whole process under my belt, including the secret recipe. I told Don Gaetano I knew the trick of his trade, but he could rest assured that no one would ever know. I never even told my father. All I can share is that they came from Columbia, Haiti, and Kenya—one for the creaminess, one for the aroma, and one for the mellow mouthfeel. I'll let you figure out which is which.

One time, though, Don Gaetano had run out on an errand and left me to watch the roasting process, since by that point he knew that I could get the job done. I was just climbing into my regular position atop the large sacks of raw coffee when I heard a sudden ripping sound. I hadn't noticed that one of the sacks was torn. When I stepped on it, my weight proved too much, and the sack gave, bursting its entire contents all over the floor. I fell face first into the beans, which were even then bouncing in every direction. Franco, Don Gaetano's oldest son, rushed into the room, saw what was happening, and came very close to giving me a beating for it. It took Bar dei Fiori's manager, Mr. Gargiulo, to come to my rescue and hold Franco back while I picked green coffee beans from my hair and checked to make sure the roasting coffee hadn't burnt. I just managed to get it out in time, and left it in the cooling bin. Embarrassed, I went out front to Papá, but I didn't say anything, too ashamed to name my downfall.

But when Don Gaetano learned of what happened, he came to me and said that the same thing had happened to *him* many times. In fact, he took me by the arm and dragged me back inside to pick up where we left off. All was forgiven.

* * *

No day in the café was complete without a bite of gelato, and in Naples this was doubly true. At Bar dei Fiori, the pastry master and head gelatiere, a Sicilian named Don Antonino, made a new batch of ice cream at least once a week, and he would often wait for me to arrive so I could keep him company while he did so. While listening to stories of his native Sicily, I would help Don Antonino separate the hundreds of egg yolks from their whites for use in the unflavored ice cream base. This base consisted of milk, sugar, and egg yolks cooked over the lowest flame possible and stirred constantly to prevent lumps or burns and to make sure that absolutely nothing would stick at the bottom of the pot. (Various all-natural flavors—banana, or coffee, or hazelnut—would come later on, after the single enormous batch of plain ice cream was finished.) Once the big pot was cooking, Don Antonino would go back upstairs to check on the rest of the *Pasticceria's* operation and would send one of his assistants down to the basement to relieve me and continue stirring the pot.

When the base was thick enough, we would set it aside to cool off before placing it in the walk-in refrigerator overnight. The following day, we would divide this cold, thick goop into separate batches to be flavored accordingly. When each batch was ready, we would pour it in the ice cream machine—a giant drum with agitating scraper fins, surrounded by cold brine. This operation always fascinated me, and I got a kick out of seeing the ice cream goop thicken into something creamy and delightful. I especially loved operating the scraper inside the ice cream drum, to shear off the already frozen cream back to the bottom, occasionally grabbing a small amount with a spoon to taste (for professional reasons, of course) and repeating the process until the entire drum was filled with ice cream.

Don Antonino always reserved part of the batch to sell as loose scoops into cones or cups at the counter. The rest we stuffed into molds of various shapes to create individual servings known as *Ge-*

lati da Passeggio, to enjoy while walking. The one *I* liked most was in banana-shaped form. Once the molds were filled, a flat wooden stick was forced in at one end, and the whole thing was placed in the freezer to harden further. Days later, we peeled the molds off and partially dipped each ice cream bar in chocolate before sticking them back in the freezer. During festivals and saints' feasts, we would roll a wheeled counter onto the sidewalk and sell bars to revelers walking by, bringing all my earnings back in to the Signora. During the Feast of Carmine in July, I would sell *hundreds* of ice cream-on-the-stick, and the Signora never failed to send me home with some of the money for my mother. Even during hard times, ice cream was one of the reliable ways to put a smile on your face.

Most of the employees seemed happy to work for Don Gaetano. He was an easygoing boss and loved to tell stories. One day, when I was about nine or ten, I was operating an annoyingly loud food mixer in the kitchen at Bar dei Fiori when Don Gaetano came in and stopped by me. Without saying a word, he began to hum a tune that—in combination with the mixer's noise—became very pleasant and musical. He seemed to want me to say something about it, and duly impressed by his talent, I said, "Don Gaetano, where did you learn to turn annoying sounds into music? That sounds wonderful!"

We all knew that he had a passion for music; in his spare time, he played guitar and wrote songs in the Neapolitan dialect. Raising his voice proudly over the kitchen din, he said, "Well now that you mention it, I *have* been taking piano lessons. Oh, and I joined a group of musicians, too.

Wow, I was impressed. Most people I knew were too busy making a living and had no time for creative pursuits. But here was Don Gaetano, owner of the Café, the next Enrico Caruso!

That evening on the trolley ride home, I asked my father, "Papá, is it true that Don Gaetano writes songs?"

He told me that yes, indeed he did.

"And that he can play many instruments?"

He pursed his lips. "Tell me my boy, was Don Gaetano bragging in front of all his workers?"

"I'm not sure, but I think so?"

"Well then, next time it comes up, ask him if he ever played the skin flute."

"What is a skin flute, Papá? I never heard of it."

"It doesn't matter, just ask him that."

One day not long after, in the pastry kitchen, the conversation once again turned to the subject of Don Gaetano's many talents. He was leaning against the counter while everyone else worked around him, telling us about the latest song he was inspired to write.

"Don Gaetano," I broke in. "My father wanted me to ask you something."

"Oh? Anything, what is it?"

"Well, amongst all the instruments you play, have you ever played the skin flute?"

To my surprise, Don Gaetano turned as white as the flour covering the counter behind him.

"Why don't you and your father just go f— yourselves?"

That answer stunned me! Suddenly, I understood what a skin flute really was. I blushed and ran out of the kitchen, hoping never to talk about it again—but laughing so hard I could barely hold it in.

Once a year at the end of August, Don Gaetano would take all the kitchen employees for a *scampagnata* (a day trip) to Montevergine, and of course, I was included. My father would come to Bar dei Fiori to see me off at 7AM, and take a seat outside the café while I climbed into a car along with all the staff. Don Gaetano would rent a "limousine" of sorts, more like just long convertible American car that carried ten persons comfortably. The outing was a sort of pilgrimage to the Madonna of Montevergine, a sanctuary built on top of a mountain in the province of Avellino. It was about fifty miles away, not an easy ride, since the road was treacherous and narrow with rough pavement and lots of curves, especially difficult in that long car. Once on top of the mountain, the driver would drop us off in front of the church. We visited the Madonna and then took a stroll, browsing the various stands outside the church that sold souvenirs and rosary beads made of hazelnuts and chestnuts.

The *torrone* nougat candy they sold there was the best I ever had. I always brought money with me to buy some to bring home to my family. My mother and Antonietta loved *torrone,* and my father would get the chestnut beads. He would pray and then eat a few chestnuts and save the rest for more prayers. (Sofia would get a souvenir, since she didn't really relish food.)

When we were all finished with the pilgrimage, we would get back in the car and go down the mountain. In a nearby town named Ospedaletto, known for its excellent wild game dishes, we went to a particular outdoor restaurant where we would eat and drink for hours. There were a couple of dishes I looked forward to particularly: *Gnocchi di Patate con Filetto di Pomodoro* and *Coniglio in Umido.* At the end of the meal, Don Gaetano would play Neapolitan songs with his guitar while the rest of us sang along.

Late in the evening, closer to midnight, we would roll into Bar dei Fiori tired but full of wine and in good spirits. My father would still be there. He waited for me all day, just so I could have some fun.

I would touch him on his hand to let him know I was back, and he would ask, "Did you have a good time, Michele?"

Together, the two of us would board the trolley, and on the way home I would tell him about all the things I had done that day, and all the delicious food I had eaten.

During the Christmas season, Bar dei Fiori would set up a stand on the sidewalk in front of their show windows and load it with panettoni, sparkling wines, and other homemade holiday treats. Whatever we put out there would sell out by the end of the day. I had two jobs: the first was to watch that no one walked away without paying, and the second was to bring large bills in to Signora to make change. Christmas was always fun, especially when people had the money to spend.

When I was a child, even people who were always broke (and I speak from experience) would allow themselves to enjoy a sumptuous meal. In December, everyone with a job or collecting a pension would receive what was known as *tredicesima*, or a thirteenth month salary, a sort of end-of-year bonus. People on disability, as well as the unemployed, would also receive the *tredicesima*. This added benefit enabled every family to celebrate Christmas.

Throughout the year, whenever I was on the trolley, I would often notice the *struggles* on people's faces—drooping skin and weathered brows, distant looks. It made me sad to see those gloomy expressions. So many times I questioned the fact why so many people were sad. However, during the Christmas holidays it was different, I was happy to see people with smiles on their faces and the satisfaction of carrying bags filled with holiday shopping.

Every year, in the days leading up to Christmas, Signora Esposito would send me home loaded up with all kinds of goodies, not just sweets or sparkling wine but meat and fish as well. One of Naples's traditional Christmas foods is eel, four feet long and about one-and-a-half inches in diameter. It has to be alive to guarantee fresh taste and aroma when you cook it. When Signora would order eel for her holiday dinner, she added some extra for my family.

As a child, and probably still today, I was fascinated by the eel, a sort of snake of the sea and rivers. Eels are very stubborn creatures that move constantly in the tank. Once purchased, the merchant wrapped it in a thick paper bag. The experienced buyer would then place it in his or her own cloth shopping bag. (Plastic bags weren't introduced until the 1970s, almost twenty years later.) The novice buyer might just take the paper bag and go. Inevitably, the wet paper bag would crumble and the eel would escape. Once out of the bag, it was virtually impossible to catch the eel as it is a very slippery fish. If the bag broke while you were on the *trolley* the eel found refuge somewhere on the trolley floor and the passengers would go crazy trying to catch it.

In *my* house, it was Antonietta's job to kill the eel. Her technique was to wrap it around her fist and, with one shot, bang its head on the marble counter. Than she and my mother would fry it in popping hot oil, to get its skin nice and crispy.

My father liked traditions, and for him Christmas was not complete unless *Capitone In Umido* was part of the dinner. He was actually the only one who ate it! No one else cared for it.

A few days before Christmas, my father replaced the normal dim light bulbs with stronger ones saved in a drawer in the bedroom. He would leave them in until after New Year's Day. The cost of electricity was exorbitant, and we all were very careful not to waste energy, but during the holidays he liked to keep the place nice and bright.

Every evening during the approach to Christmas, my mother would spend additional time in the kitchen with Antonietta's help, preparing all the treats that we ate throughout the holiday season, up to New Year's Day. On the Eve there were three dishes that we never failed to have, besides our usual bread: *Spaghetti alle Vongole*, *Scarola Monachina*, and of course, *Insalata di Rinforzo*, or *Giardiniera* as we call it in the States. The difference is that here we get it directly from the jar, while in Naples it is all made at home. The traditional dishes for Christmas Day dinner began with a *Minestra di Natale*, followed by *Ruoto al Forno con Patate*.

On Christmas Day, according to tradition, each one of us wrote a letter to our parents and placed it under my father's dinner plate. In our letters, we would list all the good and bad things we had done in the course of the year. Before taking a bite, we had to wait for my mother to read the letters out loud to my father. If he liked what he heard, he gave us a pat on the back and a little bit of money.

Dinner was always followed by an assortment of dried nuts, dried figs, fresh apples, and tangerines; but the highlight was always *Struffoli* and roasted chestnuts.

At the end of the meal, we would clear the table and invite our neighbors, particularly the Pelillos, to join us for coffee and home-made liquor and then sit around the table to play *Tombola*, a sort of 90-number bingo. The smaller children—Gigino, Dino, Sofia, and I, along with a few more children from the building—would play "golf" in the hallway, gambling our dried nuts by rolling hazelnuts in a small hole that had formed over time in a cracked tile on the floor. We still couldn't afford proper toys, even on Christmas (or, in the case of Ne-apolitan children, toys came on the Feast of the Epiphany, on January 6). As a child, I had never seen a Christmas tree or even heard of Santa Claus. The only one who got anything special was Sofia, who some-how managed to get a doll year after year after year.

Every December we built our Christmas Crèche. Mario and I bought the bark, moss, wood, and glue, and for days we worked at creating a scene that was not too different from the year before. I don't know why we always painted the background with Mt. Vesuvius, prob-ably because we didn't know what Bethlehem looked like. We glued clay figures into the Nativity scene. This included a four-inch-tall Mary and Joseph and other figures, from previous years. Anything that had gotten damaged in the storage box, we would replace. The only figure we left out—until Christmas Eve, was Baby Jesus.

Starting on December 15 (my birthday), we displayed the complet-ed Crèche sans Baby Jesus in our dining room on a small table placed between the two windows. On Christmas Eve, we set the table with our holiday tablecloth and shiny silverware, waited until minutes be-fore midnight, placed the dishes filled with food on the table in front of each of us, and then had to sit and wait. We weren't allowed to eat until midnight struck, so that my father could say a few prayers. Then all of us took turns kissing Baby Jesus before placing him in his man-ger. Only then we could begin to eat.

The day after Christmas was the day I most looked forward to, because dinner that day was always *Mafalde al Ragu con Ricotta*, one of my favorites. Every meal during the week from Christmas Day to New Year's Day was finished with the remaining fresh and dried fruits.

Fast forward to New Year's Eve in Naples, and there was always a big celebration. The only traditional dish that evening was *Zuppa di Lenticchie*. The lentils represented gold coins; therefore, it was a way to wish good fortune for the new year by eating them. For the main course, we had a fish dish. If I had a choice, I would always pick *Spigola alla Marechiaro*.

For weeks leading up to New Year's Eve in the Porta Nolana vicinity, fireworks stands would appear on every block, and my brother somehow managed to acquire a rocket from every single stand. Another tradition was to save all the chipped dishes, cups, and bowls to throw out the window (out with the old, in with the new) along with the lighted fireworks to make as much noise as possible. The Pelillos would set their fireworks off from our windows as well, because our windows were better positioned for maximum chaos. Anyone who could afford a car always made sure that on New Year's Eve it was parked well away from any building. Those who failed to do so woke up the next morning to find their cars looking like they'd been through a war zone.

One New Year's Eve almost ended up in tragedy. We had placed our box of fireworks on the floor near the Nativity Crèche, the easier to shoot them from the nearby window for the night's merriment. As we were all busy lighting our flares and firecrackers, one of the flares from the apartment *above* ours—the upstairs Espositos, here they come again—screamed in through our window, tangled in the curtains that hung over *our* box of fireworks, catching the fabric on fire. Smoke filled the room, thick acrid stuff, burning our nostrils and eyes. This prevented us from seeing where the burning curtain was dangling. Before we realized it, it was too late: The curtain brushed the fireworks inside the box, and suddenly pops and flares started shooting off, scaring the wits out of most of us. Then the *Crèche* started to burn. Without wasting any time, Mario and Don Tommasino grabbed the fireworks box and threw it out the window, right into the street below. They did the same with the burning curtain and the Nativity. We watched out the window in horror as the centerpiece of our Christmas celebration and the product of all our hard work—to say nothing of Mario's precious stash of fireworks—went up in a howling pile of pops and sparks.

Porta Nolana

Via Cesare Carmignano was the street behind Bar dei Fiori, one of the arteries coming off of Piazza Nolana just outside the wall. It was also where the water refill station for the water trolley was located. Full of potholes, it was a narrow street lined for four or five blocks with fish stores and a single fried-food shop. Food connoisseurs in Naples knew this street, since it was here that you came to buy any type of fish from anywhere in the world. In addition to its imported fish, Naples boasted an abundance of its own *fresh* fish. Area fishermen who had gone out onto the Tyrrhenian Sea the night before would bring their catch to the vendors on Via Cesare Carmignano to sell. The granite roadway of the street was always wet because the storekeepers kept their fish on crushed ice and often sprinkled them with sea water, to keep them well salted.

A block away from Piazza Nolana there was (and, last time I checked, still is) the one take out fried food shop, Friggitoria. On the sidewalk next to its entrance, there sat a big glass case where freshly fried delights were frequently replenished. It was a busy place, and no matter what time I went there I had to stand in line half an hour or more waiting to order, my mouth watering the whole time. (Not even Papá could jump the line here!) When my turn finally came, it always proved worth the wait. They made *Panzarottini*, small potato croquettes with just a touch of mozzarella inside, that were absolutely divine. There were *Zeppole*, succulent morsels of fried dough, not to be confused with the oily kind you find here in the United States at Italian street fairs. Another delicacy was *Scagnozzi*, small polenta triangles. Let me not forget the delicate zucchini blossoms, or the strips of fried eggplant and small fried pizzas filled with ricotta, mozzarella, and black pepper. These treats were served in brown bags with extra absorbing paper to remove the excess oil, and after you paid the quite affordable prices, you walked away with one hand holding the bottom of the bag and the other digging in. For people who love fried food, this was the place. For my money, there was no better.

Once you walked through the arch of Porta Nolana, you would find yourself inside the wall on Via Sopra Muro, which translates into "Top of the Wall" Street. The first stop my father and I would make was always at the corner, directly across the arch, at Eugenio's lemon stand. He and his brother Armando made the best ever lemonade, using fresh lemons squeezed right in front of you into large glasses and filled with sulfuric water (I'm not sure if this water is still approved for consumption nowadays), which was poured out of a giant clay urn, with a bit of bicarbonate of soda. It was quite the thirst quencher, especially in hot weather.

Both sides of Via Sopra Muro were lined with food shops, many of them arranging their goods on large tables placed directly in the street directly out front. During the day, Via Sopra Muro was closed to traffic, transforming into a pedestrian area. Shoppers would thread in and out of stores, taking their time to haggle for the best quality and the best price and watch that they weren't cheated on the weight. Every store had employees tending to their goods, constantly adjusting the displayed items to make them more appealing. Every few minutes, they would hawk their items to whoever was passing by.

There were half-barrels filled with different types of olives, nuts, capers, and dried beans of every type and color. Eventually we came to the fresh mozzarella shop, where mountains of wet white cheese loomed, attended by smoked mozzarella balls at their base. A few feet beyond, we would arrive at the *baccaleria*, a store that specialized in dry cod soaked in huge vats filled with running water. On Friday, that was the store where we bought *baccalá*. My mother cooked what we called *Stocco alla Siciliana,* which I absolutely loved. This was *baccalá* Sicilian style, cooked in a red sauce with capers and Gaeta olives. Beside *baccalá*, they also kept barrels with salted herrings, fillet of anchovies, and capers. All these stores were close to each other, looked out for one another, and were proud of the products they sold.

I also remember the open drinking fountain that ran day and night. The water there was always so cold that I could feel my teeth about to fall out. After taking a good long drink, it took a few minutes of severe brain freeze to get my bearing before I could resume my walk.

As I've said before, cars weren't allowed on Via Sopra Muro, but kids on bicycles and motor scooters (*motorini*) would wiggle their way in and out as they pleased. One had to be on alert every time two boys rode by on a scooter, because in many cases they were a team of petty thieves looking for easy prey: snatching handbags and jewelry from their victims, then disappearing down the narrow alleyways.

Even so, Via Sopra Muro was the place to be, especially at lunch time. You could get great sandwiches made with delicious crusty Neapolitan bread, filled with *Salsicce e Friarielli*, or *Salsicce e Peperoni*, or with fresh juicy mozzarella and prosciutto with a drizzle of olive oil and a touch of salt. Still, my favorite sandwich was a simple piece of whole wheat bread filled with pitted Gaeta olives and olive oil—just the way I enjoyed it on days at the beach with my buddies.

After about four blocks, just before Via Giacomo Savarese, new delights awaited you. Here, vendors carted goods in daily and stayed until late in the evening, or until they had sold out. Depending on the season and availability, you could pick up any of several possible treats, all right out of the hot vat—corn-on-the-cob, boiled chestnuts, tripe soup, or octopus broth. A few steps away you could get tripe salad—a crunchy assortment of boiled belly, snout, cheek, or pig feet—dressed with just a squeeze of lemon and salt, and *taralli* (Italian snacks similar, but really not even *close*, to breadsticks or pretzels), dried sausage in various thicknesses and lengths, and roasted chestnuts. Never mind America; for us, Porta Nolana was the land of opportunity.

Continuing along via Sopra Muro, you would come to via Giacomo Savarese, the street where my father was born. Here was the building where his mother had run the bakery (which eventually was bombed), and near where my father suffered his fateful accident with the army motorcycle. At the corner still stands a crucifix that has been there for centuries. Whenever I passed by with my father, he had to pause and light a candle and say few prayers. Just before the crucifix there sat a store that, decades *before,* had been my Uncle Michele's shoe factory. I can still hear my father's voice telling me the story of Uncle Michele when he came to America and left my father in charge of the shoe factory. My father didn't do as well as his brother had expected, failing to keep up with the management of the factory. My father had been more interested in chasing girls and racing his horse-and-sulky down Via Caracciolo than running his brother's business.

The former shoe factory had become an olive and nuts store that was owned by Alessandro Vollaro, a distant cousin of my father, who always addressed him as "Uncle Salvatore." Whenever my father and I stopped in his store to say hello, he would drop whatever he was doing and come to shake hands and talk for a minute. That was a common phenomenon all up and down the street; whenever I was in the neighborhood with my father, every storekeeper recognized us. But what I *really* loved was walking down Via Sopra Muro by myself, incognito, so I could take my time and observe and treasure everything that went on around me without the interference of my father's popularity.

He was very proud of the fact that his ancestors had been in that more civilized district for centuries, living "inside the walls," as he would say. Even though I had never met his relatives (with the exception of his brother, Uncle Vincenzo), I was told over and over again where they had lived, the kind of work they did, where they hung out, and whether they had money or, like us, were *morti di fame,* "starving people." Every kind of store you could think of was there—food, wine, pastry shops, bread shops, tinsmiths, craft shops, cabinet makers, barrel makers, and, of course, restaurants.

There were also many shoe shops—no, not just shoe shops and shoe repairs, but craftsmen who, like my uncle many years before, created the most beautiful works of shoe art out of their own home workshops. You could smell the goodness of the leather alone. Shoes were made to order in the most beautiful hides. When you wore those shoes, you knew you were wearing a one-of-a-kind pair. Even on my incognito trips, I always stopped to gape at their industry when passing by one of those miniature factories. I was always taken by the natural way everyone worked in unison to create such high-quality products. It was all done right there in the open, near the door where the sunlight came in. Past that, deeper inside those spaces one might see the beds where they slept or a woman cooking, because this was where they lived and worked to produce the shoes, working from morning to night as long as the sun was up.

The same was true of the tailors. I'd see the same scenes over and over—boys and men of every age sitting on chairs or stools, with one leg crossed over their knees, their heads hunched over, one hand letting the garment hang over their legs, while the other held a threaded needle, sewing.

Via Sopra Muro was the main street in that ancient neighborhood. On one side, it gave access to a web of narrow alleys called *vicoli* where only small carts could pass. The buildings on both sides were tall— five, six, even seven stories high, depending on which century they were built, and all had balconies. They were so narrow that from one balcony to the other, a person could shake hands and mingle in comfortable conversation. Everyone knew everyone's business, it was all open; as a matter of fact, it was offensive to close the balcony doors in good weather, so as not to give the impression that you were hiding anything.

The balcony railings were used to run clotheslines from one balcony to the other. With narrow alleys, tall buildings, and clothes hanging on lines going across to the facing building, the ground was always wet and dark, even on sunny days.

Once day, while walking down one of those alleys with my father, he turned to me. "Miché, is it raining? I feel rain drops hitting my hat." I looked up and saw that, from the balcony a few flights above us, a little boy about three or four years old was peeing down into the street.

What a position I was in. If I told my father what was really happening, he would have yelled out like a madman for the parents to "Give that kid a *sculacciata!*", or a hard slap on the ass. But the poor kid didn't know any better. Thank God above, He gave me the inspiration I needed to lie in that moment.

I answered, "No Papá, it's not raining. The lady on the balcony above us is hanging wet clothes on the line."

An American Visitor

One sunny afternoon, my father and I were at Bar dei Fiori, sitting at our usual outdoor table, next to Vincenzo, the shoe shine man. Right by the curb where we were sitting, a beautiful American convertible automobile stopped. It was very unusual in the early 1950s in Naples to see such a car. Who could afford it? The driver was a man, about thirty years old. I was telling Papá about the car when the man got out and went over to Vincenzo. I was following the man's movements as he was talking to Vincenzo, who then directed him towards my father. The fact that Vincenzo would send people looking for directions over to my father was pretty common, as it was recognized by my father's friends that he was knowledgeable about the area. The man started to speak to my father in broken Neapolitan dialect.

"Excuse me, Signore, is your name Savarese Salvatore?"

My father answered, "Yes."

Smiling broadly the man reached over to shake my father's hand and said, "You must be my uncle! I am Tony, your brother Michele's son."

My father asked, "Have you come here from America?"

"Yes. I came to see the beautiful Napoli, as my parents call it. I will be here for a while to check the situation in Naples. I would like to move here one day."

My father said, "Wow, that is great news. Please sit with us and let me offer you a drink."

So Tony sat and talked about his parents and about his brothers and sisters. He asked me my name and age, and if I went to school. My father introduced his new-found nephew to some of his friends and to Don Gaetano, who had come out to look at the American car.

Tony stayed with us for a while and seemed interested to know about the rest of our family. He was telling Papá about his business in America and about his new bride. However, as he was talking, he was doing strange movements with his face and hands. I was wondering why he was doing that, and later realized that he was tricking my father to test his sight. Of course, my father was not aware of what Tony had been doing. Finally Tony asked my father, "Uncle, is it true that you can see a little?"

Staying silent for a moment my father said, "Tony, I wish I could. But why do you ask?"

Tony said, "Because my father is very interested in you and wishes that he could do something for you."

My father said, "That is nice of my brother, but what can he do for me when some of the best eye specialists in Naples have told me that I'll never regain my sight?"

"Uncle, in America, we are doing well with my father's shoe factory, and your brother would like to bring you there, so that he can have you get another opinion. But Arturo, my father's childhood friend in Naples that he corresponds with regularly, told him that you are 'playing the blind card' in order to fool the system and receive your disability pension. In a few words he wants to be sure that you are not putting on an act."

My father's face became stern. I saw him clench his teeth, but he kept in control. He then said to Tony, "You are my nephew from far away. You don't know me. You can assure my brother in America that I am not playing games here in Naples with my life and that of my wife and children. However, when you go back to America, please tell your father that I appreciate what he wants to do for me, but I am satisfied with my doctor and I am not leaving my family. As far as Arturo, I'll deal with him when the time comes."

Before leaving, Tony said, "I'll come by again, and together we will go to your house. I want to meet the rest of your family." That night, I was anxious to get home from Bar dei Fiori so I could tell Gigino about my cousin Tony and the big American car.

On the trolley, my father told me about his brothers, Vincenzo and Michele. Vincenzo worked for Circo Togni, a popular circus, where he was a leather craftsman, specializing in whips and saddles. That job took him throughout Europe, returning to Naples whenever he was on break. His brother Michele, looking to expand his shoe business, traveled to New York in 1923. One year later he decided to move there with his wife Teresina and his three sons, Gennaro, Giuseppe and Tony, and their daughter Nancy. However, he had to leave behind his two sons, Gennaro and Giuseppe, who failed to pass the physical at the American Consulate. Giuseppe eventually followed his parents to America, while Gennaro, who suffered with various health issues, stayed behind with Aunt Consiglia, his mother's sister. She lived a block away from my father and Gennaro remained very attached to my father. When my parents got married, he moved in with them for a short time. Eventually, in 1941, Gennaro got on a ship as stowaway heading for New York, where he went on to become a successful restaurateur.

My father continued…Shortly after I was born, my Aunt Teresina upon learning that my mother and father had a baby boy, began sending boxes of baby clothes, gifts and sometimes even a bit of cash. Four years later, when Sofia was born, she continued with the tradition and began to include things for her as well. She never failed to include a considerable amount of candy. I can still remember those times when the mailman would deliver the large box wrapped in canvas. If kids were around at the time of delivery, they would come to our door and ask for candies. "Signo', can we have some American candies?" My parents never refused, but would ask them to return later after they had opened the box. My mother would dress me up every chance she had. The dollars from my aunt helped her a lot during that period.

I liked to listen to my father and to learn about his family.

A couple of weeks later, Tony came to my house. He arrived in his beautiful car, accompanied by a mutual cousin, Gennaro Grieco (my Aunt Nunziella's son), who knew where we lived. A crowd gathered, as in my poor neighborhood no one had ever seen such an extravagant car. I often fantasized that maybe one day I might go to America and become a wealthy man, and just like my cousin, travel all over the world on beautiful ships and own beautiful cars. Tony was shocked to see how we lived and asked Papá if he could help in any way. My father felt a bit humiliated, and as the proud man that he was, said "Tonino," as we all got to call him, "have a good time here in Naples. Don't worry about us. We have all that we need." A couple of years would go by before we saw Tony again.

In the spring of 1954, Tony returned to Italy to help plan the wedding for his brother Giuseppe, who would soon come to Naples to marry Anna Esposito (yes, another Esposito), a young brunette, and a real Neapolitan beauty. Tony had come back to Italy with his mother, (my Aunt Teresina), his wife and their baby boy. He planned to settle in a beautiful apartment on the hill of Vomero overlooking the bay of Naples. They had arrived on a big ship named the SS *Independence*. I was there to greet them, along with my brother Mario and my two cousins Gennaro and Totonno. I was fascinated with the ship—the porters hauling big trunks, suitcases, and all kinds of wrapped boxes, but most of all the American cars. The line of people getting off the gangway snaked like the fuse on a firecracker.

Some of the passengers had brought their cars with them. I was impressed watching the operation of unloading the cars from the ship. The cars would hang from a crane and then placed on the pier. I wondered if my cousin had brought *his* car, and if so, which one it might be. Then I heard someone yell out, "There it is!"

Whoa, what a car. It was a big white convertible car, with red interior. A crowd of curious bystanders had gathered around it. I wondered if I was ever going to be allowed to ride in that car. As I was wondering, I asked Mario if he had ever been in one of those cars. He looked at me for a while before answering, "In a car like that, no, but during the war when the American soldiers liberated us, as we were greeting them they would throw us candy and occasionally let some of us ride with them for a block or two."

At that, Tony came by, greeted us, and took us to meet his mother, his wife Elaine and his baby son Anthony. Zia Teresina reminded me a lot of Signora Esposito, the owner of Bar dei Fiori: tall and heavy, a bit stern, with a beautiful face. After meeting Tony's family we left, promising to visit them a week or so later at their new address in Vomero. He yelled to me and Mario, "And make sure to bring your parents!"

A week or so later we went to visit. To get there we took the Funicular up the side of the mountain and got off at Via Palizzi. It was the first time I had ever been on a cable car, and I liked it. It was better than the trolley; you had a vision of height, an overview of the bay, rather than the street-level view from the trolley. I was taken by that ride and by the view of the city as we climbed the side of the mountain to get to our destination.

Aunt Teresina was so surprised to see my Papá. She had known Totore, as she called my father, (Totore is the Neapolitan nickname for Salvatore), ever since he was a small boy in their old neighborhood. She had always liked her brother-in-law. In a way, she let Totore do the errands for her the same way Signora Esposito did with me fifty years later. Aunt Teresina was sad about my father's misfortunes, but happy to see him.

When my father asked her about his brother, she said that he had been busy with the shoe factory and would be in Naples in a few weeks. She had never met my mother, but seemed truly happy to meet her. My mother, with her hand on my shoulder, introduced me to Aunt Teresina saying, "Teresina, this is the boy to whom you sent so many boxes of diapers and baby clothes. Thanks to you, my son was the best-dressed baby in Naples, and thanks to you, the dollars you put in the boxes helped me with my kids."

Aunt Teresina said, "Maria, during the war you went through hell here and we, on the other side of the ocean, were so preoccupied with what was going on that it kept us on edge. The first letter we received from you, was after the war when you had your son Michele. It was than that we learned about the loss of your baby and Totore's accident."

My mother replied, "Thank God, that war is just a memory now, even though we are reminded of it every day, particularly when I look at my husband. I still have to convince myself that he is the same man I knew before his accident. He always took charge, and no matter what the situation was, he would make it better."

While the adults were talking over coffee, I went on the balcony to look at the view. I could not believe my eyes. I kept asking myself over and over if the real Naples was the one I was looking at now, or the one I knew. The city was below, and I could see all those buildings that my father and I had walked by so many times. I was fascinated to see all the domes and bell towers of the churches. The advantage that I had from that observation point was that I was able to move from one street to another very fast, without having to deal with traffic, people or noise. From up there, everything looked smaller, even the ships in the harbor.

That day, the SS *Constitution*, the sister ship of the SS *Independence*, was in town. From my cousin's balcony I was analyzing it. I stopped looking when I heard the details of Giuseppe's upcoming wedding. I heard that Uncle Michele would soon be coming to Naples with the groom-to-be, so I jumped in the conversation and asked, "Will I get to meet him? Papá always talks about his brother. On Easter Sunday, as he blesses all of us with the holy water and then dips the olive branch back in the water and turns in the direction of America to send his blessings to his brother."

Tony said, "I don't see why not, he is going to be here for a month, then he has to go back to America to tend to his business."

My parents were so excited to learn about Uncle Michele coming to Italy. As we were leaving, my aunt gave my mother a small envelope with money, and insisted she take it. We left wondering if we were going to be invited to the wedding, and if so, where were we going to get money to buy a present for the newlyweds and new clothes to wear to the party?

Uncle Vincenzo, in Naples on a break from his job with the circus, came as usual to Bar dei Fiori to spend time with my father. As my father was bringing him up on the latest family news, I spotted the beautiful white American car when it was a block away, and I said loudly, "Tony is coming, and he has two other people in the car!"

When the car stopped by the curb, Uncle Vincenzo stood up and went toward one of the men, saying in a subdued but excited voice, "Michele, let me hug you. It has to be thirty years since we last saw each other." And the man, Michele, said ,"You are right. Thirty years!"

Michele let go of Vincenzo's hug to embrace Salvatore, who by now was also standing. Tony and I were just observing the three brothers together for the first time in thirty years, when Tony kind of turned to me, upset that I had not greeted the other man they were with.

"What's the matter little boy, you don't say hello to Arturo?" and my father immediately answered, "My son never met Arturo, he only heard of him. I certainly brought him up the right way, you know."

At that, my father asked me to salute the newcomers and to go spend time inside the pastry laboratory after fetching the waiter. I figured that he did not want me to be present when he bawled out Arturo for making up stories about my father's eyesight. What Tony had told him on his previous visit had bothered him a lot, and knowing my father, I knew that he would not let it go untouched. I also knew that he might wait for a time when he was eye-to-eye with Arturo to straighten him out. Arturo might have been a lifelong childhood friend of Uncle Michele, but not of my father, who always disliked him for being a Fascist.

It turned out that neither Uncle Vincenzo's family nor ours were invited to the wedding, probably because of our poverty, sparking such a rage in my father that he promised he would never speak to the "Americans" ever again. That anger did not last long. One day, not long after, Uncle Michele came by Bar dei Fiori to apologize and to bury the hatchet. He explained that he had had nothing to do with the his son's wedding invitations as they had gone out before he arrived, and that on wedding day he was surprised not to see either of his brothers there. Uncle Michele seemed sincere and so my father and Uncle Vincenzo agreed to accept the apologize and forgive (or, at least, forget).

Soon after, we went to visit them at their Vomero hill residence. At one point during the conversation, I asked my uncle if one day he would take *me* to visit the big ship. He turned to his wife Teresina and spoke "American" to her. Later I realized that whenever they didn't want the rest of us to understand, they reverted to English, a language unknown to us. Somehow their English did not sound to me the same as when Tony and Elaine talked.

Innocently, I asked him, "Uncle, why do you talk so funny?" and he replied, "If you think that I speak funny now, wait until you come to America, then you'll die laughing." With time I learned that Uncle Michele, who could understand but barely spoke English, would have to translate through his wife, who could speak it but barely understand it. Either way, I never got my answer.

When we left, on the ride back downhill on the *funiculare* cable car, I asked my father to hold me up so I could reach the high window in order to look at the view. While struggling to pull myself up I asked him, "Papá, did you hear Uncle Michele when he said to me, 'Wait until you come to America'? Do you think he was serious?"

My father said, "Come on. It was just a way of talking. Besides, I believe I would have to think about that, should he seriously ask me."

We continued to visit Uncle Michele quite often while he stayed in Naples. He spent a lot of time with his brothers. He was a lovely man. Just like Uncle Vincenzo, he would always speak softly, while my father had a tendency to be loud. When the three of them were together, the thirty years of separation disappeared. My father was the kid brother, so out of respect, he would always allow them to speak first. But when speaking about the past, God forbid if one of them would say something different from what my father remembered. He would jump right in and tell them his version, completely taking over the conversation. One day my mother, while listening to one of those episodes, yelled at him, saying, "What the hell, all the fire that is missing from your brothers came to you?"

The time came when Uncle Michele and Aunt Teresina left to go back to New York. We were invited on board the ship for a farewell party. Antonietta and I were amazed by the beauty and luxury of the ship. We wished never to get off. There were trays of different foods all over the place. Cheese, cold cuts, breads and cookies, none of which we were familiar with. For a treat, we were invited to taste an American drink called ginger ale. I turned to Antonietta and said, "It is very *sweet. I like it*."

She nodded, "I like it too. I read somewhere that if you want Americans to like anything, just add sugar, and they will love it."

The big luxurious ship, the big American cars, and the sweet ginger ale were all I could think of for a while. Did I make a good impression on my Uncle Michele? Was he serious when he said to me "One day, when you come to America"...My daydreaming continued.

As the years went by, my cousin Tony would spend a lot of time in Naples. His family stayed in Naples while he went back and forth to America to tend to his business. Whenever he was in Naples, he would often come to Bar dei Fiori to spend time with my father.

The day I graduated middle school, being anxious to know if I had passed, my father and I left our apartment in Barra early in the morning. I dropped him off at Bar dei Fiori and walked to school to read the posted results. When I went back to tell my father that I had passed, to my surprise, Tony was there.

As I approached them, I yelled out, "Papá, I did it!"

And my father replied, "Come here, let me hug you. Congratulations!"

Tony, who did not know what was happening, asked ,"Congratulations for what?"

My father explained, "He just came back from his school to check the postings. He just graduated from middle school!"

Tony smiled broadly and patting my back said, "Bravo!" And asked, "Is he getting a present?"

My father told him "Maybe in America, when one graduates, he or she gets presents! Here in Naples, when you graduate, congratulations and a handshake is all you get."

When Tony heard that, he turned to me and said, "I am American, and I am going to get you a present. Do you have anything in mind?"

I said, "Yes, I would like a bicycle, but not just any bicycle. Every day on the way back from school, I pass this bike store, and in the window they have a Bianchi bicycle that makes me drool. It is pale green. It is just beautiful."

And at that, Tony said, "Get in the car."

I could not believe my ears. Was it possible that I was going to get the bike I had yearned for for such a long time? When we got to the bicycle store and I pointed out the bike to my cousin, he looked at me and said, "I like the fact that you know what you want. Is that the best bike in the store? Are you sure you won't have it stolen on you?"

The shopkeeper was reluctant to sell that particular bike, as it was the window display and he did not have a similar one in stock. So Tony told him he would make it worthwhile for the man to sell the bike. So after checking out the bike, the man handed it to me.

I was flabbergasted. Not only did I have a bike, I had the best bike! Tony had left me in the shop to wait for the bike to be fine-tuned and went on his way. I rode my bike to Bar dei Fiori to show it to Papá and our friends. My father kept touching it, asking me all kinds of silly questions—What color was it? Was it the right size for me? Was I going to fall off?—which did not register with me, as my excitement was so high that I felt kind of numb. As we were praising my cousin's generosity, we got distracted, and lost sight of the bike for a moment, a stranger who had also been looking at the bike, grabbed it by its saddle, and tried to run off with it. Vincenzo, the shoe shine man, grabbed my bike, as a bunch of people grabbed the thief and gave him a beating. Boy, that was close. What was I going to tell my cousin if the bike had been stolen only one hour after I got it?

America Becoming a Reality

The summer of 1961 was a turning point in my life. Uncle Michele came from New York with his son Gennaro. During his stay in Naples, Gennaro visited with us constantly, staying for dinner, since he remembered my mother's cooking. As a teen he had suffered severe headaches, and when the pain was unbearable he would go over to my parents' apartment to relax, since that place was very quiet. My mother would make him lay down, and while he rested she would cook his favorite soups, *Zuppa di Verdure* or *Zuppa di Friarielli*. He and I became very close.

At the end of the summer, before Gennaro went back to America, he promised me that he was going to do everything possible to get *me* to the United States so that I could continue with the schooling that my father intended for me—schooling that would put me behind a desk one day, earning a salary with my mind rather than with my hands. This was something we could not afford in Italy. But in America, my family could help. I believed him. He had not struck me as a charlatan.

In the spring of 1962, we received a package from the United States containing a number of documents and a pre-paid one way ticket for the ship's passage to America. Was it possible that another one of my dreams was about to come true? The Italian bureaucratic system required significant documentation, and it took months to get all the paperwork in place. There were many visits to the American consulate. When the documents were finally approved, I had to go back for a physical, and if all was good I would receive my student visa. Thankfully, I didn't have any of the health concerns Gennaro did, so I passed with no problem.

At the beginning of September, when the medical exam was finished, I was escorted to a large room, along with other applicants, and lined up to be greeted by an American official. When we were all gathered up, a small group of men entered the room and one of them, a very tall man, walked by everyone of us, shaking hands. Because of my shyness, I was looking at the floor and never took a good look of him. The only thing that I remember was his big shiny black shoes. He murmured a couple of words and moved on. Once we were out, one of my fellow applicants asked me if I had recognized that man. I said, "No, who is he?" He told me that the man's name was Lyndon Johnson, the Vice President of the United States. Thinking that I was being put on, I said, "Why, President Kennedy could not make it?" Then I asked, "And what is Signor Johnson doing in Naples?" My buddy then told me that he had read in a local newspaper that he was in Naples on an official visit.

Only when it became official that I was going to America did I let my friends know—including my girlfriend. Many of my friends were envious, but Lucia was not. In fact, she was crushed, even though I kept insisting that I would be back. But our relationship was irreparably broken after that. (Years later, when I went looking for her, I found out she had married while I was gone. I couldn't blame her. I never saw her again.)

Upon learning the departure date, my Aunt Teresina wrote to my mother asking for one of her homemade *Tortano Dolce* cakes, those giant doughnut-like poundcakes that my mother was known for. My father had saved a US $10 bill and gave it to me so that I could spend it on the ship if necessary. With that money I bought the picture that the ship photographer had taken of my family and friends standing on the pier to see me off. I would eventually mail that picture to my parents and not see it again for many years, not until 2012. That year I went to Italy to mourn the death of my brother Mario. Nunzia, his daughter, came out with a box full of pictures. While we were reminiscing, she came upon that picture and asked me if I knew anything about it. Fifty years had passed since that photo was taken. In it I pointed out some of the people that had accompanied me to the pier, including her mother, Titina, who was Mario's girlfriend at the time and would later become his wife. Nunzia asked me to point out her father, but I told her that Mario was not in the picture because he had left Italy four years earlier to work in Germany.

My parents were happy for the opportunity I was getting, but not happy to see me go. I was, after all, my father's best friend, I was his eyes, his buddy. To my mother, I was a necessary help, as I took care of accompanying my father, leaving her to her own chores. We had a very close bond. I was the one to help her every Sunday to prepare the meal. I would stir the *ragu* while she and my sisters made the beds and did laundry. Occasionally I would go to the store to do her shopping. I would break the long ziti, and grate the cheese to sprinkle on top of the pasta. I loved to roast coffee for her, as she could not take the smoke but loved the aroma of fresh-roasted coffee beans. She enjoyed my silly jokes, they made her laugh.

August 1962, my sister Antonietta married Giovanni (Gianni) Sabatino and moved to San Giorgio a Cremano. With me going to America, it meant that Sofia would be the only child to live at home with our parents. The mood around my home had become a bit somber. My excitement was such that both my parents, when questioned, always would come out with a different excuse for their sadness like, "We have not heard from your brother in a while," which was true, because many times we would not hear from him for months, or, "Antonietta is having problems with her landlord." They were always trying to give me the impression that the fact that I was about to embark on such a far-away destination had nothing to do with their misery.

About a month before my scheduled departure date, my father had a brilliant idea. He had been preoccupied for weeks by the thought that I might get seasick on the ship, and so he decided to send me and Gigino for a day trip to the nearby island of Ischia. In his experience, he knew that the sea between Naples and Ischia was always rough. If I did not get sick on *that* trip, there was a good chance that I would not get sick on the big ocean liner either.

Ischia, however, turned out to be a very interesting experience. When we got off the ferry, we noticed that every woman was dressed in a Roman toga and every man was dressed in a Roman centurion costume. Gigino and I looked at each other, totally intrigued, and kept walking towards the Castello Aragonese. Again, every single person we encountered, young or old, male or female, was dressed in Roman clothing. We were also surprised that there were no cars, no bicycles and no Vespas. Curious as we were, but inexperienced with such an island, we asked a street vendor why everybody was dressed like that. His quick response was, "What's the matter, when you got off the ferry didn't anybody tell you that in Ischia, during the summer, everybody goes around in Roman clothes?" Like two jerks, we believed the man until we found out the real reason—that summer, the movie *Cleopatra* with Elizabeth Taylor was being filmed, and every person in Ischia was an extra in the movie. By the way, the boat trip to and from Ischia did not affect me in any way. I was ready for the big ship! (Or so I thought.)

It was not long after that that I visited the Cianos' house for the last time and heard Mrs. Ciano utter her fateful criticism. In fact, her words—*If you were my son, I would not send you to America*—echoed through my head all throughout the final day of preparations and made me doubt whether I was making the right choice. Could it be possible that my decision to go to America was because I had been blinded by the beautiful American cars, the opportunity to become a rich man like my cousins? That one day I would come back with my pockets full of money and move back to Naples and help my family improve their standard of living? Was I that naive?

But then there were my mother's words, equally powerful in my ears: "*To me, your future is more important than anything. So don't listen to anybody and go without turning around!*" I wanted to believe her. But the doubt remained.

October 2, the day of my departure arrived. As we were packing my suitcases with my clothes and the tortano dolce (and bottle of sweet vermouth) for Aunt Teresina, my mother stopped me coming out of my room, squeezed me close to her chest, and pulled out a thin gold chain with a crucifix on it. She reached up and hung it around my neck. "Promise me that you're not going to change over there." I felt the cold metal on my skin, and looked her in the eyes. "Mama, I'll never take this off." And I never did.

After several hours of packing and reminiscing with family and friends (about thirty people altogether had showed up!), we left for the port, myself, Antonietta, Gianni, Gigino, and Sofia in Gianni's Fiat, along with my two suitcases.

And then suddenly, there was the big white ship, right in front of us.

After a few hugs, I started for the gangway and went down below to look for my cabin, which was equipped with four beds, two on the floor and two hinged to the wall, in which myself and three other strangers—two Italians and one Lebanese—would berth. It was decided amongst the four of us that I would get the upper bunk, and I was OK with that. Quickly, I stored my two suitcases and went up on deck. Everyone was talking loud. From the ship, I could see the beautiful white administration building surrounded on three sides by piers where many ocean liners were docked. The ship was separated from the pier by just a few feet. I could almost touch my family and friends.

Looking at my father, wearing his characteristic Panama hat and black glasses but staring completely in the wrong direction from everyone else, I knew at that moment that this man would be lost without me. Yet my future was so important to him that his personal feelings were completely secondary to him. I could see this in his expression; for a man whom I was so used to listening to all the time, he was now remarkably quiet. Seeing him like that, a feeling of guilt rose up and threatened to take over all the excitement of that moment. What a tough thing for me it was to deal with this. I had spent most of my life at his side, and now here I was about to embark on this ship that would take me away to a far away land and leave him—possibly forever. What kind of son does that to a man who has leaned on him so much? Even when that man is *telling* him to go?

With so much going on, it was difficult to register the whole situation. I kept calling out their names and telling them that one day I was going to be back in Naples with a big long American automobile. It wasn't clear if I was trying to reassure them or myself. The ship had not moved yet. I could still jump off, if I'd wanted to. We were all together, separated only by those few feet. Nothing permanent had happened yet.

But just then, the smokestack let off its three loud blows to announce imminent departure. I looked again at my parents, and the pain I saw on their faces was indescribable.

The loud belch that came from the smokestack sent a jolt through my body. The deck under my feet vibrated vigorously. A cold feeling overcame me—we were ready to sail. All I could do was watch sadly as the big vessel pulled slowly away. I grasped the rail with one hand while with the other I waved furiously, occasionally jumping up and down to get a better view of that fleeting scene. Then I remembered Mr. Sorrentino's promise and ran towards the rear of the ship. When I heard the two blows coming from the tugboat, I looked and saw my friends' father waving and screaming from the top of his lungs, "Good luck Michele and God bless you!" As the ship began to accelerate, everyone and everything I had ever been familiar with slowly disappeared.

I held my composure as long as I could, then went below to my empty cabin and burst into tears. I did not know what was happening to me. I knew what I had left behind and at the same time I did not know what was ahead. I had never been away from those people, who most likely were still on that pier, hoping to get another glance of the ship.

One of my new cabin companions, who I had noticed earlier sitting on the deck by himself smoking a terribly smelling cigarette, came in and introduced himself to me in a foreign language. At first I didn't understand anything, then I realized it was French, the language I had taken in school for the last four years. I asked him to speak slowly so I could understand him.

"You left many people on that pier, I understand why you feel so bad." With that, he patted me on my arm and added, "You will be OK."

That friendly pat, in a moment of discomfort, made me feel somewhat reassured. The language barrier forced me to concentrate more on the conversation. So the man continued to talk. "In Beirut, Lebanon I left behind my wife and my two year old daughter to join my brother in law, who has a job lined up for me in Paterson, New Jersey."

When I finally understood him clearly, I said to myself, *This guy must be really desperate to leave his loved ones to find a job.* I tried to comfort *him* now.

"You must be a strong man to have taken such a decision. Hopefully within a year or two you will have your family join you in Paterson."

After a while I was feeling a little better, so the two of us went out to explore the ship. Since we were 3rd class passengers, we weren't allowed to go beyond the 1st class doors, so we went out on the deck instead. All I could see was water, water all around me. I went back down and fell asleep in my clothes.

When I woke up, it was 6:00 AM. I went up on deck to see the coastline. It was beautiful as we passed the towns of Lavagna and Rapallo, nearing Genoa.

A million things were going through my mind. I kept questioning myself if I had made the right decision. Could I be making a mistake that I would regret for the rest of my life? After having a cup of coffee (or at least that was what they called the brown hot water with milk and sugar), and some type of pastry, I went back to my cabin to shave and shower. Mrs. Cianos' words bounced in my head. I put on my gray suit, put all my documents in my pockets, and went up on deck to watch the docking operation into the Port of Genoa, the last port in Italy and the first of three Mediterranean stops before heading out into the Atlantic for good. I saw some people get off the ship, and a brilliant idea came to my mind: *What if I got off here and went back home, to Naples?* Would my parents accept my decision and forgive me for putting them through such hardship for the past few months? Or should I squeeze my teeth and continue on to America and possibly to a better future?

As these thoughts continued bouncing in my head, I found myself at the bottom of the gang plank. I started to walk, just to look around, curious and eager to explore. I saw a taxi and hailed it. Once in the cab the driver, an older gentleman, turned to me. "Where to?"

"The train station, please."

As the cab was moving, the driver kept looking me over and studying me. He asked me, "Which train are you going to catch?" and I told him, "To Naples." In his accent, he said, "Bellin! ["dick", a typical Genoese expression] That train leaves at the 14th hour (2:00 PM)."

I told him it didn't matter, I would wait.

The driver asked me, "Didn't you just get off that ship?"

I told him that I had.

He then asked, "didn't that ship originate the trip in Naples?"

"Yes," as he continued, "I can't figure this out. You are going to Naples, you just came from there and you are not even carrying a suitcase?"

I told him, "If you really want to know, I was on my way to New York, and I changed my mind. I am going back to Naples. I had a change of heart and left everything on the ship."

The taxi kept on moving as the driver blurted, "Wait a minute, you look like a smart kid to me and I am old enough to be your grandfather. What are you doing? You have an opportunity to go to America and you are telling me that you changed your mind and want to go back to Naples? I bet you anything that your parents are probably not happy with you leaving them, but they also know that you have a better chance in life than what they can offer you."

We continued our conversation as we drove along. I had been in that cab for about 15, maybe 20 minutes. When looking at the road ahead, I suddenly noticed the big white ship and my cab moving toward it. When the taxi came to a stop, the driver turned off the engine, got out of the car and opened the rear door and saw me holding the $10 bill. Looking straight at my face, he said, "Son, you are my first passenger today, and I have no change. This cab ride is on me. Just go back on that ship."

The old man convinced me, so I headed back to the ship. When I got up on deck, I turned around to wave at him—but the driver and the cab were gone. No vanished!

(A note: Four years later, on my first trip back to Italy, I made it a point to go back to Genoa and go to the port; and from there I walked to the train station. The walk took about 10 minutes, which was less than the time I had spent riding around in the cab. This confirmed a suspicion I had carried for years - the cab driver must have taken me for a ride just to convince me that I was about to make a big mistake. I often think about that taxi driver—where had he come from)?

Back on the ship, still confused. I came upon one of my cabin mates, the man from Calabria, who told me that the Lebanese man had been looking for me, as he had not seen me all morning and was worried. When I met up with him, I told him in my halting French that I had gone for a walk around the port. After we left Genoa, the next two stops in as many days were Cannes and Casablanca. In each instance, I stayed on the ship to mingle with the other passengers, deciding I had seen enough of the mainland for now. I befriended a few guys my age, but took particular interest in a girl from Calabria, a girl whose name I've since forgotten but whose huge green eyes I'll never forget. She was traveling with her family, who were emigrating to somewhere in America. She told me that she was going to America against her will. Her parents had waited years to get the visa, and when it finally arrived they had to borrow money to buy the passage. She had fought long and hard, along with her two little brothers, but in the end they had to succumb to their parents. I had found a kindred spirit.

One or two days later, the ship slowly passed by the Azores, probably to allow the passengers to enjoy the beauty of those islands. The ship sailed close to the coast. It must have been a tradition, because hundreds of fisherman were already out there waiting in their small boats to wave at us, and the people on the ship waved back. All along, the weather had been perfect. Every place we passed was more beautiful that the last. Now I was happy that the Genoese taxi driver had convinced me to continue on my journey.

A few hours after the Azores, the weather changed completely. The clouds got thick, and the waves began to punch the side of the boat. The ship bounced continuously, and the passengers were barred from the deck because of high winds. The next five days I spent indoors, exploring the many areas of the ship. I was already familiar with our 3rd class dining room, which was always crowded at meal time, reminding me of the dining room when I was in Castellammare di Stabia with my school mates. But even in Castellammare, the dining room always had a pleasant food smell, while on this ship all I could smell was the odor of burned butter that emanated from the unfamiliar dishes that came out of the ship's kitchen. It made me sick to my stomach and I ended up feeding myself nothing but slices of bread and drinking Coca Cola.

One day I snuck into the 1st class area of the ship and found it spaciously designed but in actuality much smaller than the accommodations of 3rd class (or "Tourist class," as travel agents kindly referred to it). I later discovered that there were fewer than fifty 1st class passengers on the ship, out of a total of several hundreds. Their dining room was absolutely beautiful, filled with statues and paintings, very elegant table settings and matching draperies. White-gloved waitstaff stood on their toes ready to serve their 1st-class customers, to whom they had each been previously assigned. There was even a card room and library. Most of the passengers *here* sported beautiful clothes and jewelry. My own trousers and home-made sweater must have marked me out pretty clearly as an interloper, because within a few minutes, a gentleman dressed in a black tuxedo approached and ordered me, quietly but in no uncertain terms, to leave. Realizing I was caught, I apologized and quickly made my exit.

One place I did spend a lot of time was the deck just outside the Captain's bridge, hoping to catch a glimpse of how the ship was run. The benches that lined the foredeck outside the bridge were the perfect place to sit and hope for the chance to get in, even if it meant perpetually putting up with the cold wind and salty spray. Eventually, one of the officers must have taken pity on me, because I was allowed inside and given the chance to watch the crew run the vessel. A bit more complicated from the trolley! For example, it took several officers at a time to maintain the ship's course, helming the ship's wheel or poring over giant paper charts of the ocean. For someone who had always loved cars and speed, the ship's bridge was an entirely new but nevertheless thrilling experience for me, even if they never actually let me touch any of the equipment. Just being there was enough to get me through the rest of the journey.

Often, looking through the porthole out on the gray sea with no horizon, I would think back to some of the stories my father told me about my cousin Gennaro and his first trip to America. With all his health problems, I couldn't imagine how Gennaro would have survived the journey on a ship similar to this one, or in his case the even worse conditions of a stowaway. Was he able to roam? Where did he sleep? Where did he wash? And, more importantly, what did he do for food?

Because there was something I could not get past on the ship: the food. I couldn't even get accustomed to the bread—plain, no crust and no taste. I had never tasted butter in my life, and when I finally tried it, I found it disgusting. Every dish served on that ship had butter. It made me sick to the point that I would vomit at least once a day. I was

Postcard of SS Atlantic

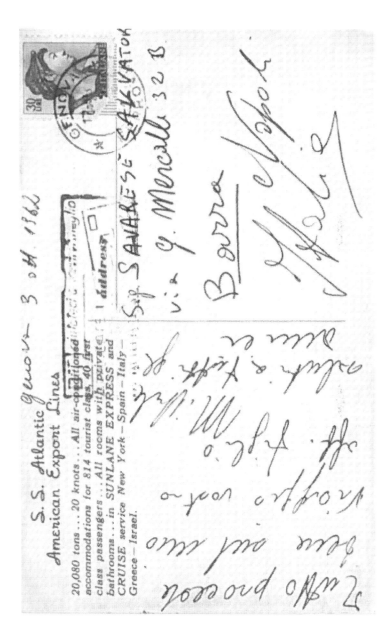

Back of postcard mailed from Genova

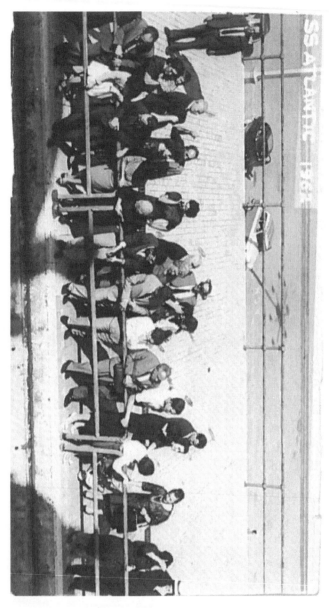

Naples: The pier with my friends and relatives seeing me off to New York

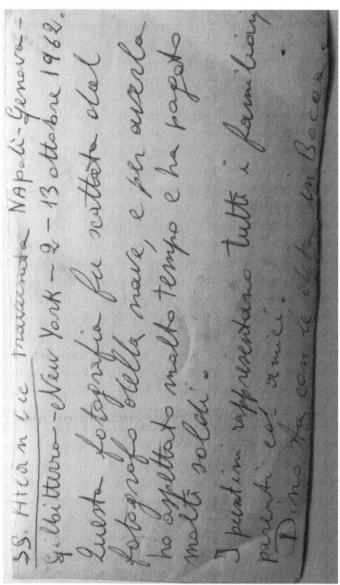

Back of photo: S.S. Atlantic crossing between Naples and New York with stops in Genova and Gibraltar. October 02 to Oct 13, 1962. This photo was taken by ship photographer and for me to get it I had to wait a long time and spend a lot of money. The dots indicate friends and relatives. Dino is the one biting his nails.

a skinny kid to begin with, and I knew that if I did not eat by the end of the ten-day trip, I would probably arrive in New York a skeleton.

A brilliant idea came to my mind—Aunt Teresina's tortano dolce, in my suitcase! It would keep me going for sure. She would understand. She was after all a generous Neapolitan, just like me. She must have been in a similar situation many years before, when she traveled to America for the first time. Surely she wouldn't mind sharing part of it with me. The tortano was a nice size after all, and it would definitely keep me fed for another four to five days until we got to New York. I took a knife from the dining room and cut off a small wedge. Oh boy, was it good!

I wrapped up the remainder of my newfound delicacy and went on my way. The next day I cut another chunk, and soon realized something: Aunt Teresina would likely not be the person I'd be sharing the rest of this tortano dolce with. When I told my green-eyed Calabrese friend about my problems with the food on the ship, she told me at once that she felt the very same thing. I proceeded to tell her about the tortano dolce, and she did not hesitate one moment to ask for a taste.

I happily shared some of my Aunt Teresina's tortano dolce with her, as well as swigs of my sweet vermouth. As the days passed and New York grew closer, so did we. I spent much of those final days on the ship just talking with her. We both knew that once we were off the ship, we might never see each other again, but for the time being, we behaved as if no one else existed.

For the second time in as many weeks, I found myself torn between wanting to reach America and wanting to stop the boat from moving another inch. But either way, America was becoming a reality. My last night on the ship, all my newfound friends and I stayed up late, celebrating our successful crossing. The green-eyed girl sat with her parents across from me in the deck circle. All I could do was lock eyes with her as the night wore on, knowing that this might be our last night together. The long trip was almost over; in the morning we would be in New York and would be passing the Statue of Liberty. Even as we talked and told jokes, I felt time's inevitable passing. I waited for everyone—including the girl from Calabria and her parents—to go back to their cabins for the night before I did the same, falling asleep in my bunk, one last time, alone.

The next morning, I woke up and noticed that the ship was not moving. I looked through the porthole and saw that we were already docked. I had missed seeing the Statue of Liberty. What a disappointment!

The American Experience:
The Pompeiian

Up on deck, still wearing my pajama bottoms and a sweater, I searched in vain for my green-eyed friend from Calabria and for my Lebanese friend as well. Hundreds of passengers were lining up to debark, but I saw no sign of my closest travel companions.

The weather was cloudy and cold. In just a short while I would be stepping onto American soil. Though I was excited, the view in front of me was not the pretty postcard I had left in Naples - a beautiful port with marble walls and tiled floors despite the poor economic conditions the country was in. In New York City, Pier 88 (where the SS *Atlantic* had docked) looked run-down. The green paint that covered the pillars was peeling off, and the concrete floors and ceilings were cracked and looked ready to fall at any moment. I did not get a feeling of care, of wealth. An elevated highway that ran close to the port was also in decrepit condition, looking as if it had been abandoned.

I felt that I must be missing something. Was I really in America? Or was this an unexpected stop the ship had made in a third world country? How could *this* be the land of opportunity and wealth? It was the depressed and gritty condition of the port that had blurred my view of what lay behind it. After my eyes had adjusted to the scene, I noticed that the ugly elevated highway was hiding many beautiful skyscrapers, but the one that stood out was the Empire State Building. A knowledgeable passenger had told me that it was the tallest building in the world. I believed it. Back in Naples, the tallest building was probably only ten stories high. Then I saw big cars, even longer than the ones my cousin Tony had brought to Naples. The place was booming, with taxis coming and going in every direction.

I went down to my cabin, cleaned up, picked up my suitcases, and started to make my way off the ship. Uncle Michele was going to meet me and help me proceed through customs and the passport office. As I was about to pass through the customs office, one of the agents there pointed to his badge and motioned for me to follow him into a small room. I made him understand through gestures that I did not want to leave my suitcases out there in the open. He shoved me, I yelled at him in Italian to watch his manners, and I refused to move. A handful of passengers started to yell at the agent. Then I spotted Uncle Michele, who upon hearing the commotion had come over to see what was going on. In his broken English, he explained to the customs agent that he was my uncle, that this was my first time in the United States, and that I had all the necessary documents. The agent insisted that I go in the small room to see if I was hiding anything on me. Uncle Michele was not allowed to come in, but just knowing that he was waiting out there for me calmed me down. Even still, my treatment at the hands of the customs officer was degrading and dehumanizing. I immediately wished I could go back to where I'd come from. Once this ordeal was over, however, I was able to finally set foot on American soil.

Uncle Michele and I got in a taxi and set off on our way, between the tall buildings of the avenues. Aunt Teresina was happy to see me and asked if I had anything for her. I gave her the gold bracelet her sister Consiglia had sent her. She looked at it, put it on her wrist and then said, "Come on, open the suitcases and let me see the Tortano Dolce your mother sent me."

Oh my God! What was I going to tell her? That the food on the ship was lousy and that I actually survived thanks to the Tortano Dolce? I did not have the guts to tell her the truth, that I had eaten the entire Tortano Dolce. I answered instead, "Zia Teresina I am sorry to disappoint you, but the Tortano started to smell bad and I tossed it out."

To that, Zia Teresina exclaimed, "What do you mean? Do you know that every time I returned from Italy, your mother would make me the Tortano Dolce to take back to America with me?"

Seeing the disappointment in her face, I said, "I know! Remember, I always helped my mother to bake it for you. Evidently, this time something went wrong and the Tortano Dolce went bad, I am sorry."

I believe that I started on the wrong foot with my aunt. In that moment, I regretted having eaten the tortano. The degree of disappointment was evident on her face, and made me realize how much she had looked forward to that treat from the old country, that taste of home. I felt so bad for her. But there was no going back. I had already made up the story. That dry cake fed me for four or five days. But in my mind, I decided that one day I would tell her the truth about the Tortano Dolce.

After that initial disappointment, Aunt Teresina eventually warmed up to me. I knew she liked me. We talked about everybody back home. After lunch, she took me for a walk just a few blocks from her apartment, to Bleecker Street. Back then, Bleecker Street was noisy, bustling, full of stores selling Italian specialties. There were vendors lining the street with push carts, shouting over each other at passing customers—Don Alfonso with his truck of chunky artichokes and boxes of grapes as big as plums, other trucks loaded up with pots and pans, household knives and shiny silverware, cotton smocks and children's shoes stacked in layers like loaves of bread. Aunt Teresina introduced me to the various storekeepers and vendors. Everyone she talked to was kind to her; she had shopped those blocks for decades, and her sons owned a beautiful, popular restaurant nearby called Cafe Pompeiian. Everyone spoke Italian and some even spoke Neapolitan. I felt like I was back in Italy. The only difference between Bleecker Street and Naples was that everything here was big: eggplants the size of footballs, long trunks of celery, carrots like French baguettes, big apples, big oranges, *huge* watermelons. When I would shop in Italy, I would handle the food individually and smell it for ripeness and quality; but here, all the smells swirled together, or maybe the produce itself was too green to give off an aroma yet—too green, just like me.

Out of curiosity, I asked my aunt, "Zia, how come every vegetable we have seen is so big?"

She said, "Oh, you noticed that already? I think they give them..." and she mimicked the motion of squeezing a syringe.

From there, Zia Teresina took me to the Pompeiian, a beautiful building built to resemble the House of Vetti in Pompeii, displaying a sunken-in marble fountain and many statues of Roman characters. The Pompeiian was where I would spend most of my time for the next four or five years, and where I would get acquainted with the American experience in earnest. I didn't realize it yet, but I had found my Bar dei Fiori in New York City.

That afternoon, at the Pompeiian, I spent time with my cousins Gennaro, 42, Giuseppe, 40, and Tony, 38. I was introduced to the waiters, one of whom was a young man from the Abruzzi region of Italy named Ennio Sammarone, and the bartender, a stocky guy named Francisco Aviles, a Puerto Rican who nevertheless spoke Italian quite well. The six of us got on well right from the start. At dinner, I learned that I would be living with cousin Gennaro, who lived on the eleventh floor of a tall building on Houston Street, right across the street from his parents. I had always lived on the ground floor, so I was trying to imagine what it would be like to live all the way up there. But I was happy to be moving in with Gennaro. The year before, when he had visited with my family in Naples, he had made a good impression on me and we seemed to get along well.

After dinner, Gennaro, his plump American girlfriend CG, and I walked to his apartment. It was a one-bedroom, so I was shown to the convertible couch, which was going to be my space in the living room. I went across the street to my Uncle Michele's apartment to pick up my belongings, and when I got back to Gennaro's I was told that CG was not going to live with him anymore. I wondered, *Did my cousin make that decision because of me? Was CG disappointed?* I told Gennaro that I did not want to come between him and his girlfriend. Like the gentleman that he was, he reassured me that CG had her own place in Brooklyn, and that she used both places regularly. So with his blessing, I had my first address in New York: 241 W. Houston Street, Apt 11E right across from the elevator.

A week later, CG brought me a pocket Italian-English dictionary (that I still have) and began to show me around the city. She was very well mannered, knowledgeable, and a very good guide who knew the city well. Her name was Harriet, but my American family referred to her as CG. She did not speak Italian, and Gennaro had asked her to teach me to speak English. Using the dictionary she had given me, the two of us started to converse. One day I asked her, in my broken English, what "CG" stood for, and to my surprise she said *"Culo Grosso,"* Italian for big ass. I blushed when she said that, but then inconspicuously I took a look at her behind and had to admit there was truth in a name.

Gennaro had never recuperated from the illness that had plagued him since he was a young man in Naples. In fact, this, along with other medical issues, may be what had denied him entry to the United States with his family the first time.

He told me that he'd had another brain surgery just two months before I got to New York. He walked with a limp and used a cane. He was epileptic, and when he had a seizure someone had to put a taped stick in his mouth to depress his tongue so he could breathe. We rarely left him unattended. CG was originally his nurse and in time became his girlfriend. Gennaro was a small person with a very big heart, and with time I would learn that no one ever had anything bad to say about him. My father, whenever he talked about Gennaro, never failed to tell me how he loved this particular nephew.

When Gennaro failed his physical to enter the U.S. back in 1924, his parents (my aunt Zia Teresina and Uncle Michele) had to leave him behind to live with Zia Teresina's sister Consiglia, who lived in my father's neighborhood. Consequently, Gennaro ended up spending a lot of time with my father. My father spoke to me so often about Gennaro that I felt close to him even before I met him. In 1936 when my parents got married, they gave Gennaro his own room so he ended up spending even more time with them. The closeness he had with my father was a good thing, but he still missed his family in America. During WWII, Gennaro took advantage of the war-time chaos and stowed away on a ship bound for America. Once in New York he worked in a couple of restaurants, and in 1953 he took over management of the famous Caffe Reggio at 119 MacDougal Street. He stayed there until 1957, then joined his two brothers in opening their own restaurant, the Cafe Pompeiian, at 136 West 3rd Street, in Greenwich Village.

My second day in America was a Sunday, and my Uncle Michele decided to show me how to get to the high school that I was to begin attending the following day. The two of us got on the Seventh Avenue subway at Houston Street. My uncle had already been in New York for thirty-seven years, but told me, "You'll have to bear with me, I don't know thirty-seven American words."

The experiences I had had in Naples—dealing with traffic, riding the trolley, and constantly being pushed by my father to lose my shyness—were suddenly helpful again. Even though I knew even less English than my uncle—just "yes" and "thank you"—I took the paper with the name and address of the school and told him to let me lead the way.

I went over to the train man who operated the doors at each stop and showed him the paper. He must have repeated himself ten times before taking us over to the map posted inside the subway car. He pointed to our stop, which was called "West Farms." Once we arrived at our stop, I looked around and realized that I needed to go into one of the stores to ask for more directions. I went into a donut shop and I was told to get on the Q44 bus and to show the slip with the address to the bus driver. Bingo, we got to St. Helena's Business High School. My poor uncle could not believe it. After walking around the school building for a while to familiarize myself with it, we went back downtown the same way and returned to my uncle's apartment.

High school was not easy, especially for me who only knew two words of English. But with the help of Principal Sister Mary Richards and some of the teachers, I began to adjust. I knew that in order to succeed, I had to learn to read and write English. I enrolled in additional evening classes at the Greenwich House on Barrow Street, just few blocks away from where I lived. The Greenwich House, a settlement house, was started at the turn of the century to assist Italian immigrants settling in the neighborhood. For the next year, I read and spoke only English, pushing myself to the limit. I did not frequent any Italian cafes, no easy feat given how many of them there were in Greenwich Village at that time. In order to increase my exposure to English and immerse myself in the language, I read books and newspapers in English rather than Italian.

Even though Gennaro and Giuseppe together ran the Pompeiian, it was their youngest brother Tony who owned the property. Gennaro was the one who really knew every aspect of the restaurant business. Those few times I had the pleasure of dining with him at the Pompeiian or some other restaurant, he always managed to point out the positive and negative aspects of the dining experience. He taught me a lot: How to deal with employees, how to speak to the salesmen, and most importantly how to treat customers. Giuseppe, on the other end, had a beautiful family and prior to my arrival worked at the Pompeiian just during dinner hours. During the day he worked for his father as a shoe salesman. With Gennaro's prolonged sickness, the Pompeiian became Giuseppe's only occupation.

Gennaro decided to give me an allowance of five dollars a week. Back then, the round-trip ride to school was only thirty cents a day; the remainder I could use to buy a sandwich, a soda, or a French cruller from the donut shop near the bus stop. After two weeks, I found my daily routine: get up at 6:00 AM to get ready for school, take the combined train and bus one hour and forty-five minutes each way, and by 5:00 PM, be back at the Pompeiian for dinner. I always ate whatever the restaurant crew had eaten: pasta, chicken or veal trimmings, nothing expensive of course. Mr. Silvio, the chef, always held my dinner on the side, but if dinner that day had been *Spaghetti with Calamari*, he would make me a fresh batch, as I would not just throw reheated spaghetti down my belly. I would wait for my uncle and aunt to come in, and after they had coffee, we would all walk the short distance home together.

There were many times when Gennaro did not feel well enough to come to the restaurant; in that case I would quickly make him *Tortellini in Brodo,* a dish he enjoyed. We always kept a few cans of Swansons chicken broth in the cupboard and few bags of tortellini in the freezer. After settling Gennaro with dinner, I would walk to the Greenwich House for my two-hour English lesson, return home to do my homework, and go to sleep. This was my typical day during the school week.

On weekends, I would hang out at the Pompeiian doing restaurant chores—filling up the ice bins, loading the glasses behind the bar, and refilling the shelves with liquor and soda bottles. Who knows how many times I had to walk the fifteen blocks to Uncle Michele's shoe factory on the Bowery to pick up a box of sugar packets or canned tomatoes, or whatever else might have been needed in an emergency. The Pompeiian restaurant did not have a basement, so storage space was limited; therefore, the bulk of supplies were stored at the shoe factory. If during business hours the restaurant workers realized that they were out of something, one of the porters or busboys had to make the trip, but if I was around they called on me to run to the factory and bring it to them instead. Once in a while, I would even get tipped.

* * *

Weeks went by, and with my combined income streams of allowance and tips, I eventually saved thirty-five dollars, which I hid in one of Gennaro's books. I don't remember how he found out, but one day he confronted me. Holding the book in one hand and the dollar bills in the other, he asked me, "Michele, do you know anything about this money?"

I told him, "Yes, it's my money, I put it there."

He said, "Can you tell me where you got it from?"

I explained, "Every week you give me five dollars for school, but I only use three dollars and save the other two. As you know, when your employees at the restaurant run out of something, they ask me to pick it up from the shoe factory, and once in a while they give me a dollar for getting it. Christmas is coming and I want to send it to my mother."

Gennaro was touched. He hugged me as if I were his own son and said, "I never thought I could find a person with a bigger heart than mine. You spend these thirty-five dollars on yourself and send your mother this money." He then handed me double the amount I had saved, seventy dollars, and told me to buy a money order and mail it to her.

Somehow, Aunt Teresina and my cousin Giuseppe learned that Gennaro had been giving me five dollars every week, and that from that, I was putting away two dollars. Zia Teresina came into Cafe Pompeiian one night and sat down at the table by the fountain in the middle of the dining room where Gennaro was having his dinner. "Why do you give Michele $5.00 a week? Three dollars a week is plenty!"

Gennaro, who himself was very respectful of his mother, smiled and asked her, how did she know that?

"I know everything," was her answer.

Gennaro became a bit nervous, but defiant nevertheless. "Ma, what I do with my money is my business. And besides, five dollars or three dollars make no difference to me. But two dollars means a lot to that boy."

Later that night, to calm him down, I told my cousin that he shouldn't be angry with his family. In order to keep the peace, he should only give me three dollars. But he didn't want to hear about it, and told me to stay out of that discussion. The following week, when Genaro handed me a five dollar bill, I pushed his hand back.

"Please, from now on, just give me $3.00."

He got very angry and threw the money at me and told me that they should all butt out. After that, I kept my mouth shut, and the $5 a week kept coming.

Gennaro and I spent hours and hours together every week. When business was slow, we would talk at length. He told me things I would never have known otherwise, including many stories about my father, whom he called "Zi Totore," in true Neapolitan fashion. He told me that after my father married my mother, he was the happiest man in the world, because she was a sweet girl and very beautiful. Gennaro was as fond of my father as my father was of him. He told me that even though his parents had left him in Aunt Consiglia's care, he preferred to be with my parents. He was also fond of my mother, who

Cafe Pompeiian

My cousin Gennaro

he called "Zi Mari." Whenever he did not feel well, or if he had a headache (which was often), he would go over to my mother and she would give him aspirin and let him lie down in her bedroom so he'd be more comfortable, as that room was in the rear of the building and away from all the street noise.

I enjoyed listening to these stories, particularly when they were about my parents. He was aware that I missed them, and talking to me about them was his way to alleviate the situation.

Gennaro's health deteriorated rapidly, but still it did not change his attitude; he was always an amiable person. No matter who you talked to, you never heard a bad word about him. Once in a while, he would crack a joke to make people more comfortable around him, as by now his physical appearance had changed dramatically. He had become extremely thin, walked with a cane, and drooled most of the time. Being with Gennaro felt a little like being with my father; though his problems were different, they both benefited from my help, which made me feel useful and even necessary.

I was in the United States on a student visa and was not allowed to work, yet I had so much energy. I thought of getting into sports, but my school didn't offer any. I did not want to be a financial burden to my cousin. During the Christmas holidays I worked at the restaurant full time, and I loved it. When school resumed in January, I decided to ask Sr. Mary Richards, the principal, if it would be possible for me to get a work permit. In all this time I had been in America, she was the only authority I had known. She promised to look into it.

Weeks later I was told to report to her office the next day and bring my passport. She opened it to the last page and wrote a serial number, followed by her name and the school's information. She told me that I could get a job, but I needed to apply for a Social Security number. When I went to the Social Security office, I was just asked for my name and address. I was not asked to produce any documents. A few weeks later, to my surprise, I received my card in the mail.

Trials and Tribulations

My first winter in New York was cold and very long. Back in Naples I never experienced such weather; I had no use for heavy coats. But now I was worried I would freeze to death without one.

Gennaro must have read the preoccupation on my face, because one day he bought me a nice overcoat and a few sweaters. Was I glad he did that! That first winter was also when I experienced snow for the first time. It happened one morning in late November as I was sitting in my classroom. I looked up at the window and noticed all these white flakes coming down, making everything white. It must be snow! I couldn't wait for the lunch break so I could go out and touch it, to experience its feel. I must admit that my first step was embarrassing: I immediately slipped and fell flat on my back, sparking a huge laugh from my school mates. Back in Naples, I would see snow only from a distance, when the top of Mount Vesuvius would get covered in white, sparking the Neapolitan phrase *Mount Vesuvius is wearing the shirt*. Now laying on the ground, belly up and with snowflakes covering my clothes, I had become Mount Vesuvius.

At one point during that long winter, in a moment of weakness, frustrated by all the difficulties, I wrote to my parents complaining about a lot of things: school, the fact that I had become the errand boy for everyone at the Pompeiian, my cousin Gennaro's deteriorating conditions that demanded my care and attention that eventually became my sole responsibility. I wanted to be independent and live on my own. At seventeen I deserved more. Yes, at the moment I had a bed to sleep and food on my plate, but I didn't have to be in America for *that*. I had more than that in Naples. "Papá, life in America is a struggle, for the amount of work that I do and for the money that I make, when I take a dollar out of my pocket, it is like cutting off one of my fingers." Maybe I had been blinded by the way my American relatives behaved whenever they came to Naples—living large, in a beautiful apartment in the most luxurious area of the city, driving fancy cars and dining in the most expensive restaurants. The reality was that life in America—or at least my life—was anything but.

Young and naive while still in Naples, I had gotten the impression that in America, making money was easy. How naive could I have been? Now I realized how hard it was. Most of the jobs in the kitchen were held by non-English-speaking employees who worked for an average pay of seventy-five dollars per week, and the head chef earned less than two hundred dollars. After carrying cases of restaurant supplies on my shoulders for fifteen blocks in extreme weather, sweeping floors, taking out garbage of every size and weight, and running all kinds of errands for everyone, I became convinced that I had made the wrong decision. I could have done better by staying in Italy. Yes, in school in Italy I was only a passing grade student, but I was a hard worker and I would have done well anywhere. These feelings made me miss my family and my beloved Naples even more.

The response from my parents arrived in a letter two weeks later. They told me to pack up everything and come back home. That answer surprised me. Didn't they want me to try to make it work a little harder? Didn't they want me not to give up so easily? Their unquestioning validation of my complaints, combined with the couple of weeks' time that elapsed between the letters, made me realize that I had been foolish in telling them. I was being weak and childish. I also realized that my comments must have made *them* feel guilty about the decision to send me to America in the first place. That decision had been made by all of us, but by writing that letter, I was subconsciously putting the blame on them. Why did I do that? My parents did not deserve that. It had been *my* choice to come as much—or more—than it was theirs; in fact I had had to *beg* them to let me go.

That letter opened my eyes. I resolved to hold on, to resist the urge to go back, and try harder so that one day I would succeed.

At the end of that first school year, I began helping my uncle with various chores at his shoe factory. I spent hours stamping the labels on the insoles of the shoes using a lever-stamp machine. I also helped deliver orders to Bonwit & Teller, Saks Fifth Avenue, and Lord & Taylor—my uncle only sold to the best of the best. He gave me fifty dollars a week for the work. In another new development, I was promoted to work every Friday and Saturday as a busboy at the Pompeiian and made an additional twenty dollars a day. Once a month I would send my mother $100 to help her pay a few debts they had made to buy me clothes for my journey. I also sent money to Sofia, who was by now a teenager, so that she could buy her own clothes and other things a young lady might need. I wanted her to fit in with her friends without depending on my parents. My thinking was that the money might shield her from the need to rely on a bad boyfriend (I couldn't imagine any other kind) to do it for her. Having spent so much time in the streets of Naples, I had seen a lot of bad things, particularly for girls. With my father's disability, Mario in Germany, and me in America, that was my way to protect her.

With the money I was earning, it wasn't long before I was able to move out of Gennaro's apartment and into one of my own. My first apartment was a walk-up flat at 50 MacDougal Street, where the rent was only fifty dollars a month. I lasted there only three months, because the place was infested with roaches. I couldn't live like that. I spent so much money on roach spray that *I* couldn't breathe, and still I could not get rid of them. I found a much better place at 255 Sixth Avenue, at Houston Street. It was a clean one-bedroom apartment well worth one hundred dollars a month. I fixed it up nicely with used furniture I bought at a store on Cornelia Street.

Proud of my new apartment, whenever I could I would have friends over. I still didn't have a steady girl yet, but that didn't mean I wasn't looking for one. One evening, as the restaurant opened for business, two beautiful young ladies about my age came in for dinner. They had the attention of all the waiters and busboys. I approached their table to take the order, and soon realized that that was no easy task. The taller of the two girls had many questions, and not just about the menu. When she asked my opinion about our *Spaghetti al Pesto,* I told her that I had never tasted it, but that everyone who ordered it seemed to like it. She went for it. When I placed the dish in front of her, I waited for her to take her first bite and then asked, "Miss, what do you think? Do you like it?"

"I love it. I never tasted anything better in my life!"

At that, she took a forkful without rolling it and handed it to me to taste. It was absolutely delicious! I was thrilled. The fact that she had me eat from her fork told me that she liked me, so I spent a bit of time at her table teaching her how to twirl spaghetti while thinking that I needed to know more about her and the pasta she was eating. It turned out that in addition to my Genovese taxi driver who convinced me to get back on the ship, I had found something else Genovese that I liked—*Pesto alla Genovese.* And it seemed that the girl with the questions, whose name I learned was Anne, had found something *she* liked too, besides the pasta. From then on, Anne and I dated steadily and my new apartment had its first patron.

One rainy Tuesday evening in February, 1964, I was sitting with my Aunt Teresina at her usual table by the door. The restaurant was almost empty, and the few waiters were in the back by the service bar, having a conversation, completely forgetting to keep an eye at the door. Two gentlemen walked in. My aunt asked me to greet them, something that I had done in the past, even on days I was not working. I approached them and said, "Good evening gentlemen, will you need a table for two?"

One of them said, "No, we are looking for Michele Savarese."

"Oh, you are looking for my uncle. He went to the supermarket and will be back in a few minutes."

The gentleman then said, "Can you tell me your name?" and innocently, I answered,

"My name is also Michele Savarese."

One of the men took out a badge and showed it to me. They were from the Immigration Department. He said, "Come with us. You are in violation of the law."

Pointing to my aunt, I tried to explain, "Sir, actually I am not working. I was having coffee with my aunt who is sitting right there. She asked me to greet you, because the waiters are in the back and had not noticed when you came in."

He said, "I am sorry, we caught you working and you must come with us."

I started to get nervous. This was not fair. First of all, I was not working that evening, but even if I were, I had a permit given to me by Sr. Mary Richards. So remembering my father's admonition, *When in trouble do not react immediately. The first thing you do is to take a deep breath, count to ten and then continue,* I said, "Sir, I have a permit. It is in my passport at home, just a few blocks away from here, please allow me to get it."

Somehow, they realized that I was not lying and gave in to my request, but asked my uncle, who by then had returned, to go to my apartment and get my passport. When he came back with it, I showed the last page with the number and Sr. Richards' information. They were not convinced, and it was too late in the day to call the school, so they kept the passport and told me to report to the Immigration Department in the morning.

That night I had trouble going to sleep. Those officers had come into the restaurant looking for me! How did they know I was working there? They did not ask to see anyone else's documents; they were just interested in me. The Pompeiian, as most other restaurants, employed many illegal workers; how come they did not bother to check anyone else? I convinced myself that once I was able to prove my honesty in the morning, everything would be fixed. I had been in this country fifteen months, I had new friends and finally felt comfortable living in this country, as my English was getting better and better, despite my accent. Could someone have spied on me and reported me to the authorities? Cousin Gennaro's girlfriend CG was the only person I suspected. I was convinced that she might have resented me from my very first day in America, when Gennaro told her to go back to her place in Brooklyn, because I would be moving into his apartment. Again, it was just my suspicion. I had no proof.

Early in the morning, my uncle and I went to the Immigration Department. It was 10:30 AM, and we had already been there for two hours when my name was finally called. I jumped right up and walked over to the official, who was sitting behind one of many desks in a very large room. My uncle followed slowly behind me. The official, pointing at my uncle, asked me if he was my lawyer.

"No sir," I said. "He is my uncle! Why do I need a lawyer? I didn't commit any crime, and I am sure I'll be able to explain."

"It's not that simple," he said. "I have looked at your passport and these numbers in the back mean nothing to me. I want to send you in to see my boss. It will be up to him to decide. Go out and wait."

After another hour, I was called back. This time my uncle and I were taken to a small private office. We sat at a desk as the official behind it, with a pen in his hand, looked down at some notes. I spotted my Italian passport, which was opened to the page with my picture. He looked up and asked me for my name and how long I had been in this country. When he heard my answer—"Fifteen months"—he dialed the phone to his left and without asking me anything else, I heard him say, "An Italian."

We waited until a man arrived who looked at us and addressed me in Italian. He was our interpreter.

The official explained to me that I was in violation of the law and that I was to be deported. Without giving the interpreter a chance to translate, I answered in English, "Sir, I did not violate any laws. I got permission to work from the Principal of my school. Look at the back of my passport and you'll find her name and phone number. Please call her and ask her. I am not lying to you."

The official shouted, "You speak English and you let me order an interpreter? What's wrong with you!"

I meekly answered him, "Sir when you looked up, you asked me for my name and asked me how long I have been here. You did not ask me if I spoke English, and when you dialed your phone, all you said was 'an Italian.' How was I to know that you were ordering an interpreter?"

His face was changing to all colors and expressions. He stood up, leaning on the desk looking at the bare wall behind him and said, "There is nothing I can do for you. You will be detained until your departure is arranged. It may take a few days. Case closed."

I could not contain myself. "You know, sir, with all due respect, if everybody in this country is like you, then I'll be happy to go back, but you will have to take me out of here, because I am not leaving your office on my own. Who are you anyway? I met President Johnson at the American Consulate in Naples, and he welcomed me. Why can't I talk to him now? This year I was going to graduate, and now I'll be left back because you won't do anything to help me. Well, sir, is there anyone in this office who can make such a decision? Because if there is, I'll wait as long as it takes until I see that person."

Without saying a word, the man who had been interviewing me left the room. When he finally returned, he told me to go for lunch and return at 2:00 PM. He handed me a card with directions to one of the upper floors. During lunch, my uncle told me that he was amazed at my courage. Even though he didn't speak much English, he had understood everything. "Anyone in your place would have been terrified!"

But I simply felt that, at that point, I had nothing to lose.

At 2:00 PM, I walked into a big office with just one desk. I was alone, as my uncle had not been permitted to enter, and was waiting just outside the room. Behind the desk sat a short, balding man reading some documents while holding his head in his hands. Next to him, an American flag and a New York State flag stood side by side. Through a large window I could see the Statue of Liberty right below us. The two skyscrapers of World Trade Center weren't built yet, so from that window I had a clear view of the statue. The gentleman behind the desk got up and extended his hand to me, and I shook it with dignity and hope. He invited me to sit in a chair that was positioned sideways to his desk, from which I could still see the statue.

In a low tone, as if I was talking to myself, I said, "When my ship went by that statue, America took on a bigger meaning to me. Liberty was no longer just a word to me, it had a shape and a face. It meant hope, work, honesty, freedom. Yes, I came here as a student. I wanted to work, so I asked the Mother Superior, the principal of my school, who gave me permission, I honestly thought that I was working legally."

The man stopped me with a wave of his hand, saying, "I spoke to Sr. Mary Richards a few minutes ago, and she confirmed everything you have been saying. She also said that you are a good student and a hard worker. Not only does she see you graduating, but she remembers the first day she met you, when you did not even know one word of English. She says she wished that she had more students like you."

He continued, "We are going to waive the fact that you were caught working and allow you to stay until June, which will give you time to graduate. Your case is different than the ones we come across every day. I am glad we were able to remedy the situation." He paused, then said, "Tell me, do you have a girlfriend?" I told him that I did, and he continued, "Are you planning to marry her?"

Surprised at his question, I said, "Sir, I am only eighteen years old. I don't think I am ready to be married. Besides, I am not sure my parents would agree."

He nodded. "Either way, you have a lot of time in front of you. Good luck."

I thanked him with all my heart and left. When I told my uncle the outcome, he embraced me and said, "I can't believe you beat them!"

He had wasted his whole day because of me, but it'd been worth it.

* * *

Through correspondence, I explained the situation to my parents. Their firm response was for me to graduate and to return to Naples. I respected my parents' decision, but it did not sit well with me. I was not ready to go back yet. In the time that I had been here, I had made many friends, I was working, I had learned the language, I was living independently in my own apartment, and I had Anne. She was from Massachusetts, and her family had been in America for many generations. That weekend, I told her of the problem I'd had with the Immigration Department and that the only way for me to stay here for good was to get married. At first, she had a big laugh, until she realized that I was serious. We were good together, but it was too soon. We were inexperienced. However, after a couple of months, we decided we would get married but would wait until the current school year ended. Neither my parents nor hers were happy with our decision, so we decided to find a state where a young man could be married without parental consent. We were told that in Washington DC we could do it.

At the end of May, once the school year was over, Anne and I went to Penn Station and boarded a train, which arrived in Washington DC about lunch time. At City Hall we learned that I still needed parental consent there, and were suggested to go to South Carolina. That night we slept inside Union Station, because early in the morning we had to catch *another* train for South Carolina. We decided to get off in Florence, SC. How appropriate! I had never been to Florence Italy, but soon I would be in Florence SC, which I hadn't even known existed. Yet something told me that in this Florence, there was no chance I would meet Michelangelo, Leonardo or Lorenzo dei Medici.

We arrived in Florence that evening and began to ask for information at the station. We were directed to a taxi driver who knew the city well. We explained that we were there to get married. He knew exactly where to take us. We hopped in his cab and he drove us to this fancy-looking house in the suburbs. We stayed in the taxi as the driver went up the stoop and spoke to a heavy-set man in his house robe. When the driver came back, he said quite a few things, but I could not understand his Southern accent. Anne nervously yanked me out of the car and up the stairs.

The Judge took us into his study and spoke to us for a while. Anne was doing most of the talking. The Judge called on his wife and the cab driver to be witnesses as Anne and I took our oaths. He then asked us to stay for a bite to eat. It must have been evident that we had not eaten in a while and the nice lady brought us sandwiches and coca cola. When we finished, the judge gave us a signed document and told us that the next day we needed to go to city hall to pick up our marriage license. He gave the taxi driver some information to make sure he knew where to take us. We left that house completely flabbergasted by the way we were treated—southern hospitality, I suppose.

The driver took us to an inexpensive hotel back in the city. We paid him well and begged him to pick us up in the morning and stay with us until we got our license. I don't even know what Florence, SC looks like, because we were there less than twenty four hours. As soon as we got the license, we were back in the cab on our way to the train station to return to New York. Quite an adventure. And in the end, our marriage was just that as well—an adventure, exciting in the moment, but over fast.

About a month later, I received my green card. I started to work full-time as a waiter at the Pompeiian, and shortly thereafter I became the dining room captain. Giuseppe was running the restaurant by himself as Tony had moved permanently to Palm Springs tending to his own business, and Gennaro was confined at home due to his illness. Over the next few months, Giuseppe tried to break in a couple of guys to help him manage the Pompeiian, to no avail. When he offered me that position, I accepted immediately, as I was always eager to take on new challenges.

Winter of 1965 was another important paragraph in my life. Usually January and February were bad months for business, due to the weather, though restaurants in Greenwich Village rarely noticed the difference, doing business as usual. However, that winter was so bad that we had to lay off a few employees. One was Francisco, my friend the bartender. In the weeks that followed, he would drive by in his Chevrolet Impala to check if business was improving, maybe stop for a bite to eat and a chat. On one of these visits, I noticed that he was in pain and looking unusually pale. At one point he made a face and put his hand on his belly.

"Francisco, you need to go to the hospital."

"But my car!"

"Leave the car here. I'm taking you there right now."

We got in a cab and went to St. Vincent's emergency room, a few blocks away. Thank *God* we did that, because they admitted him immediately with what they termed as "Peritonitis." I had no idea what that meant, but I felt better knowing that he was in good hands, so after moving his car to his apartment, I went back to work.

A day or two later, I went for a visit and found his wife sitting there next to him. Apparently they had operated on him the day he arrived, and discovered that he was in serious medical jeopardy. So when his wife saw me, she said, "Thank you so much for forcing him to do something! This idiot would have gotten himself killed if it wasn't for you!"

He was laying in the bed, all wrapped and unable to bend. But he was all smiles. "Thanks, *amico*. By the way, what did you do with my car?"

I joked, "I sold it!"

He laughed, and winced, and I laughed more. But his wife has more complaints.

"Look at him, Michele! He needs a shave...I can't look at him the way he is."

I laughed, went out, and got him a shaving kit. When I got back, we gave him a nice shave, and I continued to do so until he was able to shave himself.

"By the way," I told him, scraping off his beard one day. "My cousin says as soon as you get well, you can have your job back."

He smiled. I thought he was happier about that than the fact that he was going home soon.

Francisco was back at work before too long, but it took a lot longer for business to pick up sufficiently to welcome the rest of the laid-off staff. In particular, we'd had to let go the second chef in the kitchen. But we still needed someone to do the job. I had always been front of house until then, but out of necessity I jumped into that spot and worked side by side with our chef, Silvio, a nasty guy with an even nastier mouth. (The funny thing was that Silvio's brother Ervi was the sweetest man you could ever meet, so *he* got to work up front with all the customers.) But by virtue of Silvio's short temper, (he didn't allow mistakes in the kitchen), I learned a lot from him, so much that I would eventually replace him on his days off. I would cook dishes like *Spigola alla Livornese* and *Pollo alla Paesana* so well that our customers couldn't notice any difference. As spring grew, so did the business. We re-hired our errant employees, and I went back to my job as dining room captain. The experience I got working in the kitchen those months was incredible, though, working side by side with one of the best chefs in Manhattan.

That spring, after divorcing Anne, Gennaro took a turn for the worse; he could no longer afford to pay rent due to his health problems and dwindling savings. I took him in to live with me and gave him my room, while I slept on the couch. A group of us, his New York based family, chipped in to watch him throughout the day, but in the evenings he preferred to be alone, so he could enjoy his favorite TV shows.

One night in late May when I got home from work, I found Gennaro sprawled on the bathroom floor, clutching his toothbrush in one hand. I thought he was dead. "Gennaro! Gennaro, what's going on?"

His eyes flung wide open, desperate. He was unable to get up. But even though I could tell he was relieved to see me, the first thing he said to me was, "Why the hell are you so late tonight?!"

"Gennaro, this is the time I always get home when I lock-up."

"Oh, sorry." He seemed more surprised at his confusion about the time than anything.

"How long have you been on the floor?"

"I don't know, half hour, one hour? Help me up."

I felt so bad for him, he was all skin and bones. He couldn't even lift himself up, and I was afraid to, for fear of hurting him further. I called his brother Giuseppe, who rushed the four blocks to my apartment. A few minutes later, my downstairs uncle and aunt appeared with Giuseppe, and together we all processed the seriousness of the moment. Meanwhile, Gennaro remained on the floor, toothbrush still in hand.

We called the ambulance, and they took him to Lenox Hill Hospital. In the last five or six years after his brain surgery, he had been to that hospital many times, but on this particular visit it seemed that there was not much that doctors could do. In fact, all they did was to make him comfortable (this was before the concept of palliative care). He wouldn't eat. Thinking the reason was that he didn't like hospital food, I would have Silvio prepare him some of his favorite dishes and, because my cousin was such a ladies man, I had Silvio make extra for his nurses too. Every evening I brought it over, and we would have dinner in his room together.

In those three weeks that Gennaro was in the hospital, I made eighteen trips there, carrying boxes of his favorite foods and becoming familiar with his favorite nurses. And so it was the middle of June when one of them pulled me to the side and, in confidence, said, "I don't think he's gonna make it too far, Michael. He doesn't look good at all. He weighs only 57 pounds, and his eyesight is going. It's probably just a matter of days. I'm sorry."

Gennaro passed away on June 19, 1965, and with him, I lost my best friend in New York. He was my mentor, my motivator, and the only person that truly loved me in America. I will always miss him.

My Turn To Buy Gelato

In the summer of 1966, in a letter to my parents, I told them that I was thinking of taking a trip back to Naples, but did not specify the exact date because I wanted it to be a surprise. September 26 that year was a beautiful sunny day. I took a taxi to Kennedy airport carrying two very full suitcases; I was bringing something for everyone. For my father, I brought a braille watch and a white retractable cane that I bought at a store on Eight Street that specialized in accessibility supplies. For my mother, a beautiful pearl necklace.

This was to be my very first time on an airplane. The first leg of my trip, from New York to Rome, was beautiful, I loved it. The second leg, from Rome to Naples, was horrific. It was a small propeller plane, and the air pockets *en route* were so bad that my stomach was in my mouth the whole time (but thankfully I never vomited on my dress shirt). I was very relieved when we finally landed in Naples.

It felt good to be back on Italian soil. By that point I had been away four years. It was a beautiful sunny morning and I was excited. When I got behind the wheel of my rental car, I realized that it had a standard transmission, which I was not familiar with. I tried to negotiate for an automatic, but there were none available. While sitting in the car with the door open, stumped by the clutch, I noticed that a taxi driver was looking in my direction with curiosity.

I went over to his taxi, ducked my head inside the window, and said in Neapolitan dialect, "I don't know what to do with the clutch, can you help me?" That Good Samaritan spent an *hour* teaching me how to shift gears and the use of both feet and hand coordination, free of charge. With him sitting in the passenger seat, I drove around the airport quite a few times, and finally I was ready for the traffic in Naples. At least that's what I *thought*.

From the airport to the center of the city, I had no problem. But once I left the highways for the denser street grid and its heavy traffic,

I stalled so many times that my left knee was nervously shaking from working the clutch. On one of the hills, I had to come to a stop to allow the cross traffic to pass by. When I released the brake pedal and engaged the first gear, the car began to roll back. The cars behind me honked madly, as if that would get me over the hill. I needed space to roll back, but I didn't have it. Instead, I had an idea.

"I'm driving a clutch, and I don't know how to do it!" I yelled out the window at the car behind me. "How 'bout you let me just roll into your bumper nice and slow, so you can stop me, and then I can engage and get out of your way?"

He actually helped guide my back slowly so I wouldn't cause any damage to his bumper. From my resting spot against the front of his car, I was able to let out the brake and engage the first gear and get up and out of his way. Finally, I made it over the hill. Sweat was coming out of all my pores. I was drenched, but grateful. Once again, Naples proved it could come to the rescue when needed, even if it was part of the problem in the first place (steep hills and traffic congestion).

As I approached the outskirts of the city, the roads lightened up, and with less stop-and-go traffic my manual transmission driving improved. It was "high noon" as I turned onto my street. When I was about one block away from my building in Barra, I spotted a familiar-looking couple walking in the middle of the Street. It was my parents returning from a morning of shopping, (by the way, this was the exact spot where the bomb that killed my brother Pierino exploded 22 years before).

My mother was carrying a bag with her right hand, and with her other arm she held my father, who was carrying his own bag with his free hand. I thought of having a little fun, so as my car closed behind them, I tapped lightly on the horn. This sweet, mild-mannered lady who I had not seen in four years turned around and, in my dialect, nastily yelled: "Hey, Just go around!"

I couldn't believe my ears. I put the car in neutral, pulled the hand brake, jumped out of the car, and cried, "Ma!"

My poor mother - the shock was too much. Her legs gave, and she grabbed onto my father while muttering my name: "Miché? Miché…!"

My father was trying to understand what was happening while he was doing his best to keep her from falling.

"Papá! It's me, Michele!"

I grabbed my mom, hugging and kissing her for a long while. My father put the bag down and squeezed himself to us in a tight embrace. Vincenzo Pesce, a neighbor who had been standing there observing the scene, offered to drive the car to our building so I could walk with my incredulous parents the final block to our apartment.

As soon as we were home, my mother picked up the phone (yes, to my surprise, not only did they have a telephone, they also had a *refrigerator*. A lot can change in four years) and made a couple of calls. Within half an hour, our house was filled with people. Mrs. Pelillo and Dino, my cousin Michele and his wife Assuntina, Mrs. Oliviero from across the street and her daughter, Pinuccia, and my sister Sofia, who had become a beautiful young lady, though now with a sixteen-year-old skinniness. Then came Antonietta and her husband Gianni, along with their little daughter, Mena—a brand new addition to the family. A while later, Don Tommasino and Gigino arrived. I asked about Mario, since he had just moved from Mannheim back to Naples to raise his family there. My mother told me that he and his wife, Titina, were living in an old building in the historic district, a very popular neighborhood known as *Quartieri Spagnoli,* or the Spanish Quarters. Mario didn't have a telephone yet, and my mother thought it would be fun to surprise *him*, the way I had done with *her*. But first: Food.

With the help of my sisters and Mrs. Pelillo, my mother put together a nice dinner, and once the curious neighbors left, we sat down to eat. Because of the excitement of the moment, that was one of the few times in my life that the food I was eating was not my main focus. There must have been twelve or fourteen of us, including the Pelillos. My mother was ecstatic. Normally she was a quiet person, but now she could not stop telling Antonietta and Don Tommasino how I had surprised her and my father on the street. Everyone wanted to know how I was settling in America, and whether I would eventually move back one day. I deflected their questions as best I could, because the truth was I didn't know.

By the time dinner was over, I was exhausted after such a long and exciting day, but I was too wound up, having a great time and just could not think of sleep. While having an espresso and without consulting with my mother, I told everyone to come for dinner that very Sunday, and that I was going to cook the entire meal. My mother looked at me bewildered as I started to make arrangements to get what I needed to cook that meal. When I said goodbye to my brother-in law, I told him to come a bit early and bring a good amount of clams. I told Sofia to get butter and heavy cream, and told Antonietta to bring a few pastries.

After dinner, it was time for another surprise. Along with my parents and Sofia, we drove to Mario's apartment, about twenty minutes away. When we got there, the younger ones—Sofia and I—ran up to the front of the building and rang the doorbell. We heard the fourth floor balcony door open up overhead, but we were hidden by the balcony itself, and we heard Mario's wife Titina call down to see who it was. My mother waved up, and Titina buzzed them (and us) in.

Sofia and I bounded upstairs, racing each other up the four floors of spiraling stairs. Mario stood outside his apartment door looking down. When he saw Sofia with me right behind her, he realized who I was. What a shock! He started running downstairs, and when he reached us he began to sob uncontrollably, something I could not believe. When we had lived together in the projects, before he had emigrated to Germany, he never showed any type of affection for me. When he left in 1958, I was only twelve, then four years later I left for America and he was still in Germany. We had not seen each other for eight years. He was looking at me in disbelief. I had grown much taller than him. I was no longer the boy who shined his shoes on Sundays. I was a man.

"Look at what this *little shit* has become! Let me look at you." He pulled me in for a hug, and his tears were so strong they wet my shoulder and brought tears to my eyes as well. My parents were euphoric; they could not contain their happiness. My mother would not stop telling Titina how I had surprised everyone. It was a moment I'll never forget.

That Sunday, I took my dad on a trolley ride to Naples and brought him to an early mass at Madonna del Carmine Maggiore, in his old neighborhood. After shopping for ingredients for my grand meal that afternoon, we stopped at Bar dei Fiori, where I was received like an exiled monarch. Don Gaetano Esposito and his wife could not believe their eyes at how much I had grown. Their sons were happy to shake my hand. Mr. Gargiulo, the manager, joked, "You came in just in time. I need a hand to redo the display case."

I told him, "Mr. Gargiulo, I know you're joking, but you wouldn't believe how many times in America I wished that I had been here helping you with your chores instead."

Papá and I got home in early afternoon. My mother was frantic and instead of greeting us cried, "Miché! When are you going to start cooking? Everyone is going to be here within an hour!"

"Ma, relax! By the time everyone's at the table, I'll be ready."

Sofia came in and brought me the heavy cream and butter. Gianni arrived carrying a bag of clams. Mario and Titina brought veal from their neighborhood butcher. I thanked them all and then ordered them out of the kitchen, and only then did I start to prepare the meal of *Clams Oreganate*, *Fettuccine Alfredo* and *Veal Scaloppine al Marsala*.

The day before, I had done my *own* shopping and preparation for that meal. Now, with all my ingredients spread out before me, I put on my mother's apron and began to cook. I made good use of the new (to me) refrigerator and set to preparing my *oreganata* filling for the clams. I sautéed the onions, washed and boiled the mushrooms for the Veal Marsala, and hand cut all the fresh fettuccine to size.

Now that I had sent everyone out of the kitchen, I started to bang things around to get everything going. Antonietta walked in and said,

"Brother. You really are serious, aren't you? But do you have to be so *noisy?*"

"My dear sister, when I cook, I always imagine that I'm inside the kitchen of a restaurant. Who cares about noise? I need to produce."

"C'mon, are you telling me that your customers don't complain about all the clatter? Man, I'd run out of there in a minute."

I paused, looked at her from top to bottom, and said, "You are clearly dying to see what I am doing. So put on an apron and start helping me."

Immediately she pulled up the sleeves of her dress and dug right in. We were done in less than one hour.

As I dished out the clams, Antonietta cleaned herself up. I walked into the dining room to announce, "Come and get it! I made it for you, don't think I'm going to bring it to you too."

They all looked at me with the sweat rolling down my face like I'd just run a marathon, and Gianni, Antonietta's husband, said: "Yeah, and if my wife hadn't come in the kitchen, we'd be lucky if we ate by midnight!"

We all laughed and began to stuff our mouths. They all enjoyed the food, except my sister Sofia, who was still a finicky eater. Butter and cream were decidedly *not* part of her diet. As my cousin Michele was wiping his plate with a piece of bread, he looked at me and exclaimed, "American food is delicious!"

All gathered at the table agreed, and they all spontaneously clapped their hands. This was the moment I had been waiting for. Throwing my fingers down and shaking them in the excited Neapolitan gesture for, *What are you, stupid?,* I exclaimed, "What American food? In America, they call this *Italian* food!"

I cannot describe the surprised expressions on their faces.

You see, until that very moment, my family had never experienced any foods outside of Neapolitan cuisine, which is made up primarily of olive oil, tomatoes, fresh herbs, pasta, pizza, and, of course, fish.

During my first week back in Naples, my mom cooked all of my favorite dishes— *Bistecca alla Pizzaiola, Stocco (Baccalà) alla Siciliana*, Eggplant *Parmigiana, Spaghetti alla Puttanesca, Pasta e Fagioli*, and Ziti with *Ragu*. Those were the days when I was spoiled the most. "Ma" I said, "one day you have to make me *Mafalde con ricotta*."

Over coffee each morning my mother would ask me what I wanted for lunch and dinner, and she and my father would then go food shopping. Every afternoon, after lunch, I would take a nap. She would wake me up with the smell of espresso. While I was drinking it, she would ask me to take her for a car ride to her new favorite *gelateria*. After a quick rinse, I would throw some clothes on and off we went. I'd take her and my father to Piazza St. Luigi overlooking the bay of Naples from the hill of Posillipo. She was so thrilled to be up there with me, when I said, "Mamma, this is my turn to buy gelato." From her facial expression, I could tell how proud she was. Then we would take a stroll across the street to admire the view from up there.

Leaning on the wall, looking down at the Bay of Naples, we would talk about so many things. My mother wanted to know all about the last four years away from home, my experience being on the ship crossing the Atlantic Ocean, if my father's precautions to keep me from getting seasickness had worked. She wanted to know how I got along with our relatives, but she was particularly interested to know about the horrible sickness that led to Gennaro's death. She asked how I spent my days, about my school, my work, and about Uncle Michele and Aunt Teresina.

"Did she like the Tortano Dolce I made her?"

"Ma," I said, feeling uncomfortable, "the Tortano never made it to America. I ate it!"

She covered her mouth in disbelief. "What? How come?"

"Ma, I couldn't eat the food they served on that ship, it was *awful*. Your Tortano saved me from starving." I paused. "By the way, you know how much I liked your Tortano, but out there on the ocean it tasted even better."

She gave me a faint smile and in a passive way she said, "Oh my, she must have been very disappointed about that. It's okay, I will make her a small one so you can bring it to her when you go back."

Then in her usual, mild-mannered way she grabbed my arm. "Miché, you have to know that your father has you on his mind all the time. When I bring him his coffee in the morning, after the first sip, he never fails to say, 'Maria, now Michele is sleeping, because he is six hours behind us.' At lunch, before he takes the first bite, he stands, looks west in the direction of America, and sends you his blessings, and he does the same every Sunday and every holiday. He sits constantly by the radio hoping to catch news of America, to hear the weather conditions in New York. Often he asks Sofia to read your letters over again. He keep every one of them in their original envelopes and carries them in his coat pocket all the time. You are *always* with him. Lately, he has been playing lotto more aggressively than usual in hopes that he'll win lots of money so you will move back."

While my mother and I leaned against the parapet in conversation, my father would sit peacefully at one of the outdoor tables of the corner coffee bar across the street. He would sip his Campari and soda happily, knowing that I was there, just across the road and not across the ocean. When my mother and I joined him at his table, we would all have an espresso, and he would proudly light a cigarette from one of the packs of American cigarettes I had brought for him. Those were unforgettable moments.

After a week, I returned the rental car and used my sister Antonietta's Fiat 600 to get around. I asked Gigino to take a few days off and come with me to Rome. I had never been there, and though we didn't have much time to tour the city, I wanted to visit the Vatican. When I walked past Michelangelo's Pieta into St. Peter's Basilica proper, I was astounded not just by the beauty of the space, but by the sound. There was a hum, the collective texture of all the visitors' whispers lifting up into the cathedral space and becoming something not quite of this earth. I could have stood there forever, but unfortunately we only had ten minutes.

After Rome, we drove to Genoa. I needed to spend time in Genoa to find out the distance between the port and the main train station. I had to know. So many times I thought of the Genovese taxi driver and how he, a total stranger, had been instrumental in my future that day of indecision on (and off) the boat.

It was only now that I discovered the distance was only about ten blocks, and that the cab driver had done me such a deed in keeping me close to the ship. Afterward, Gigino and I went to a small trattoria near the port, and I finally had the chance to try some real *Spaghetti al Pesto*—Anne's favorite—straight from its Genoese motherland. We returned to Naples a few days later, and I spent two more delicious weeks with my family before my inevitable return to New York. When I said my goodbyes, my mother uttered a phrase she would repeat to me each time I returned to America:

"Miché! Am I going to see you again?"

And my answer to her was always the same:

"Si, Mammina, you are."

On the plane back to New York, I made a promise to myself that I was going to make it my business to go back once a year. With time I was able to keep that promise.

Back and Forth

When I returned to New York, I resumed work at the Pompeiian. I learned that Giuseppe wasn't getting along with his brother Tony. The loss of Gennaro had affected the two brothers a great deal. Giuseppe went off on his own and purchased a restaurant in Greenwich Village, The Chez Vous on Carmine Street, just a few blocks from the Pompeiian. (It was *called* The Chez Vous, but the only two French things about it were its name and the *Coque au Vin*. In all other respects, it was as Italian as they come.)

Tony had actually moved to Palm Springs, California a few years prior. He became tired of making the trek to New York and decided to sell the Pompeian. I took this as an opportunity to jump ship and enroll in technical school to further my education. I had harbored notions of going back to school for a while to achieve something more than the restaurant business. One year later I graduated from the Albert Merrill School certified in computer programming.

However, immediately after graduating I realized that I had no passion for technical work. I was a 'people person.' I could not sit at a desk looking at the wall while working on some giant sheets of paper. I missed the glamour of the restaurant business, the experience of serving people, and the opportunity to make them happy. I loved the fact that I didn't have to be at work early in the morning and could stay out late and enjoy the city nightlife. Staring at spreadsheets all day would not have given me the opportunity to interact with show business personalities, prominent politicians, and important Wall Street executives.

When I wrote to my parents about the fact that computer programming was not for me, my father's response was: "It is your life, and you are capable of making the correct decision. Throughout the time you were in computer school, I always had dreams of you inventing the next generation of computers that would change the world." I was sorry to disappoint him, but that future wasn't for me.

Word got to my cousin Giuseppe that I had changed my mind about my programming job search, and he offered me a turn as a waiter and part time manager of his restaurant. I was happy to take it. I helped him run all aspects of the restaurant business, ordering supplies, doing the bills and the payroll. I rented a studio apartment in the same building, directly above the Chez Vous. In the five years I had been in New York, I had already lived at six different addresses. I moved so often my cousin Giuseppe teased me by asking if I lived out of a suitcase. Now I was living and working in the same building.

The Chez Vous did a good lunch business, but dinner was kind of slow. I was of the opinion that the stretch of Carmine Street where the restaurant was located was too dark and remote. Customers with reservations were often late for their table because they could not find the restaurant. I discussed the situation with Giuseppe and convinced him to let me take a crack at it. I designed and built two electrical signs to make the place visible from a distance. Papá would have been proud of my electrical skills. Dinner trade improved significantly as the facade now could be seen from Seventh Avenue to the west and Bedford Street to the east. I wasn't making as much money as I had been at the Pompeian, but I didn't mind. Life was good. I had my new home.

In March of 1967, as I was coming out of Minetta Garage in Greenwich Village, I tripped on a piece of broken sidewalk and broke my knee. I also hurt my back so badly that I was hospitalized in St. Vincent's for ten days. While in the hospital, my cousin Tony sent one of his lawyer friends, Peter Canevari, who was interested in the dynamics of my accident. He told me that my injuries suggested that I might be away from work three to four months; he was sure this merited a case against the garage, even though it might take years to settle. I signed the papers to begin proceedings.

My hospital room was known as "the cage room," as every one of the ten or twelve beds there was equipped with a sort of cage-structure to help the patients prop up limbs in casts. All I could think was the fact that I would be out of work for three to four months—and would not get paid, as I made my living mostly on tips. What was I going to do for money? What about rent and the monthly check I sent to my parents?

When my friend Francisco Aviles—the bartender at the Pompeiian—came to visit me a day or two later, he was surprised to see me so depressed. He asked me if anything was wrong, besides the obvious.

"Francisco, I have so many problems. First of all, I won't be able to work, and I might lose the apartment. Plus, if I don't send money to my parents in Italy, they're gonna be worried sick."

Francisco smiled. "Do you remember when I had that bout of peritonitis? You put me in a cab, and together we went to the hospital. After that you came every other day to shave me, and even lent me money because I couldn't work"

"Let me tell Amanda that you'll come to live with us for few months, until you're back on your feet." He lived in west Harlem with his wife, and I never dreamed he would go so far out of his way and make me part of his household.

I ended up subletting my apartment for six months to two nurses who worked on the same floor as my hospital room. They liked to come by my cage to check on me, and even bring my favorite ice cream, Breyers butter almond. The problem was, whenever they brought it, I couldn't rest until I'd eaten the whole thing. Those days were some of the least healthy but most pampered in my life.

After ten days, I was released from the hospital and I moved in to the small apartment on Broadway and 107th. Francisco's wife Amanda was also Puerto Rican and like him, she loved to cook. Even though she had a job, every night we ate a very tasty dinner, thanks to her. Rice and beans was *my* favorite, along with the occasional flan. I lived with them until the sublet was finished and I could move back to my own apartment.

* * *

In the spring of 1969, two years after the accident, something miraculous happened. I got a phone call from Mr. Canevari with a piece of news. The insurance had decided to settle the case. The result was a payout of $32,000. My salary at the restaurant at that time averaged $7,000 a year. Suddenly, a vacation back to Italy sounded like a possibility. But first, I had some debts to pay.

The first thing I did was to buy a top-of-the-line console television for Uncle Michele and Aunt Teresina. This was my way of saying thanks for all that they had done for me during my transition to America. After that, I was almost at a loss of what to do next.

Besides the insurance settlement, I had saved a fair amount of money working lunch and dinner shifts six days a week, three years in a row. I decided to take a long leave of absence and go to Italy.

In fact, I considered moving back to Italy permanently. Seven years had passed since I left my home country for my American adventure. Here in New York, I had many good friends, had a comfortable apartment, a car and finally, money in the bank.

But I missed the warmth and the love of my parents. The real truth was that ever since that day in 1962 when I left Italy, I had carried with me an anguish over leaving them. My absence must have been very painful for them. Unfortunately it was one I lacked the ability to alleviate, since leaving America would have meant giving up all the things that positioned me to help them in the first place. Now the settlement money changed all that. Suddenly I could afford to leave New York without leaving behind my ability to support myself, as well as them. I calculated that, by adding my savings to the insurance settlement, I would be able to open up my own business back in Naples.

For months I went back and forth in my head over what to do. Many of my old friends in Italy had moved on to careers in Rome, Cremona, Sardinia. Only Gigino was left, but that was only because he was still in school and eventually he would leave as well. But I decided to make the move anyway. I left my apartment above the Chez Vous, sold all the furniture, sold my car and shipped my belongings to Naples. I moved in with my friends Enzo Terra and Natalino Di Lullo on Thompson Street for my last three weeks in the New York.

Just a few days before my departure, however, my roommates and another friend, Benedetto di Benedetto, approached me with a proposition. They had a chance to buy a pizzeria in Parsippany, NJ, and were short $5,000 to complete the $20,000 purchase price. I gave them the money and told them that whatever decisions they wanted to make would be OK with me, as long as I got 25% of the shares.

When I returned to Naples I was twenty-four years old. I had money in my pockets and even more in the bank. I bought a Fiat 124. Despite my love for sports cars, I was never a splurger. I traveled by helicopter to Capri two times, just to impress two girls I had been dating in New York when they visited. I took a few skiing trips with friends. I was living large. My parents had moved to a new apartment complex, built by the government to replace the old "Mussolini Projects." (It only took nineteen years!) This apartment was on the third floor of a five-story building and had two bedrooms, a dining room, a big kitchen, and a full bathroom. It even had two balconies, something I had always wanted. I loved the one by the kitchen, because of its clear view of Mt. Vesuvius.

During this time, I came to understand my mother's character even better. On one occasion, I brought one of the girls I had been dating over to meet my parents. After dinner, my girlfriend and I sat on the balcony to enjoy the beautiful view of the volcano (it was summer, so no "shirt" on the peak today), flooded by the moonlight. But I could sense my mother's uneasiness.

"Ma, are you okay? Is something bothering you?"

"Miché...I'm wandering where is this girl staying tonight?"

"In my room, why?"

"Then what about *you*? Where will you sleep?"

Her question surprised me. "Ma, in New York, this girl has lived with me for quite a long time. She'll stay in my room."

My mother was shocked by my answer, and said, "In America, you do things your way. But in *my* house? You do it *my* way. Your girlfriend can stay here with us, and you'll be going over to Antonietta's tonight. Tomorrow morning, get here early so you can take good care of her. She is our guest after all, and I want her to be comfortable."

After that, whenever I was with a girl we would disappear for a few days, just short road trips for sightseeing. Upon my return I would have to endure the same rant from my parents each time: "How long do you think your money will last? At this rate, you will be broke before Christmas!"

Winter did not bring me any 'visitors,' so I was able to hold onto my money. That was a good thing, because I had ideas for it. I began to explore plans for going into business in Italy. I was told of a bar-pasticceria that was up for sale ten minutes' drive from my parents' house, in San Giovanni a Teduccio. I began to visit the area to check on the business, often with my brother-in-law Gianni accompanying me. One day, as we were engaged in conversation with the pastry shop's proprietor, someone came in through the doorway, a mobster-type with his arrogant stride and presumptive attitude. At his appearance, the owner got up and, together with the thug, disappeared into the back. Gianni and I shook our heads at each other, disappointed in this development, but we stayed seated until the two men returned, and the thug made his exit from the shop.

"My apologies for the interruption, gentlemen. So anyway, where were we?"

Gianni checked his watch, and I spoke up: "No problem, no problem! Let's resume tomorrow because, unfortunately we have somewhere we need to be. A few minutes later, we left the bar.

Walking back up Viale Due Giugno, I turned to Gianni and said, "So, what do you make of it?"

He spit. "I don't like it."

"Me neither. It's *pizzo*, I'd put money on it." I paused a moment.

"But actually, this is a good thing."

"Losing your preferred location is a good thing?"

"No, but realizing that it was a trap, it is a good thing that I didn't step into it".

After this, I couldn't shake the feeling that Naples was no longer for me. The mentality there was different from what I had grown used to in New York; people were petty, close minded, afraid to make moves. I had gotten accustomed to a different way of doing things. America was where I belonged, for good or ill.

In spring 1970, after six months in Italy, I told my parents that I had decided to go back to the United States. My parents' love was important to me, but I needed to go back to my life—and my life, I now realized, was in New York.

During this period I spent a lot of time with my parents, to make up for all the lost years abroad, and the fact that I was about to leave again. The three of us, and occasionally Sofia, would go out for dinner so my mother didn't have to cook so much. I loved anything that would make her happy, that would make her feel like a queen, and I have to say that she totally embraced that role. She was proud of her son, and she was content to let herself be pampered—for a little while, at least.

One day, sitting in a nice little trattoria in Barra, my father said something to me out of a spontaneous excess of pride : "Miché, I feel that one day you will own your own restaurant in America, and I will not die until that happens." I didn't give much thought to it at the time, but later I would look back on this moment with complex emotions and regret.

In the meantime, I had kept in touch with Natalino in New York, and learned that the pizzeria in Parsippany was doing well, and that they could certainly use my help. That was my cue. After Easter, I would return to New York.

A week or so before departing, I decided to do something I had wanted to do for many years: Buy my father a diamond ring. I wanted to replace the one that he had hung around my mother's neck. The one he had been forced to sell at the end of the war to buy few pieces of furniture for the apartment in the Mussolini projects. I took my parents to a jewelry shop they were familiar with and fitted my father for a diamond ring. It was of lesser value than his original one. But that ring made him happy and proud that I could afford to by him such an expensive present. In the very first letter I received from my parents after returning to New York, he expressed his pleasure at receiving the finished, set ring. He wrote that he would wear it as long as he lived, but that the ring was mine and would come back to me upon his death.

As usual, the flight back to New York was bittersweet. However, once I was walking on the sidewalks of Lower Manhattan again, I knew that this was where I belonged. To save money I moved back in with Enzo and Natalino on Thompson Street. I went back to work part-time at my cousin's restaurant The Chez Vous, and worked two days a week at the pizzeria in New Jersey. A year later, my partners and I sold that pizzeria and made a good profit. The decision to move back to NYC had been the right one.

As if to validate my decision, one evening my friend Ennio Sammarone came in the Chez Vous for a drink. I had known Ennio since first setting foot in the Pompeiian almost a decade earlier, and we'd been friends since then. His story wasn't too different from mine: Ennio, along with his father Federico Sammarone, had immigrated to the United States in 1960, when he was just 18. His first job had been as a busboy at the Pompeiian. Two years later, as his English improved, he had jumped up to a waiter spot. Our friendship started when I found Ennio to be the only Italian-speaking waiter working the Pompeiian dining room. He left the Pompeiian in 1963 for a job at Joe's Restaurant on McDougal Street, which was certainly a career bump for him. Back then, Joe's was the best Italian restaurant in Greenwich Village, and spots on staff were famously competitive amongst the restaurant world. Now, sitting at the bar of The Chez Vous, he told me that a waiter position was about to open up over at Joe's. The waiters there made a *very* good salary, as the tips were above industry standard—thanks to a clientele that included actors, politicians, and local movers and shakers. When I went to my cousin Giuseppe with news of this opportunity, he was disappointed but understood that he couldn't keep me forever. I was 25 years old, and ready to strike out on my own. Or at least take one more step in that direction.

Carol

One day, visiting my friend and former business partner Benedetto's pizzeria in Little Neck, Queens, I stopped cold in the entrance to the store. Standing at the counter, waiting for her fresh pie, was the most beautiful brunette I had ever seen in my life. In fact, I had seen her there previously, from the kitchen, but this was the first time we were both on the same side of the counter. I struck up a conversation and told her that I'd seen her in the pizzeria before, and was wondering if she would go out for a drink with me. She didn't even answer me and shyly left the shop.

I was no stranger to rejection, but this one hurt. There was something special about her that I couldn't get out of my mind.

"What'd I do wrong, Joe?" I asked the pizza man.

"Don't worry, my friend. Sometimes a woman behaves this way when she doesn't like a fella. But sometimes she behaves this way because she *does*. And I think this is one of those times."

"Really? You think so?"

"Yes! Take it from me. The pizza man knows."

"Then how about this. You have my number, right? Next time she's in, why don't you give it to her, and tell her I'd like a call?"

He laughed and said he would, and I left feeling pins of anxiety needling me all up and down. But a week later, my phone rang, and there was Joe on the other end.

"Michele? Wait a second! Someone wants to talk to you!"

I couldn't believe my ear; a moment later, a girl's voice came on.

"Hi," she said. "Your friend here in the pizzeria is saying lots of good things about you."

"Really? But I don't know anything about you. Could we meet at the pizzeria next week?"

She said yes, and we set a date, and that was that.

* * *

Her name was Carol Pizzuro. She was a nurse at North Shore Hospital in Manhasset, Long Island. We met at the pizzeria as planned. Joe made sure to keep the slices coming, while still managing to keep his distance to allow the two of us to get acquainted. After a few more dates, I learned that she was twenty-five years old and that she had a two year old son, also named Michael. She had been previously married, but her husband had died the year before from diabetes (after first going blind), and she and her son had moved in with her parents, in Queens.

Her parents were eager to meet me, so they asked Carol to invite me to dinner at their house one autumn evening. Mrs. Pizzuro, a second generation Italian, had prepared lasagna in an attempt to make me feel at home. But when the huge lump of pasta, cheese, and sauce landed on my plate, I almost fainted. It wobbled side to side! It *certainly* didn't look anything Mammina would make, but I managed to eat more than half of the portion nevertheless.

Apart from little Michael, all eyes in the room were on me. Mrs. Pizzuro, who had clearly spent hours creating this monstrosity, exclaimed, "Whatsamatter, you don't like lasagna?"

I answered quickly, "No, of course I do. It's delicious! I'm just, just—just taking my time with it, because it's so good."

Mrs. Pizzuro said, "Thank God! For a minute there, I thought you didn't like it."

After a few kicks from under the table and some sharply encouraging looks from Carol, I managed to finish the rest. From that moment on, whenever I was invited to dinner, I made sure to starve myself for the whole day beforehand, so that I would be hungry enough to gulp down whatever Italian creations my potential mother-in-law thought would make me "feel at home". To my surprise, Mrs. Pizzuro veered off into some of her "American specialties" too: beef stroganoff, baked ham, macaroni and cheese. However, I always looked forward to the coffee and her *Homemade Italian Cheesecake,* because that *was* something she made extremely well.

* * *

My relationship with Carol continued for about a year. We liked one another, but as far as getting serious, I didn't give it much thought. We had fun when we were together, but both our jobs were demanding and prevented us from spending more time together. Carol's schedule at the hospital was from four in the afternoon to midnight, four days a week. I worked at the restaurant six days a week and my only day off was Tuesday, when the restaurant was closed. Most of our encounters had to wait until 1:00 AM when I finished working. I would drive to Queens to pick her up and go out to a diner or whatever we could find open at that hour. Once in a while, if toddler Michael happened to be awake when his mother got home, we would take him with us (he was usually the only toddler at the diner at 3 in the morning).

As time went by, Carol and I grew closer, but when she began to talk about moving in together, like many thirty-something men I got cold feet. First, I wasn't ready to cross that line; and second, I respected her too much to lead her on. If we moved in together she would definitely think it meant I was ready for even more commitment. I told her that I needed time and that we should take a break from each other. I decided to take *my* half of the break back in Naples. I bought a round-trip plane ticket, returning in a couple of weeks. It overlapped nicely with the annual two-week break that Joe's Restaurant customarily took, so all the personnel, including the owners could go on vacation. I landed in mid-August, to my parents' great joy.

One afternoon, leaning on the parapet up in Posillipo enjoying *gelato*, I told my mother about my new girlfriend. In the past, my mother had repeated many times that I should think seriously about getting married and raising a family, rather than flitting between different women in brief relationships that went nowhere. She reminded me that I would soon be thirty years old—old enough to start a *family*. She told me again for the umpteenth time the story of her and my father's meeting, and about the ten years it had taken him to ask her to marry him. "If it hadn't been for your grandmother Maria Sofia pushing your father to make his move, nothing ever would have happened! Do you want that for yourself?"

"Ma, ma, ma, I know your version of the story by heart."

My mother's version was that, while it was true that her own mother was protective of her, my father had always looked at her with fervent desire, and Grandma Pierina did not trust him enough to leave him alone with her daughter. "If he wanted me that much, how come he never proposed to me? Instead, one day he disappeared without saying a word. We kept seeing each other on rare occasions, when he came by the tailor shop where I worked. One day I grew tired of waiting and told him not to come by anymore, I had enough! Boy, was he surprised! Even though he never came back to my shop, every so often some of my girlfriends reported that they had seen him walk by in my neighborhood."

Things continued this way for a number of years, until Salvatore's mother became very sick. Afraid that she would die leaving her youngest son a bachelor, Grandma Maria Sofia ("the broker") asked her son Vincenzo to come up with some kind of story in order to convince Salvatore to get back with Maria. They both felt that Maria was the right woman for Salvatore and couldn't understand his reluctance.

One afternoon, Vincenzo told his brother, matter-of-factly that he had met Maria and had learned that she was dating another man and was soon to be engaged. When my father heard that he went crazy. He rushed to his friend's jewelry shop, picked up the most beautiful diamond ring, went over to his beloved's apartment and asked her mother's approval to be engaged right then and there. My mother was totally bewildered. Whatever had made Salvatore take that decision? Either way, they engaged and married within the year. Unfortunately Maria Sofia died a few months before the wedding, but she died knowing that she had brought her son to make the right decision.

Then I began to tell her about Carol. She was married and that her husband had died two or three years before, leaving her with a son. I also told Mammina that I loved the girl and *would* marry her, but I was concerned about having a ready-made family.

Mammina looked at me, with a surprised look. "Is the little boy your problem?"

I replied, "Perhaps."

She said, "Do you really have feelings for her? What about her feelings for you? Am I to understand that you don't love her enough, or is there something else?"

I told her, "No, no, Ma. I do love her. I'm just not sure."

She cautioned me, "Then don't make your decision based on the fact that she already has a son. Do you feel she's a good mother?"

"Oh, no doubt. She is so good with him, and she's responsible and a hard worker."

Mammina said to me sideways. "You're not stupid. Ever since you were a child, you always made the right decision. I'm not going to tell you what to do. *But*, make your decision based on the two of *you*, and *not* on the boy."

I had been in Naples for nearly a week when, one morning, the phone rang. My father answered and told me to pick up, as the person on the other side was speaking "Americano."

I said, "Hello, who is this?"

Carol answered, "It's me. I'm in Rome, waiting for the plane to Naples. Can you pick me up at the airport?"

Thinking it was a joke, I said, "Are you teasing me? Come on! You just got off work."

She said, "No, I am really in Rome. I'll be in Naples around 11:00 AM. Pick me up!"

I couldn't believe my ears. While getting ready, I told my parents what was happening. My mother was looking at me with a sort of smile and could not resist asking the question, "Was all this planned?"

"No, Ma, she decided all by herself! I honestly had nothing to do with it."

Driving to the airport, I still could not believe that Carol was about to land in Naples. Had she planned all this by herself? She hadn't hinted anything to me when I was in New York! She was flying to Italy just to be with me? Carol was a girl of few words, yes, even a bit shy, but this was a gutsy move, no doubt. One that I hadn't expected.

"Carol." I approached her, took her bags in one hand, and threw my arms around her. "I'm glad you are here." I stepped back. "Even though you *really* shocked me."

She looked at me like she was just as surprised as I was. "Is this alright? You want me to turn around?"

"Are you crazy? Come on, get in my car, I'm going to bring you home to my family."

I introduced Carol to my parents, and my mother was pleased as punch right from the start. The first thing she did was run to the telephone to tell Antonietta and Titina about my "new girlfriend." In the meantime, I took Carol on a sightseeing ride around the neighborhoods and right up to the crater of Mt. Vesuvius. That evening, Mario and Titina and Antonietta and Gianni came over to meet Carol. For this special occasion, we had a complete Neapolitan meal cooked by the boss herself: my mother. I got the impression that my mother liked Carol, even though no words had been exchanged because of the language difference. But my mother didn't need words, because she could communicate with food: *Spaghetti Puttanesca, Veal Scaloppine alla Pizzaiola* and *Broccoli Rabe Sautéed*. Antonietta took a liking to Carol too, and after dinner a few of us went out for a ride to the Mergellina for gelato. Antonietta showed herself to be very affectionate toward Carol, even though she also spoke no English, grabbing her by the arm and walking arm-in-arm behind me and Sofia. After gelato, I dropped Carol and Sofia off at my parents' apartment (I had learned my lesson) and went over to sleep at Antonietta's.

The next morning my sister told me that she'd had a nice conversation with Carol. I said, "How could you? You don't speak English and she doesn't speak Italian. What could the two of you have possibly talked about?"

She pushed me away and said, "We are women, we understand each other!"

A few days went by, and my mother approached me saying, "I have had many opportunities to observe Carolina [as they called her at first], and even though we can't speak to each other, she strikes me as a nice girl. If you are staying with her for fun, I think you should leave her alone and find someone else for you to have your fun with. From what you've told me, this girl doesn't need more grief. She's had enough of that. Personally, *I* feel you should marry her."

Throughout her stay in Naples, Carol and I were not allowed to sleep together—not just in the same bed, but the same *house*. However, we made up for it once we were on the road to Rome, Florence, and Venice for the requisite road trip (or, perhaps, an early honeymoon?). I always knew that I loved Carol, but I needed a push. My mother's blessing was that push. (And Carol flying to Italy didn't hurt.)

Carol and I rented a house in Flushing, Queens, and moved in together with little Michael. In the back yard, I started to teach him to play soccer, and we spent lots of active time together that way. One day, Carol had to work overtime and asked me to drive him to pre-kindergarten, which was not far from where we lived. He sat next to me and did not say a word. When we arrived at school, as parents were dropping off their children, he looked at me and asked, "Michael, can you walk me to the door?"

I got the message. He probably wanted to show the other kids that he also had a man in his life, a father, so to speak. I grabbed him by his small hand and slowly walked him to the door, kissed him on his forehead, and sent him on his way. When I turned around I saw him waving at me through the glass pane, while looking around to make sure that other kids had seen me. I was touched. This four year old boy, with that small request, single handedly transformed my uncertainty into our future as a family. Carol and I were married a few months later, in June 1976.

My Father's Desire

Another significant event happened in November 1977 while working at Joe's Restaurant, which really opened my eyes and gave me a lot to think about. It was when Ennio broke his ankle. That injury was devastating since a waiter who can't walk is a waiter who can't work. I had experienced that in 1967 when I broke my knee. Ennio had a wife and three children to support and no other source of income. How was he supposed to survive?

Together with the other two waiters, we decided to take a percentage from our tips to help Ennio. He had worked at Joe's Restaurant for fifteen years, and wouldn't be receiving any compensation from the management. Working in a non-union establishment was a 'no work, no pay' situation (The same exact thing had happened to my mother many years before.) If a long time employee like Ennio, wasn't getting paid , imagine what would happen to *me* if I were in his situation. I had only been working there *five* years. So I began to think about how to solve this little problem and decided that the best solution would be to go out on my own somewhere, somehow, by myself or in a partnership. I adopted Michael, our daughter, Maria, was born in May 1975 and her sister Cristina in November of 1977. Carol had stopped working at the hospital to take care of our family. I had become the only breadwinner. I had to be more than just a waiter. I didn't want to do to my wife what had happened with my mother and father, or now with Ennio and his family.

Ennio had been an integral figure of Joe's. When regular customers came in, not only did they expect to see Ennio, they wanted him to be their waiter. The questions "How come Ennio is not here?" or "What happened to Ennio?" became as common as "How are you?" or "Good evening!" We waiters had no problem telling them about his injury and the fact that he had a family to support and no money coming in.

Most of our customers were very generous, the moment they heard of Ennio's accident they took cash out from their pockets and handed it to us; or the next time they came in, would leave envelopes addressed to Ennio to put away for him. As Christmas was just around the corner, we made sure that Ennio and his family could celebrate the holidays the way they always did, with plenty of food, wine, and toys for his kids.

Two days before Christmas, I went over to his house and gave him the money and all the envelopes. One generous customer went as far as putting $500.00 in his envelope. Later I learned that Ettore, one of the two owners of Joe's Restaurant, had also visited Ennio and given him $100. Only $100, for a veteran of fifteen years - I couldn't believe it! Ennio had been such a loyal employee. Never an argument, always available, often running errands that had nothing to *do* with waiting tables. Was that how the owners were rewarding him in his time of need? This became the eye opener for me! I realized then that I had to plan ahead for a future. As long as my legs were good, I had a job; but what would happen to me and my family if one day I got an injury and was unable to work? Who was going to feed my children? So I began to look for ways to open a restaurant.

New York City from the late 1950's and onward was in many ways similar to Naples, especially Greenwich Village. To do business here, you might have to deal with more than just the city and state permit and license offices. There were also the neighborhood chieftains and their gangs, dividing up the territory of the city for their own profit. Memories of petty shakedowns on Corso Garibaldi and *pizzo* payments from small business owners had left a bad taste in my mouth. However, unlike back in Naples, I was familiar enough with the organized elements running the neighborhood here that it was no longer an impediment to my venture. Still, I knew I would eventually need to clear the air and set things in order with the men who mattered most—especially the man on top, who we all called Big Boss.

But first, I needed to find a place. In May 1978, I took a look at Café

Magda, a restaurant that had shut down during the winter from lack of business. Nicola Di Laurenzio, one of the cooks at Joe's Restaurant, had invested money in that café, but was not involved in its operation. Nicola was an old gentleman, about five feet tall, he was thrifty for petty things, but as I later discovered, he was generous and he was a man who always kept his word. In confidence, Nicola told me that he owned fifty per cent of the shares in Cafe Magda. I proposed to him that I would buy his partners' shares, if he was willing to go into business with me and hopefully Ennio. Nicola was all for it, which made me very happy.

Nicola had left his tiny town in the mountains of Abruzzo at the tender age of nine. Along with an uncle he settled in Naples and began working in various restaurant kitchens as a dishwasher. As he got older he moved up in status, preparing antipasti and salads. Eventually he began to work at the stove. He became a cook and was hired by Hotel Paradiso.

In his early twenties, he migrated to Caracas, Venezuela, where through a friend, he found a job in a restaurant where he eventually became the chef. In 1963 he married Maria De Vita, a native of Altavilla Irpina, in the province of Avellino, not too far from Montevergine, (where Don Gaetano took us every year on the scampagnata).

That same year Nicola and his wife emigrated to New York City and rented an apartment on MacDougal Street, directly above Joe's Restaurant.

In 1970 Nicola landed a job as preparation chef at Joe's Restaurant. As a prep chef, Nicola made less money than what he had been earning, but he preferred it that way. He was comfortable working in the same building he lived in, therefore he had no commute and the owners and the two chefs were all from his native Abruzzo.

Nicola and I became good friends and whenever Carol and I had family gatherings at our house in Queens, I never failed to invite him and his wife Maria, (who happened to be an extremely annoying woman). I'd drive into Manhattan to pick them up and drive them back. We loved Nicola - his wife not so much, but we never failed to respect her.

Years later when they retired to Italy we kept in touch by telephone, and when my family and I went back to visit my "Italian" family, we would go to Altavilla Irpina and spend one day with them.

On Our Own

Now I had a bigger job to do: Convince *Ennio* to join us. Ennio had been working as a waiter for a very long time. He felt that the money he was making at Joe's was good enough, and he didn't want to risk to go on his own. Ennio and his wife, Cristina, had raised a nice family and had recently bought a house. But still, what if he was hurt again? What if he wanted more out of life? I was surprised by his lack of ambition.

To convince him to see it my way, one day after lunch we went to Caffe Reggio for an espresso, something we did every so often.

"Ennio," I said to him, "Nicola owns fifty per cent of Magda's Café. I'm willing to put up the money to buy the remaining shares. I would like for you to come in with us. What do you say?"

He took a sip and looked at me. "How much would I have to put in?"

"No money. But I need you to work with me. I can't do this without you."

"Why not?"

"How many Ennios beside you do you know?"

"None..."

"Exactly!" I shouted. "If I put my name on the sign, who's gonna know it's me? I got it all figured out. Nicola and I will do the demolition of Magda ourselves to save money, and Nicola will advance the construction money. You and I will repay him along the way, a little at the time."

"What about me? What do I need to do?"

"For now, nothing. Just keep your job at Joe's. Only promise me, when we're ready, you'll come over."

He smiled. It was an unbelievable offer. "You mean I don't have to put any money upfront?"

"None at all."

"Okay, but I'm still worried about a couple of things. One, you already know I make all the tips I need at Joe's. I'm putting the food on my family's table and paying for the roof over their heads. I'm a comfortable guy. *Two*, what are our neighborhood *friends* gonna think about the idea of us opening a restaurant just around the corner from Joe's? I don't think they're gonna take too kindly to us hurting business at their favorite spot."

"Ennio, I've thought about all this already. We'll ask the Big Boss. If he doesn't like the idea, we'll just drop it. I'm not looking for trouble. But I think it'll be okay."

He grimaced over his cold espresso, clearly not convinced.

I crossed my arms on the table. "You know what, Ennio? You worry too much. I get it, you've got a family to support, so I understand where you're coming from. But think about just a few months ago, when you broke your ankle. Was any money coming in then?"

"I know, I know..."

"And when you get older you can't run yourself ragged the way you do now. You know what the owners will do to you then?"

"Yeah, they'll kick my ass to the curb."

"So then think about it. Take some time, talk to Cristina. We need the wives on board, since going into any kind of business is always risky. Just talk to her the way I have discussed it with mine".

He nodded his head slowly, weighing my words. I could tell he liked the idea in the abstract; I just wasn't sure I could get him to take the plunge for real.

We paid for our espresso and walked out onto MacDougal Street, me full of vigor, Ennio looking at the pavement and lighting another cigarette.

"You have a name, too?" He puffed and waited.

"Yeah," I said, pointing first at him, then at me, I repeated "*Ennio and Michael. Ennio and Michael Ristorante.*" He looked at me, a little perplexed. "Come on" I said, "you and I have been serving Joe's customers for years. They'll follow us *anywhere*, especially if we're just there on Bleecker Street. But they have to know it's us. Customers who love me would just walk right past a sign saying *Michael's*. Michael who? But with *Ennio* on the sign, they will know it's me and you. And they *love* me and you."

He dragged and exhaled. "When do you think this will happen."

"Once I have your okay, I'll get moving. But until then, not a word to anyone—*no one*—understand?"

A few days later, he bumped my shoulder passing by in the restaurant and leaned in to whisper, "I'm in." I finished the day with a smile splitting my face, and my head full of plans.

But there was one final detail left in order for us to go on our own, and it was a big one.

Over the years, Joe's Restaurant had grown into *the* place to go for people of status: actors, politicians, mobsters. The fact was, half of the time I didn't even know who the actors or politicians were, but when it came to the mobsters, I always knew. Having worked in the Village for fifteen years, you learn where the power lies. Still, I didn't let it affect my service. Anyone who sat at my table was treated with the same courtesy, whether they were petty criminals or Wall Street hotshots. And no one was more important than the Big Boss.

The Big Boss was respected throughout the community, but it was a respect borne out of fear. You could never really know for sure exactly what he had *done* to inspire such fear, but the hearsay sure was convincing. People who you waved to on the street every day suddenly disappearing, broken storefront glass. Little explosives left on the sidewalks just as warning shots. The message was clear, you don't cross the Big Boss.

I knew the Big Boss well. He was a regular at my table, and Ennio's too. He loved us, and had made it clear that if we ever needed anything, we should come to him for advice.

And so one day, when he came in for dinner with five guests, we were ready. At the end of their meal, Ennio and I went over to him and humbly asked to have a word. Being the gentleman that he was, he asked us if we were comfortable talking in front of his table guests. We knew everyone at his table already, and so we nodded yes.

He asked, "What seems to be the problem?"

"There's no problem. Only that—well, you've known us for a long time. You know that we're hard workers and good family men. Recently, we've come across an opportunity to go into business on our own, and we need your advice. The spot we want to take is just around the corner from here, on Bleecker—a few doors down from the Little Red School House. Ennio and I wouldn't want it to be a conflict of interest with this restaurant. If you tell us it's not a good idea, we'll understand and will respect your suggestion and keep working here, until we find another opportunity somewhere further away."

He listened carefully, and when we were done he said, "You two are good people. You've always treated us with respect. I see no problems here. You have my blessing." My heart swelled up, and I felt waves of relief washing through. But he wasn't done yet:

"Furthermore, should you have any kind of trouble, feel free to come to me." He got up from his chair and, while shaking our hands, continued, "As a matter of fact, even if a total stranger to us decided to open a restaurant in that same spot, who are we to oppose them? All men are free to do what their hearts desire."

To be honest, I was barely even listening to his performance of humility. I was more focused on the fact that we had just cleared the final hurdle to starting our restaurant. The Big Boss sat down and resumed his conversation with his dinner companions, as we disappeared back into the dining room for the rest of the shift.

Not long after that, Nicola and I left our jobs at Joe's to start the renovation of the new space. Ennio continued to work at Joe's, but after few weeks, he also left to be with us, because another pair of strong hands was needed. He just couldn't resist. By doing most of the work ourselves, we saved a lot of money up front. I had an old Volkswagen which we used to pick up most of the construction material in Queens. Every morning on the way in from home, I made the various stops for supplies at the lumber yard, the tile shop, or the hardware store, because they were cheaper in the outer boroughs. Back then, it was a lot easier to open a new business, and in six weeks we were ready to open. Now it would take months just to get the permits.

However, an incident we had not anticipated kept us from opening when we thought we would. A ruthless, local bully well-known to us (I'll call him 'John'), was interested in buying the wet bar that was in Café Magda. We had no use for it and were just going to throw it out, so we agreed on a price with him. We also told him that he had to remove it as soon as possible so we could lay down a new floor. He said, "I'll have it out of here in two days." We shook hands in agreement.

Two days later, he let us know that he needed two more days to get a moving a truck, which was still okay with us. But another week went by, and the wet bar still had not been picked up. Ennio and I marched over to his 'office' (the cafe where all his friends hung out) and asked him when he thought the unit would be removed. Boy was he pissed!

His answer was dry and nasty. "*I'll* decide when it's going to be picked up. Understand?"

I stood my ground. "In that case, I won't sell it. The deal's off."

He started to scream all kinds of insults at me, and pushed me toward the back of the room, near the toilet. He said, "Here, we call the shots. If I decide to wait a month, I'll do it. I even decide if you open at all. I am the boss here!" Those words left a bad taste in my mouth, a taste I remembered from my life before, as a kid in Naples. At that moment, he put his right hand under my chin, as if to choke me, and with his left hand grabbed the back of my head. He screamed, "I thought you were a smart guy, eh? You'd better not say a word or I'll shove your head in the toilet bowl!" I knew better, I kept silent.

Ennio begged him to let me go. 'John' let me go with the repeated threat: "I'm the boss here, and don't you forget it."

I remember it was a Saturday in the middle of July, 1978. I was hot, dripping with sweat, and humiliated. As Ennio and I walked back to Café Magda, I was speechless; all I could think about was how to make that bastard pay for the way he had treated me. One of the thoughts that kept rolling in my mind was to run him under my car on Houston Street. The cars there are known to go pretty fast.

All of a sudden, we ran in one of the gentlemen who had been at the Big Boss's table the night when we asked for his blessing, a man in his sixties, and highly placed member of the family. He said to us, "Hey fellas, when's that restaurant of yours going to open?"

I told him, "Soon, hopefully in a month." But he was looking at the red mark on my neck.

"What's going on here? Were in a fight?"

I told him, "No. Everything is good."

"Mike, I've known you a long time. I have never seen you like this. What's the problem?"

Standing in front of such a respected man in the Village, I had a choice: Tell him the truth, knowing what that would probably mean? Or keep it to myself, and let 'John' run me into the ground? I decided to tell him what had just happened then and there.

He was shocked. "Look, it's Saturday and already 2:00 PM. Nobody is around. Go back to your restaurant and continue getting it ready."

That same day, at around 6:00 PM, a man I knew who did various tasks for the "organization" came in and told me to follow him to the Big Boss's 'office.' When I got there, six men were sitting at a large table. Our friend the Big Boss asked me to tell the whole story, without leaving anything out.

Upon finishing, the Big Boss was incensed. He even lost his composure a little, raising his voice to scream vulgarities and curses onto 'John's' head, and ordered me to give him until Monday to remove the bar. The Boss said, "If by Monday, he doesn't get that bar out there, remove it on Tuesday and finish your floor. If he picks up the bar, demand he pay you all the money you have agreed to. Keep me posted, and let me tell you something else: If anyone comes to eat in your restaurant, I expect them to pay full price. If anyone tries to bully you, you know where to come."

On the following Monday afternoon, a truck stopped out front of Café Magda, and 'John' and three men got out and came inside.

'John' said, "Listen, Mike, about the other day, I got carried away. It was hot, I wasn't thinking straight. Can we forget about it?" He took out a roll of money and handed it to me. "Take the money, it's half the amount, the rest I'll give to you next week, if it's OK with you!"

I agreed. I couldn't get rid of him fast enough. All I could think of was the feel of his fingers squeezed around my neck over the public toilet. His men took the bar out and put it on their truck. Ennio and I walked over to the Big Boss's 'office' to update him on the news. A week later, at the agreed-upon time, I went over to 'John's' new café to collect the remainder of my money. A few friendly eyes happened to be nearby to make sure that everything went as planned.

We announced August 10 as opening day for our new restaurant: Ennio & Michael Ristorante. While Nicola and his kitchen staff did all the food prep, Ennio and I set up tables in the dining room. Suddenly we noticed a leak in the ceiling, smack in the middle of the dining room.

We took it to the landlord and were told that a broken waste pipe had to be replaced, and that it could only be done *from* our dining room—by breaking the ceiling open. We were forced to delay our grand opening by another four days, until all repairs were done. To open this restaurant, I had exhausted all my money. On the morning of August 14, I left my house with two dollars in my pocket, which I needed to buy gas. As I kissed Carol good-bye, she asked me to give her money for groceries.

"Honey, if you want to feed the kids you have to take them over to your parents." I started the engine and drove away.

Papá's Prophecy and Promise

The restaurant was an immediate success. The first week we had a line outside every day. Several of our highest profile patrons did indeed follow us from Joe's and become our new regulars, and with them came the press, the publicity, and the public. It was such a great feeling, seeing something that we had dreamed up ourselves turned to life. The moment we opened the door for dinner, the sidewalk was already full of people waiting to come in. I would bring baskets of fried zucchini out to the people waiting, and the smell would stop even *more* people on the sidewalk just walking by. One day, I asked a woman in line, a woman who I knew quite well, "How many in your party?"

"Five," she answered.

I looked back over my shoulder at the packed dining room. "Signora, it's gonna be at least an hour and forty-five minutes until I can seat you."

She said, "That's fine. I'll wait."

I looked at her. "Ma'am, if someone told me that I had to wait that long, even if it was the best food in town *and* free, I wouldn't wait that long."

"Well that's you. For me? I love to wait for your food. Nothing could be more worth it."

Nicola's food was better than ever. He was using mostly recipes he had brought over from Naples. And one of our most popular dishes was the cheesecake I had stolen from my mother-in-law. I had thought of putting my *Pasta e Patate* on the menu, but both my buddies objected, so I kindly refrained from using it. In 1986, Ennio & Michael Ristorante was chosen among the top 25 Italian restaurants in New York City to participate in a contest sponsored by the New York *Times* and *Gourmet Magazine*. It was held at the famous Romeo Salta Restaurant on 56th Street. The competition consisted of each restaurant introducing a dish either from the menu or indigenous to our homeland.

For days following that invitation, we struggled to come up with a concrete idea. I was looking for something totally different, something that would make us stand out from the other twenty-four restaurants in the competition. I didn't want to just bring something basic like Manicotti, Lasagna or Veal Scaloppine al Marsala.

Pasta e Patate! It had been at least twenty years since I had eaten that dish, but I remembered exactly how to make it. I called Naples long-distance and asked my mother to go over the recipe with me. I can't remember my mother ever laughing as much as she did on that day; she couldn't stop reminding me about just how much I had hated to eat that dish. As soon as I hung up with her, I started to practice.

After a few tries I was able to achieve the taste exactly as I remembered it. There was one big difference—now I found that I loved it! It brought me back to my youth, back home. When I told my partners about my idea, they weren't thrilled, since they weren't familiar with that dish. Ennio had been involved in the restaurant business longer than I had been, and he had never even *heard* of it. He wasn't impressed with the idea.

On the day of the event, however, I prepared my *Pasta e Patate* and put it in a large to-go container. When I got to Romeo Salta's, I realized just how big of an affair this was. Big-name restaurants were there with servers, maitre d'hotel's, and sommeliers, displaying beautiful chafing dishes and fancy plates. I had never participated in such an event; I had no experience and didn't know what to expect. Thank God I had dressed up for the occasion!

I saw a couple of people I knew from the business—Mario Gattorna, the owner of Il Gattopardo, a beautiful, luxurious restaurant also located on 56th Street. He was surprised to see me there, since our restaurant was a simple storefront with only 40 seats and no wine or liquor license (because of our proximity to the Little Red School House).

In his Genovese accent, Mario asked me what I had in the bag.

"*Pasta e Patate*," I told him.

With a smirk of derision, he repeated the name: "*Pasta e Patate?*" In that moment, I felt small. I even thought of leaving.

I decided to tough it out though, and asked him to introduce me to the lady who owned the restaurant where this event was taking place. After greeting her, I told her that I had not realized this was such an elegant affair, and that I had brought a very simple dish. She was a Neapolitan like me, so when I told her she said, "Ah, Michele! What a good idea!" I immediately felt better.

She then took me into the kitchen and introduced me to her chef, asking him to help me out with anything I needed. I heated up my *Pasta e Patate,* poured it in a beautiful silver bowl, and sprinkled fresh chopped parsley and grated Parmigiano on top. Taking a deep breath, I went back into the dining room, placed the bowl on one of the tables, and put my restaurant's business card in front of it, where I wrote the name of the dish. After that, I disappeared, hiding myself among the crowd, too afraid to be seen next to my uncertain concoction.

A while later, I heard someone yell out a name: "Ennio & Michael Ristorante!" I went up to the judging platform, where I was asked a few questions about my dish. I answered very simply, then waited nearby to see if anything else was going on. Ten minutes later, I got one of the shocks of my life: Our restaurant had won the award for most original dish. My *Pasta e Patate* had done it! We proudly displayed the award in our restaurant, along with another one from the James Beard Foundation.

It turned out that Ennio Sammarone and I had created a gem of a place, where everyone that came in for dinner was served by either—if not *both*—of us. We worked our small dining room with the help of a busboy, Giorgio, a young Argentinian man who did his job with tremendous passion. We knew most of our customers and their dining habits, and did our best to spoil them. Our second week after opening was just as good as the first, but with one major difference: My father's ability to prophesy would be proven right one more time.

That second Friday after our grand opening, I got home around 2:00 AM and went right to bed. About an hour later, the phone rang. It was my brother, Mario.

I could tell that something was wrong, not only from his voice but also because, in all the years I had been in America, he had never called me. I said, "Mario, is there something wrong?"

He said, "It's Papá. He's slipped into a coma, and I don't think he'll make it."

I said, "Mario, I've got to wait until 6:00 AM for the airline office to open. I'm reserving a flight first thing, and I'll be in Naples as soon as I can."

"For the time being, make your reservation, but don't do anything else."

Around 7:00 AM, I called back and Mario answered the phone. In a very sad voice, he told me that both our sisters had made an emergency return from their August holidays and were entering the bedroom just as my phone call came in. It was then, at that very moment, that our father took his last breath. Salvatore died surrounded by all of us.

Even though I wasn't physically there, I was together with my father, mother and siblings in an emotional and spiritual bond. I could hear their cries, so I started to cry too, as Carol sat at the edge of the bed next to me. Mario put my mother on the phone, who between sobs told me not to travel to Italy. I wouldn't make it in time for the burial. To convince me, she said "Miché! We all know what you were to your father, and I know what he meant to you. I would feel better if you stay there. You need to take care of your family and your new restaurant."

I so wanted to be near them, to share this devastating loss, but my mother insisted that my father would not have wanted it. It was hard, but I listened to her. She was right—my father would have wanted me to stay at the new business. He died just two weeks after it had opened, so in the end he *did* live long enough to see his prediction come true.

I had been away from home for sixteen years, but never had I felt further away than at that moment.

Surrounded by Carol and my children, I sat on the bed crying; in my mind I could see the film reel of my youth turning round and round, and in every little frame I could see him or hear his voice. In those little frames, I could see those afternoons that I spent at Porta Nolana—the trolley rides, the various jobs at the Café, the strolls in my father's native neighborhood, the shops, the smells and aromas, how he protected me from being squished when the trolley was crowded, how he knelt and prayed before the crucifix on the corner. I could hear him telling me all the stories about his neighborhood, and of the Church of Madonna del Carmine. I could see him wipe the tears from his eyes when he was on the pier waiting for the ship to take me away.

That Saturday, I went to work anyway. Ennio had urged me to stay home, that he could handle things by himself. I knew he could—but I needed to be busy. I needed something to help me not think anymore.

So I went back. And then I went back the next day. And the next day. At some point, I realized that, 16 years after getting off the boat, I was not just the owner of another generic Italian restaurant in Greenwich Village, but was the *proud* owner of Ennio & Michael Ristorante, one of the "in" spots of the New York restaurant scene. My dream had come true.

But was it possible that, perhaps, had I not opened my restaurant when I did, my father might not have died so soon? The words he had said to me so many years before—"Miché, I feel that one day you will own your own restaurant in America, and I will not die until that happens"—revealed themselves to me as his prophecy.

Had I given up something infinitely more precious just for the sake of owning a restaurant? Had he really waited to die so as not to distract me from the goal that he had imagined for me?

Of him, now, I was left with only a piece of the past, the diamond ring I had bought for him to replace the one he was forced to sell at the end of the war. He had kept his promise—as he always did—to wear it as long as he lived and to have it returned to me upon his death.

I received it in a box delivered to my restaurant in 1978.

My Turn to Buy Gelato

Epilogue:
The Gold Chain

Throughout her life, my mother faced many struggles and dealt with many losses. When I think about my childhood experiences and those of my siblings before me, I am filled with so much gratitude for her strength, her resourcefulness, and the many sacrifices she had to make to provide the best she could for our family. She was a very strong woman, never shrinking from the adversity of the times. I often think about the hardships in her life and the grief that, at times, must have felt impossible for her to bear. And yet she did bear it. Her courage and her resiliency have been an inspiration for me.

My mother's father had died when she was barely six years old. The home she had shared with my father after they married, on via Giacomo Savarese, was destroyed by bombs, making war refugees out of herself, my father, Mario, Antonietta, and Pierino, and forcing them to flee to Sarno, where they lived for almost two years. They were not able to return to Naples until 1944, when their application for an apartment in "Mussolini's Houses" was accepted.

Even as World War II receded into memory, there remained reminders of it everywhere. My father's head injury in 1945 and the gradual loss of his eyesight had forced my mother into work as our family's breadwinner. That accident profoundly changed my father's life, and hers. Before the accident, *she* had relied on *him*; afterward, their roles were reversed. She eventually became the foreman of over one hundred seamstresses. My father's needs made it possible for my mother to realize her potential in a different way and to carry us through those very tough times. My father's needs also made it possible for me to form such a close bond with him and to free my mother to embrace her new role in the family.

The death of a child is always an unspeakable loss for which there are no words. But as an adult and a father now, I appreciate so much more profoundly what my mother lost the day Pierino died. And this becomes an appreciation of the raw, physical terror of war, and especially the War that spared no one.

In 1958, when my mother's eldest son and first-born child, Mario, was twenty, she watched him leave home to emigrate to Germany to work in the coal mines in Mannheim. At that time, so many young Italian men were expatriating to foreign countries to find work, and he was just one more. His letters home were infrequent because of the terrible winters and impassable conditions where he was working, and he wouldn't return to Naples for many years. My mother missed him terribly during that time, and even though he returned to her, she never got those years back.

On the other side of the scales are the many wonderful memories I have of my mother. One of her favorite things to do in the summer, when the weather was nice, no matter how tough things were, was to have us kids dress nicely on Sunday afternoons, and together with my father take us on the trolley for a *gelato*, a small ice cream. Sometimes, my good friend Gigino would come along. These are memories I treasure. My mother, despite very hard times, would manage to find ways to provide us with the simple experiences that all children should have. That allowed us to feel a sense of normalcy in our lives.

I remember the times when I would suffer from the smoke as I fanned the coal fire while she cooked, and she would take the paddle from my hand to relieve me. I remember her re-stuffing and fluffing up the corn leaf mattresses in our apartment so that we could have a fresh place to sleep every night. I remember roasting coffee for her, how much she enjoyed the aroma, and how she took pleasure from simple things like that. I remember the many hours she would spend making our clothes, her funny gold-rimmed eyeglasses, and how I would thread her needle for her when she had trouble seeing it.

My mother was a quiet woman, a woman of a few words—but firm and direct. If one of us misbehaved, she didn't have to wait for my father to come home. But she stood up for us too. One incident I remember vividly when I was about eight or nine years old: She had taken me along to go food shopping, and we were in front of a fruit stand when the vendor accused me of stealing an orange. My mother grabbed my head and pulled it back to expose my face, looked at me, and then at him, and said, "Does he look as if he stole anything from you?" She raised us to be good, and taught us many life lessons that guided us as we got older. I found myself teaching these same lessons to my own children as they were growing up, and I would think of her, as memories from long ago would bubble to the surface.

In her old age, my mother suffered from diabetes that caused her to gain a lot of weight. One day, in early January 1983, as she was about to water her plants on the balcony, she fell and broke her left hip in a few places and was taken to the hospital. My sister Sofia called me in New York to ask my opinion on what to do, as our mother's diabetes had caused her many other health problems. I raced to the airport, flew via London, and arrived in Naples as soon as I could. When I got to the hospital, I saw she was in bad shape, in a lot of pain. Because of her weight, it was a problem to move her. After a consultation at the hospital, it was decided that rather than operate, which would have been extremely risky, she would be in a cast from her waist down. It hurt all of us to see her suffer so much.

The few days I stayed in Naples I spent entirely with her at the hospital. As she improved a little, I was able to return to New York. Eventually my mother was able to return to her home as well. She was in that cast for three months, but never really recuperated. At the age of eighty-five, her condition had deteriorated enough that she had to be placed in a nursing home. Along with my daughter Cristina, who was fourteen at the time, I flew to Italy.

From the airport, we drove directly to the nursing home. Antonietta and Sofia were there. My mother was sitting in an armchair. She looked up at me and asked who I was. She had not recognized me, and I felt an empty feeling inside. I bent down to embrace her and whispered, "Mama."

She called out my name—"Michelé"—and grabbed my hand. She made a happy face when she realized that the girl with me was my daughter. We asked the nursing home director to allow us to take her home for few days while I was in Naples, so that she could be at home surrounded by everyone who loved her. We had some wonderful dinners and gatherings there, with the whole family. I know that it gave her great comfort, in the waning days of her life, to be surrounded by her children and grandchildren. We took her back to the nursing home on Sunday.

The following day, on the way back to the airport, we stopped by the nursing home to see her and say our goodbyes. I told Cristina to hug her tight, because this was probably the last time she would see Grandma Maria alive. It was. Two weeks later, on May 18, 1992, she died. She is buried in the crypt that she shares with my father and Pierino, in the San Giovanni Cemetery in Naples.

On the day that I left to come to America, my mother hung on my neck a thin gold chain with a crucifix. She held me tightly to her chest and whispered, "May He guide every step you take". To this day, I have never removed it. Even now, in my mind's eye, I can still see her on the pier in Naples, on that sharply beautiful autumn day in 1962, standing there watching me about to set sail, as clear as if it happened yesterday. Always stoic, she tried to maintain her composure, but I caught a glimpse of her wiping tears from her eyes with her familiar kerchief as she leaned on Mrs. Pelillo's arm. At that moment, *in* that moment, I was and am still overwhelmed by what she had endured for my father and for our family.

She wanted me to have a better life. And, above all, she wanted me to enjoy all the life that was served on my plate.

RECIPES

A Note on Recipes

I have listed recipes from my native city, as well as recipes that I learned in America. I have also included dishes from my restaurant and a few of my own creation.

When I got off the boat—literally—I immediately noticed differences between Italian and Italian-American food. I learned from other Italian immigrants about dishes that were completely unknown to me, one in particular being "veal parmigiana." In Naples, we did make a delicious eggplant parmigiana, but it was entirely different from the one we make here. Often I wonder if those differences were due to the language barriers or the limited availability of imported ingredients.

Growing up in my family, I was exposed to purchasing, preparing and serving food. Because of the scarcity of funds, I had to learn to bargain, especially at the market. No one paid the posted price for anything. To haggle was not a sport, it was a way of life. However, paying less did not mean you had to settle for less quality. I also had to demand that the merchant throw in some complimentary samples.

More importantly, I learned about food from these daily visits to the market. In most cases, low prices for fish, fruits and vegetables meant abundance and peak flavor. I loved to see the intensity with which the shoppers, in most cases neighborhood women, would engage one another while sorting through the products and exchanging opinions on how to best use them for that evening's meal. I can still see clearly the scenes from my youth; women lugging shopping bags and their small children clung to their skirts.

Since I retired from the restaurant business, I have become even more passionate about cooking. I always shop for the best quality. Most of the time, my menu for the day depends on my finds. I never shop for a full week as my motto is: "Don't buy fresh and serve it stale." When I cook I always take my time. For me, cooking is never a job; it is always a joyful event. Every dish has to be a creation, no matter how many times I have made it. If I try a new recipe, I don't expect it to come out right the first time, but I persist until I am completely satisfied. When you cook, make sure you put your heart into it. The best way I can say it is, "Always place one hand on the pot and the other on your heart."

Michael Savarese
New York City, September 2018

Indice delle Ricette

Recipe Index

Tomato Sauce

Ragu

Ragu is the most common tomato sauce in Italy and beyond. Other popular red sauces are: Filetto Di Pomodoro, Marinara, Tomato and Basil and Amatriciana. In my house Sunday was "Ragu Day." My mother, and her mother before her, kept that tradition alive.

Early on Sunday my mother began by gathering all her ingredients, and once the sauce was simmering, each one of us would take turns monitoring its cooking, stirring and whiffing, in order to give her a chance to get dressed and do other chores. Ragu is a very important sauce. With it, we make Lasagna and Baked Ziti, and here in the States we use it to make Veal or Chicken Parmigiana, and so many other dishes. To make a good Ragu takes time, depending on the quantity you need to cook, but never less than three hours. In many cases, the sauce tells you that it is ready when that wonderful aroma starts to fill the room.

Ingredients:
2 oz. olive oil
1 stalk celery (use one of the tender inner tender stalks with leaves) finely chopped
1 large onion, peeled and finely chopped
1 & ½ lbs. cubed beef
6 to 8 pork ribs
4 oz. red wine
1 tbsp. tomato paste
Two 28 oz. cans of imported Italian San Marzano tomatoes crushed in a bowl

Fresh basil
Salt and pepper to taste

Preparation:
Using a good grade pot over medium to low heat, add olive oil, celery and onion. Stir for a minute, then add cubed beef and pork ribs. The meat and onion must brown together. The meat should form a crusty shell, while the onions and celery must not burn—but wilt slowly. This is a crucial point in making this sauce, so stay by the pot. Using a wooden spoon, turn the meat cubes on all sides, and once the meat is golden brown and the onions are translucent, add the wine and continue to stir for another minute. Then add the tomato paste, stir for another minute, then add the crushed tomatoes, salt, and basil. Place the lid on the pot, leaving it a little open so steam can escape. When the sauce comes to boil, lower the heat to a minimum and stir every 5 minutes (I use a timer), lightly scraping the full bottom of the pot.

Cook the Ragu for approximately 3 hours.

Note 1:
I will refer to "crushed tomatoes" throughout my recipes. When available, I like to use cans of imported Italian San Marzano whole tomatoes and mash them myself.

Note 2:
Whenever I use chicken broth, you may substitute vegetable broth or water.

Salsa Marinara
(Marinara Sauce)

Salsa Marinara is another sauce that is used to flavor many dishes. It is quick to prepare. It differs from ragu almost entirely. Marinara Sauce is used to flavor fish dishes, Eggplant Parmigiana, Pizza, Puttanesca Sauce and of course Spaghetti alla Marinara.

Ingredients

1 oz. olive oil

4 garlic cloves, peeled and crushed

Two 28 oz. can imported Italian San Marzano peeled tomatoes, crushed

1 tsp. chopped fresh Italian parsley

½ tsp. dried oregano

Salt and freshly ground black pepper, to taste

Preparation:

In a skillet, over medium heat, place olive oil and garlic, when garlic is light brown add the crushed tomatoes. When the tomatoes come to a boil, reduce heat and add the remainder of ingredients, partially cover the pot and let it simmer for about 15 minutes, stirring every couple of minutes.

Filetto di Pomodoro
(Filet of tomato sauce)

This sauce is quick to prepare and it's delicious. It is best with gnocchi, rigatoni, penne and thick spaghetti, because it adheres best to them. Here is the trick to making this sauce work wonderfully with pasta: after cooking the pasta al dente, drain it well and bring it back to the pot where pasta was cooking. Add one tbsp. butter and one tsbp. grated Parmigiano cheese and just a little sauce; mix it well before serving. Top the pasta with the remainder of sauce.

Ingredients:
1 medium onion, peeled and thinly sliced
1 oz. olive oil
Two 28 oz. can imported Italian San Marzano peeled tomatoes, crushed
10 fresh basil leaves, chopped
Salt and freshly ground black pepper, to taste

Preparation:
In a skillet, over medium heat, sauté the onion in olive oil, until they wilt slowly, becoming translucent. Add the tomatoes, bring to boil, reduce heat, add the basil, salt and pepper and simmer for about 15 minutes, stirring frequently.

Salsa alla Amatriciana
(Amatriciana Sauce)

This sauce comes to us from central Italy, where the best olive oil and pork products are produced. The one ingredient that distinguishes this sauce is guanciale (pig cheeks), which may be replaced by pancetta or bacon.

Ingredients:
    1 lg. onion sliced thin
    3 tbsp. extra virgin olive oil
    6 oz. guanciale sliced very thin and chopped
    Two 28 oz. cans of Italian peeled San Marzano tomatoes crushed
    10 leaves basil
    Salt and pepper to taste

Preparation:
Using a deep skillet, over medium heat, sauté onion in olive oil. When onions are wilted, add guanciale and slowly brown it for about six minutes, stirring constantly to prevent burning. Then add tomatoes, basil, salt, and pepper and increase heat until it comes to a boil, then reduce it to a minimum and let simmer for 20 minutes until the sauce is somewhat thick, and not watery.

Zuppa di Pane Cotto
(Toasted Bread Soup)

Ingredients:
    2 quarts water
    3 tbsp. extra virgin olive oil
    10 bay leaves
    1 tsp. chopped fresh Italian parsley
    ½ tsp. freshly ground black pepper
    1 tsp. salt (to taste)
    3 eggs, beaten (optional)
    Toasted Italian bread
    Freshly grated Parmigiano or Romano, for sprinkling

Preparation:
Bring water to boil, add olive oil, bay leaves, parsley, salt and pepper, reduce heat and let simmer for 10 minutes. Taste for salt and pepper seasoning. Remember that if you are using Romano cheese, because it is sharper than Parmigiano, go easy with salt. Turn off heat and whisk in the beaten eggs. Put the toasted or hard bread in individual bowls and pour soup to completely submerge the bread. Sprinkle with your favorite grated cheese.

Pasta e Lenticchie
(Lentil Soup with Pasta)

Ingredients:

1 medium onion, peeled and finely chopped

1 small stalk celery, finely chopped (use one of the tender inner stalks with leaves)

1 tbsp. chopped carrot

1 tbsp. olive oil

1 tbsp. chopped fresh Italian parsley

3 oz. pancetta or bacon, finely cut (for vegetarians omit this ingredient)

1 lb. dried lentils

3 qts. water

Salt and freshly ground black pepper, to taste

8 oz. mixed pasta, or tubettini, cooked al dente, drained and set aside

Freshly grated Parmigiano

Preparation:

As with any dried legumes, it is always good to sort through the lentils to make sure to remove tiny pebbles and any foreign objects.

Using a five or six quart pot, sauté the onion, celery and carrot in the olive oil until translucent, then add the parsley and pancetta, and let it simmer until most of the fat is melted from the pancetta (about six minutes) At this point, add the lentils, stir thirty seconds and add water. When lentils became a bit soft, add salt and pepper. Then add pasta and simmer for three or four minutes. Serve topped with Parmigiano.

Pasta e Fagioli
(Cannellini Beans and Pasta)

Ingredients:
>   4 garlic cloves crushed
>   1 oz. olive oil
>   3 oz. pancetta or bacon, finely cut (optional for vegetarians)
>   1 tsp. chopped fresh Italian parsley
>   1 lb. dried cannellini beans (soaked overnight in 2 qts. water)
>   3 qts. water or chicken broth (optional)
>   Salt and freshly ground black pepper, to taste
>   8 oz. mixed pasta or tubettini cooked al dente, drained and set aside.
>   Freshly grated Parmigiano, for sprinkling

Preparation:
Sort through beans to remove tiny pebbles and any foreign objects. Drain beans. In a deep pot, brown the garlic along with olive oil, pancetta and parsley and let the pancetta cook until most of the fat is melted, making sure that the garlic does not burn. Add the beans and toss for thirty seconds, add water along with salt and pepper and bring it to a boil, reduce heat and let it simmer for approximately 60 minutes, until beans become tender. Add the drained pasta and simmer for three or four minutes. Sprinkle with Parmigiano.

Pasta e Ceci
(Chick Peas and Pasta)

Ingredients:

2 garlic clove crushed
1 oz. olive oil
1 lb. dried chickpeas (soaked overnight in 2 qts. water)
1 tsp. chopped fresh Italian parsley
2 qts. water
Salt and freshly ground black pepper, to taste
8 oz. mixed pasta or tubettini, cooked al dente, drained and set aside
Freshly grated Parmigianno

Preparation:

Sort through the chick peas to remove tiny pebbles and any foreign objects. Soak chick peas in water overnight, then drain and put aside.

In a deep pot, brown garlic in olive oil, add chick peas, parsley and 2 quarts water and let cook. Once satisfied with tenderness add salt and pepper. Add pasta and simmer for 3 or 4 more minutes. Serve with grated Parmigianno.

Insalata di Tonno
(Italian Tuna Salad)

Ingredients:

Three 5 oz. cans of Italian tuna, packed in olive oil (possibly yellowfin)*

4 tender inner stalks celery, with all the leaves, cut into 1" pieces

1 small red onion, peeled and finely sliced

20 pitted Gaeta or Calamata olives

A bit of salt and freshly ground black pepper, to taste

2 tbsp. extra virgin olive oil

Juice from a lemon

1 ripe avocado, sliced (optional)

Crusty Italian bread

Preparation:

Open cans and drain out most of the oil, place the tuna in a bowl, add
chopped celery, sliced onion, olives, salt and pepper. Toss, add extra
virgin olive oil, toss again, add lemon juice, toss again and add avocado
(if using) and toss gently a final time. Serve with good-quality crusty
Italian bread.

---

* Italian specialty stores carry imported Italian canned solid pack, light tuna, or "tonno,"
packed in olive oil. The Genova brand carries the yellowfin variety. The Pastene brand also
carries Italian tuna. In the Italian food section of many larger markets, you can also find
delicious imported solid tuna in jars.

Pasta e Patate
(Pasta and Potato Soup)

Ingredients:

8 oz. mixed pasta or tubettini

1 medium onion, peeled and finely sliced

1 small celery stalk with some leaves, finely chopped (use one of the tender inner stalks)

1 oz. olive oil

3 oz. pancetta or bacon, cut in very thin strips

1 tsp. chopped fresh Italian parsley

1 & ½ lbs. peeled potatoes, diced to 1/3 inch

2 qts. water

Salt and freshly ground black pepper, to taste

1 *only* peeled Italian plum tomato, mashed by hand

2 tbsp. freshly grated Parmigiano

1 & ½ lbs. peeled potatoes, diced to 1/3 inch

Preparation:

Cook pasta al dente, drain and set aside (it will cook a bit more once added to the soup). Using a heavy-duty pot over medium heat, sauté the onions and celery in the olive oil until translucent, add the pancetta and parsley, and simmer until the fat from the pancetta starts to melt. Add the potatoes, stir, and add 2 quarts water, or if you want a bit more consistency, 1 quart water and 1 quart chicken broth. Add salt and pepper to taste, then add the mashed tomato and its juice and cover the pot partially to allow steam to escape. After about 15 minutes, when the potatoes become soft to the touch, add the drained pasta and allow everything to simmer for 3 or 4 minutes. Turn off the heat and let the soup stand for 2 minutes. Serve topped with freshly ground black pepper (optional) and Parmigiano.

Zuppa di Pesce
(Fish Soup)

Ingredients:
- 4 cloves garlic lightly mashed
- 3 tbsp. olive oil
- 1 striped bass or red snapper, filet
- 2 branches fresh parsley, just the leaves
- 4 oz. white wine
- 15 oz. can ripe cherry tomatoes or Italian peeled tomatoes
- ½ tsp. dry oregano
- Salt and pepper to taste
- 1 lb. shrimp, shelled and de-veined
- 1 lb. Little neck clams
- 1 lb. fresh mussels
- 12 small friselle (slowly toasted Italian bread slices)
- 1 lb. linguine

Preparation:

In a large sauté pan, over medium heat, brown garlic in olive oil, add fish. Brown both sides until skin is a bit crispy, add parsley, wine and a minute later add tomatoes and cover the pot. When tomatoes are cooked (15 minutes) add oregano, salt and pepper and cup of water. Bring to boil, add shrimp, clams and mussels and cover the pot. Let simmer for another 10 minutes over low heat. The consistency of the broth should be thin but not watery. If too thin let cook another minute or two without the cover.

If serving with bread, divide the bread in four individual bowls and pour broth over each piece, making sure that every piece is submerged. Continue with the clams, mussels, shrimp and chunks of fish, that by now will have fallen off its bones.

If using linguine, boil al dente per instructions on the package; when ready, drain, put it back in the pot, pour some broth from fish soup, mix well and dish out into 4 bows, placing the rest of the ingredients as above.

Zuppa di Zucchini Cacio e Uova
(Zucchini Soup with Cheese and Eggs)

Ingredients:
1 small onion, peeled and thinly sliced
1 oz. olive oil
1 lb. zucchini washed, pat dried and sliced about ¼ inch thick
4 oz. white wine
1 tbsp. chopped fresh Italian parsley
3 chopped fresh basil leaves
Salt and freshly ground black pepper, to taste
1 qt. water
2 eggs
2 tbsp. freshly grated Parmigiano
Toasted Italian bread

Preparation:
In a large pot, sauté onion in olive oil, lightly cooking the onion without burning it. Add zucchini, and brown both sides as best as you can. Add wine, parsley, basil, salt and pepper. When wine is almost evaporated, add water and cover the pot. When it starts to boil reduce heat and simmer for ten minutes. In a separate bowl beat eggs, mix in the grated Parmigiano. Turn off the heat and add the egg mixture to the zucchini soup and stir for thirty seconds. Pour soup over dry toasted bread.

Fagioli e Scarola
(Beans and Escarole)

Ingredients:
- 1 oz. olive oil
- 1 tsp. chopped fresh Italian parsley
- 4 garlic cloves, peeled and chopped
- 1 lb. dried cannellini beans, soaked overnight in 2 qts. salted water
- 2 qts. water
- 1 head escarole, about 1 lbs.
- Salt and freshly ground black pepper, to taste
- 2 tbsp. freshly grated Parmigiano

Preparation:

Sort through the dried beans to make sure to remove tiny pebbles and any foreign objects. Cover the beans with about 2 quarts water and soak them overnight. Cook beans until soft.

Wash escarole making sure not to leave any sand or dirt, and then blanch it in lightly salted boiling water for about 3 minutes. Drain, and set aside.

In a deep pan, place oil, parsley and chopped garlic cloves, when garlic is light brown, add drained beans and toss for about thirty seconds and water. Cook until beans become soft to the touch (approximately one hour). Add cooked escarole, salt and pepper and let simmer for ten minutes. Serve with grated Parmigiano.

Rigatoni al Sugo di Carne
(Rigatoni with Meat Sauce)

Ingredients:

1 medium onion, chopped
1 small stalk of celery with leaves, chopped
½ medium carrot, finely chopped
1 oz. olive oil
3 tbsp. butter, plus 1 tbsp. reserved for later
1 lb. ground beef chuck 90% lean
Salt and freshly ground black pepper, to taste
1 cup whole milk
6 bay leaves
4 oz. white wine
28 oz. can Italian imported peeled tomatoes, chopped and strained
1 lb. rigatoni (or your preferred pasta)
4 tbsp. freshly grated Parmigiano

Preparation:

In a sauce pan over medium heat, sauté onion, celery, and carrot in the olive oil and 3 tbps. of butter, until onion becomes translucent and starts to color. Add the chopped beef, salt, and pepper. Stir the beef often to make sure it browns all over and to eliminate any sign of rawness. Once satisfied, add the milk and let the mixture simmer until the milk evaporates entirely. Add bay leaves and wine and let it simmer again until the wine evaporates. Add the tomatoes, check for salt taste, lower the flame to a minimum and let it simmer for about one hour or more. Remove bay leaves.

In a separate pot, cook the rigatoni al dente, according to package instructions. Drain and place pasta back in the same pot. Add the remaining 1 tbsp. butter, a bit of the Parmigiano and just a small amount of meat sauce. Mix gently. Divide the contents among four bowls and top off with more sauce and the remaining Parmigiano.

Scarola in Padella
(Escarole sauté)

Ingredients:

3 qts. water
1 large head of escarole
3 cloves garlic
2 tbsp. olive oil
Salt and pepper to taste
2 oz. water

Preparation:

Cut escarole in pieces of about 2 inches, soak in clean water, scoop it out of water with your hands and place it a clean bowl. Repeat this step three times, as escarole grows very close to the ground and may be loaded with sand. In a large pot bring 3 qts. water to boil, add escarole and cook for 4 to 5 minutes, drain and put aside. Squeeze excess water.

In a skillet, brown garlic. When garlic is a light brown color, turn off the heat. Add escarole, cover and the turn heat back on; add salt and pepper and water, and let simmer 3 to 4 more minutes.

Gatto' di Patate
(Potato Pie)

Ingredients:
2 lbs. potatoes
2 eggs, beaten
Salt and pepper, to taste
½ lb. mozzarella, cut in small cubes
1 oz. provolone chopped in small pieces
1 oz. ham, cut in small pieces
1 oz. prosciutto, cut in small pieces
1 tsp. chopped fresh Italian parsley
1 oz. grated Parmigiano
1 tbsp. butter for greasing the pan
About a cup of breadcrumbs
A bit of additional butter for drizzling over the pie

Preparation:
Boil potatoes, remove the skin and let cool in a large bowl. Mash them. When potatoes are cold, Add the eggs, salt and pepper, and mix well. Add the mozzarella, provolone, ham, prosciutto and grated Parmigiano, and mix well. Butter the bottom and sides of a 10" spring pan and cover the butter with bread crumbs, shaking out the excess breadcrumbs into a bowl to use for the top. Pour the mixture into the pan and level it, using the tips of your fingers. Drizzle a bit of melted butter on top and cover it lightly with bread crumbs. Heat oven to 375 degrees and bake the potato pie until the top is golden brown. Remove the pie from oven and allow to cool before serving.

Polpette di Manzo
(Italian Meatballs)

Ingredients:
   4 slices firm American bread
   1 oz. milk
   1 lb. chopped beef, preferably 90% lean
   2 eggs
   1 tsp. garlic powder
   1 tbsp. chopped fresh Italian parsley
   2 tbsp. freshly grated Parmigiano
   Salt and freshly ground black pepper, to taste

Preparation:
Remove the crusts from the bread, cut each slice into 1/3" pieces, place them in a bowl, add the milk, and with you hands make a paste, squeezing the extra milk out, or if too dry add a bit more milk, so that the bread is soft and pliable. Add the chopped beef, eggs, garlic, and the remainder of ingredients. Work the whole mixture really well. From this mix, you should be able to make eight equal size balls. Using a baking dish or tray, grease the bottom with oil, and place a bit of oil in the palm of your hand to shape each of the balls. Place them on a baking sheet without crowding. Pre-heat oven and bake the meatballs at 375 for 20 minutes, flip them over and bake for another 20 minutes.

The best way to serve meatballs is with ragu sauce. While the sauce is simmering, immerse the baked meatballs and leave them in for 15 minutes, and serve them with a bit of ragu. The sauce will make a nice combination for your favorite pasta.

Friarielli in Padella
(Broccoli di Rapa with olive oil and garlic)

Ingredients:
　　4 cloves garlic
　　1 lb. fresh broccoli di rapa
　　4 oz. water
　　Salt and Pepper to taste

Preparation:
Cut off and discard the very thick stems, soak broccoli in water and drain, using your hands to scoop it out from the water and into an empty container. Repeat this step.

In a large pot, brown garlic, add broccoli, water, salt and pepper and cover the pot, cook for 5 minutes, stirring occasionally.

Frittata Di Spaghetti
(Spaghetti Frittata)

Ingredients:

4 eggs
1 tbsp. grated Parmigiano
Salt and pepper to taste
12 oz. spaghetti cooked al dente, drained and put aside
4 tbsp. vegetable oil

Preparation:

In a medium size bowl, beat eggs, add grated cheese, salt and pepper and mix well. Add cooled spaghetti and mix well, making sure that egg mixture blends evenly with the spaghetti.

In a skillet, heat vegetable oil for two or three minutes. Spread spaghetti mixture evenly in skillet and let cook at medium to low heat, until the bottom crust becomes a rich golden brown color. Turn over and cook other side same as above. Let stand. This treat is tastier at room temperature.

Gnocchi di Patate
(Italian Potato Dumplings)

Ingredients:
2 lbs. Idaho potatoes
1 lg. egg beaten
About 2 cups flour
Salt, for boiling potatoes
4 or 5 basil leaves
3 tbsp. grated Parmigiano

Preparation:

Step One:

Place whole potatoes in a pot, add cold water to submerge potatoes by one inch, and add a bit of salt. Bring to a boil, reduce heat and simmer until potatoes are tender but not mushy. Drain and let cool. Peel potatoes and mash them your conventional way, with your knuckles, or through a ricer. Add the egg and mix well. Scoop potato mixture onto a flat surface. Knead the mixture and add the flour gradually. Add just enough flour to make a firm and delicate dough (too much flour will make gnocchi tough and hard to digest.) Knead thoroughly, then shape the dough, rolling with the palms of your hands to create a 12" log. With a knife, cut the log into 12 equal slices. Roll each slice into a long cigar shape. Cut each cigar into 20 pieces. The pieces will resemble small pillows. Flour the pieces lightly and set them aside until ready to cook.

Step Two:

Fill a big pot with water, bring to boil, and add salt. Drop the pieces of dough gradually, not all at once, into the boiling water and let them cook until they rise to the surface. Drain and quickly chill under cold running water. Drain again. This step is done.

Step Three:

When you are ready to serve, drop the gnocchi pillows into a large quantity of lightly salted boiling water. When they float the second time, drain well and return to the empty pot. Add a small amount of butter, some grated Parmigiano and basil and about 3 or 4 oz. of your favorite sauce. Toss gently and serve topped with more sauce and grated Parmigiano.

P.S. I prefer to use "Filetto di Pomodoro" sauce. Meat sauce, Pesto sauce and Butter and Sage sauce are other delicious alternatives.

Coniglio in Umido
(Rabbit with a cherry tomato sauce)

Ingredients:

2 lbs. rabbit cut, washed and towel dried

½ medium onion sliced thin

1 small branch rosemary

6 oz. white wine

3 tbsp. olive oil

Salt and pepper to taste

2 tbsp. flour

3 oz. vegetable oil for frying

28 oz. canned Italian peeled tomatoes mashed

8 oz. chicken broth

1 tbsp. lightly salted butter

Preparation:

Rinse rabbit in cold water, then place it in a bowl together with onion, rosemary, half of the white wine, one tbsp. olive oil and a bit of salt and pepper. Cover and let marinate for about one hour, tossing every 15 minutes. Drain and discard all liquid. Save the marinated onion and rosemary. Pick out all the pieces of rabbit and flour them lightly.

In a skillet, over medium heat, add vegetable oil and when the oil is hot, place the rabbit and let it brown on all sides. Remove fried rabbit and discard vegetable oil. Put the remaining olive oil and the drained onion and rosemary from the drained bowl. When the onion becomes translucent, place the all the fried pieces of rabbit and continue to brown into onion two minutes on each side. Add wine, toss meat over for one to two minutes, add peeled tomatoes and chicken broth, bring to a boil, reduce heat to medium low and simmer for 20 minutes, stirring occasionally, adding salt and pepper if needed. Just before serving add butter and toss until butter is melted.

Capitone In Umido
(Fried Eel, Naples Style)

Ingredients:
>2 lbs. eel
>3 tbsp. flour
>A generous amount of frying oil (a half-inch depth in the pan)
>Salt
>4 bay leaves
>Extra virgin olive oil

Preparation:

Wipe eels clean with a cloth, clean out and discard the interiors, wash and then cut them into 3" pieces. Flour the eel pieces and fry them in very hot oil over medium heat until the skin is nice and crispy and golden brown in color. Rest the pieces on paper towel to absorb excess oil, then carefully mix the pieces with salt and bay leaves. Place in a glass jar just large enough to hold the preparation, cover with a small amount of olive oil, and refrigerate. Use within a few days.

Mafalde con Ragu e Ricotta
(Mafalde pasta with Ragu and Ricotta)

Ingredients:

4 qts. water

Salt to taste

1 lb. mafalde pasta or wide fettuccine

2 tsp. lightly salted butter

1 lb. whole milk ricotta

Ragu sauce

3 tbsp. grated Parmigiano

Preparation:

Bring water to boil, add salt to your taste, cook pasta according to the instructions on the package, drain and put the pasta back in the pot where it came from. Add butter and mix quickly, add ricotta and about 3 or 4 oz. of Ragu sauce, mix well, and serve with a little bit of sauce on top along with grated Parmgiano.

Spaghetti alle Vongole
(Spaghetti with White Clam Sauce)

Ingredients:
   4 cloves garlic lightly mashed
   2 tbsp. extra virgin olive oil
   3 lbs. New Zealand cockles or 3 dozen little neck clams, shucked
   1 tbsp. fresh parsley chopped
   Salt and pepper to taste
   1 lb. spaghettini or linguine

Preparation:

Cockles:
Wash cockles in running water, rubbing them against one another to remove all sand. Put aside.

Sauce:
In a large skillet over medium heat, brown garlic in olive oil, add cockles and half the amount of parsley. Cover. Occasionally check that cockles are opening, when the vast majority is open (some clams will refuse to open; it is best to simply remove and discard these) add pepper. Turn off the heat.

In the mean time, have a large pot with 4 or 5 qts. water, bring to a boil, add some salt and add spaghettini, and cook al dente according to the package instructions. Drain and put it back into pot. Add a little sauce and stir. Serve in four bowls splitting the sauce and cockles equally, topping each with the remainder of parsley.

Alternate: Little Neck Clams
Shuck clams, save all the juice, and follow sauce recipe above.

Baccala all'Insalata
(Cod Fish Salad)

Ingredients:

1 lb. dry cod, soaked for two days in cold running water to soften and to remove salt, cut approximately into 2" or 3" pieces

1 inner stalk celery with leaves, roughly cut

½ medium onion quartered

1 garlic clove

2 tbsp. extra virgin olive oil

Juice of 2 lemons

1 tbsp. chopped fresh parsley

Pepper to taste

12 green olives

Preparation:

Cook baccala (cod) in a pot over medium heat, along with celery, onion, and garlic until tender. Drain and put just baccala on the side to cool off entirely, discarding all else.

When baccala is cold, break each piece into flakes and mix with Olive oil, lemon juice (to taste), parsley leaves and pepper. Garnish with green olives.

P.S.: May substitute fresh cod for dry.

Scarola Monachina
(Escarole Monk Style)

Ingredients:

2 heads of escarole

4 qts. water

3 cloves garlic

2 tbsp. extra virgin olive oil

1 oz. pine nuts

15 Gaeta olives pitted (kalamata olives may be used instead)

1 oz. golden raisins

Salt and pepper to taste

Preparation:

Remove the first few dark green outer leaves of the escaole, wash it well (two or three soakings to remove sand), and cut into 2" pieces.

Bring water to boil in a large pot and add a bit of salt. Add escarole, cover the pot and allow to cook for five minutes. Drain and let cool. Squeeze off excess water.

In a large skilled over medium heat, brown garlic in olive oil, when garlic is lightly brown remove it and discard. Add cooled off escarole and all the remaining ingredients, cover and let simmer until escarole is soft. Occasionally you might have to add a little water so it does not burn on the bottom.

Ruoto al Forno con Patate
(Baked Lamb with potato)

Ingredients:

1 & ½ lbs. lamb meat, lean, either from the leg or the shoulder

2 & ½ lbs. potatoes, peeled and cut into ¾" cubes

1 medium size onion, thinly sliced

3 oz. fresh peas

2 to 3 tbsp. extra virgin olive oil (use your discretion)

Salt and pepper to taste

4 tbsp. grated Parmigiano

15 oz. Italian peeled tomatoes or 8 oz. ripe cherry tomatoes squished

Preparation:

Soak meat in a bowl filled with water and a bit of salt for 30 minutes.

Remove from water and place it in a baking pan along with potatoes, onions, peas. Drizzle with oil, salt and pepper and grated cheese, mix it a bit. Add tomatoes and fill the pan half way with fresh water and bake at 375 degrees for one hour.

Minestra Di Natale
(Christmas Soup)

Ingredients:

One 3 lbs. free range chicken

2 lbs. beef chuck

2 garlic cloves

Salt and pepper to taste

8 oz. mustard greens (just the leaves, no stems)

8 oz. turnip greens (just the leaves, no stems)

8 oz. collard greens (just the greens, no stems)

5 oz. pecorino – 4 oz. cut in ¼" pieces and 1 oz. grated for the last step

Preparation:

Place whole chicken (remove the interior package) in a large pot, fill pot with water and let rest for an hour. Drain, rinse chicken and also rinse the pot and place chicken back in the pot along with beef. Add 4 qts. water, cover and bring to boil. Add garlic, salt, and pepper and reduce heat to low and let cook for two hours. Remove chicken and beef from the pot and put aside for your main course. Add leafy greens and chunks of cheese in the soup and let cook for one hour. Dish and serve soup, sprinkling remainder of grated pecorino. Parmigiano may be used instead of pecorino for a milder taste.

Zuppa di Lenticchie
(Lentil Soup)

Ingredients:

½ medium onion, peeled and finely sliced

1 small stalk celery, finely chopped (use one of the tender inner stalks)

1 tbsp. chopped carrot

2 tbsp. olive oil

1 tsp. chopped fresh Italian parsley

3 oz. pancetta or bacon, finely cut

1 lb. dried lentils

1 qt. water

1 qt. chicken broth

Salt and freshly ground black pepper, to taste

Preparation:

As with any dried legumes, it is always good to sort through the lentils to make sure to remove tiny pebbles and any foreign objects. Using a 5, 6 qts. pot, sauté onion, celery and carrot in the olive oil until translucent, then add the parsley and pancetta, and let it simmer until most of the fat is melted from the pancetta (6 minutes). Rinse the lentils and add water, chicken broth, salt and pepper and cook until lentil becomes soft, 25, 30 minutes.

Spigola alla Marechiaro
(Filet of Striped Bass in a Light Red Sauce)

Ingredients:

   4 filets of striped bass, about 6 oz. each
   2 tbsp. olive oil
   6 garlic cloves, peeled and left whole
   1 small chili pepper, seeded and chopped
   1 lb. ripe cherry tomatoes, halved
   Salt and freshly ground black pepper, to taste
   6 oz. white wine
   4 oz. clam juice
   2 tsp. chopped fresh Italian parsley

Preparation:

Wash the filets under running cold water and pat dry. In a large sauté pan over medium heat, place olive oil, lightly mash the garlic cloves and add them to the olive oil along with the chili pepper, and allow the garlic to brown. Add the cherry tomatoes, salt and pepper. Drown the mixture with the white wine and the clam juice, and cook the broth until it begins to sizzle. Lower the heat, add the fish filets and let them cook for about 10 minutes occasionally spooning sauce over top of fish. Serve with a generous amount of chopped parsley.

Struffoli
(Honey Clusters)

Ingredients:
2 cups flour
¼ tsp. salt
3 eggs
½ tsp. pure vanilla extract
16 oz. vegetable oil
1 cup honey
1 tbsp. granulated sugar
1 tbsp. chopped candies citron
2 tbsp. toasted almonds
1 tbsp. rainbow nonpareil sprinkles

Preparation:
In a large bowl place flour and salt, mix and make a well in the center of flour. Add one egg and mix well, follow with one more egg an mix and do the same with the third egg. Add vanilla extract and mix well to create a soft dough.

Transfer the dough onto a floured surface and knead, possibly adding a bit more flour until the dough is no longer sticky and you are able to make a square ¾" thick. Let stand for 10 minutes. Cut the square into ¾" strips. Still using the floured surface with your hands roll each strip down to a thickness of 1/3"(approximately the thickness of a pencil) until all the strips have been rolled.

Cut all the long rolls into 1/3 to ½" long.

Heat vegetable oil in a deep pan, when oil is hot place the cut up pieces of dough in oil without over crowding them. Fry for 4 to 5 minutes, until golden brown, remember to turn them to assure evenness. With a slotted spoon, transfer cooked pieces to a bowl with paper towel at its bottom, continue this way until all the dough is finished.

In a separate skillet over medium heat, pour honey, sugar and one tbsp. water. Leave for five minutes, or until the honey-sugar mixture starts to bubble. Quickly add all the fried Struffoli balls and the candied citron pieces, and the almonds. Mix until all the tiny balls are coated. Place in a serving dish and allow to cool. Garnish with non pareil rainbow sprinkles.

Panzarottini
(Fried Small Potato Croquets)

Ingredients:

2 lb. Idaho potatoes

2 eggs, separate yellow from white

2 tbsp. grated cheese (mix of Parmigiano and pecorino)

1 tsp. chopped fresh parsley

Salt and pepper to taste

8 oz. mozzarella, cut into strips of ½" x 1/3" x 1/3"

Breadcrumbs

4 oz. vegetable oil

Preparation:

Wash potatoes, and boil with skin on. Cook them until they can be pierced with a fork, but not too soft. Drain and let cool. Remove the skin, place potatoes in a bowl and mash them the best way you know how, I use the bottom of a glass or a ricer. When mashed potato is cold, add egg yolk, grated cheese, chopped parsley, and pepper. Go easy with salt. Mix well. It should have a consistency of soft Play Dough. Using your fingers, take enough mix to form a 2 ½" long and the thickness of a thick cigar. Placing each croquet in the palm of one hand, with the pinky of the other hand make a dent and fill the dent with a piece of mozzarella. Roll the croquet a bit more to cover the mozzarella and put aside. Continue until you use all the potato mixture. With a fork or a whisk, beat the egg whites, sprinkle a pinch of salt. Roll each piece in egg white then in bread crumbs, when done, put every piece on a tray and refrigerate for at least four hours (I leave mine overnight.)

In a deep frying pan, pour a good amount of vegetable oil, when the oil is hot, drop in croquets one by one without over crowding, When the bottom of each piece cooks to a golden brown color, with the help of a long slotted spoon turn them over and cook as above. When done, take them out and transfer them to a surface with paper towels, to absorb excess oil. Sprinkle with salt.

Scagnozzi
(Fried Polenta Triangles)

Ingredients:
- ¼ lb. polenta
- 1 tbsp. grated Parmigiano
- 4 oz. vegetable oil
- 2 tbsp. flour (for dredging)

Preparation:

To cook polenta, follow the instructions on the package. (For this recipe you may use either the conventional or the quick version. In some cases, I have also used the prepared version that comes in a roll.) When polenta is ready, mix in grated cheese, place in a cassarole and spread it to a thickness of 1/3" to ½". Put on the side to cool. When polenta is completely cold, remove it from casserole and transfer it on a cutting board. Cut strips length wise 2" wide, cut each strip diagonally every 2" to form so many rhombuses or triangles.

Using a deep skillet, over medium high heat, add vegetable oil. While oil is hot, flour both sides of each polenta piece. When oil is hot, one by one, carefully drop the pieces in oil without overcrowding. When a nice golden brown color is reached flip them over and cook same as above. Using a slotted long spoon, remove "Scagnozzi" to paper towel to absorb some excess oil.

Fiori Di Zucchini
(Fried Zucchini Blossoms)

Ingredients:
12 zucchini blossoms, 3" long

Ingredients for batter:
¾ cup flour
Salt and pepper
½ cup beer, room temperature
4 oz. vegetable oil

Preparation:
Look inside each blossom to make sure they are clean.

In a bowl place flour, salt and pepper, mix, add beer and mix. One of the ways to check the thickness is to stick a finger in the mix, if the batter adheres to it without dripping off, it is good. It can be used immediately as well as a while later. Immerse the blossoms in the bowl and coat them entirely with the batter.

Using a deep skillet, over medium heat, add vegetable oil. When oil is hot, drop in batter coated blossoms and fry evenly on all sides. Remove and place on absorbing paper to remove excess oil.

Another way to make this recipe is to barely fill each blossom with a bit of mozzarella and chopped prosciutto. Then follow as above.

Melenzane
(Fried Eggplant)

Ingredients:
4 large Italian eggplants, skin on and sliced length wise ¼" thick

Ingredients for batter:
¾ cup flour
Salt and pepper
½ cup beer, room temperature
4 oz. vegetable oil

Preparation:
Add flour, salt, and pepper to a bowl. Mix together, then add beer and mix again. One of the ways to check the thickness is to stick a finger in the mix; if the batter adheres to it without dripping off, it is ready. Otherwise add either a bit of flour or water to thicken or thin the mixture as needed. It can be used immediately as well as a while later. Immerse the slices of eggplant in the bowl and coat them entirely with the batter.

Using a deep skillet, over medium heat, add vegetable oil. When oil is hot, drop in batter coated eggplant and fry evenly on both sides. Remove an place on absorbing paper to remove excess oil.

Zeppoline
(Fried Dough)

Ingredients:

¼ tsp. granulated sugar

½ package dry baker's yeast (dissolve in 1 oz. warm water)

12 oz. tepid water

1 lb. flour

1 tbsp. olive oil

½ tsp. salt

4 oz. vegetable oil

Preparation:

In a large bowl mix sugar and yeast with tepid water. Gradually add flour and work well. Add olive oil and salt and continue mixing. Depending on the consistency, you might have to add either a bit more flour or a bit of water. The dough should not stick to your fingers, yet it should not be bouncy either. Cover the bowl with Saran Wrap and a towel. Let it sit in a warm spot for one to two hours.

In a deep frying pan, pour a good amount of vegetable oil, when the oil is hot, spoon in the dough, one by one without over crowding. One tbsp. should be the correct amount of dough for one zeppola. When the bottom of each zeppola cooks to a golden brown color, with the help of a long slotted spoon turn them over and cook as above. When the zeppole are done, transfer them to a surface with paper towels, to absorb excess oil. Sprinkle with salt.

Salsicce e Peperoni
(Sausage and Peppers)

Ingredients:
   8 links Italian sausage
   2 tbsp. olive oil
   4 garlic cloves, peeled and sliced
   6 red bell peppers, washed, patted dry and sliced
   1 tsp. chopped fresh Italian parsley
   Salt and freshly ground black pepper, to taste

Preparation:
Baste sausage links lightly with olive oil and place in a lightly greased pan. Poke a few holes on both sides of the links so the fat can be shed and eventually discarded. Broil for 12 minutes, turn over the links and broil for 12 minutes longer. In a skillet (with a cover handy), over low to medium heat, lightly brown the garlic in olive oil for one or so minutes. Slowly add the previously washed, sliced, and patted-dry peppers, covering the skillet after each handful to prevent hot splatters. Add the parsley and 1 oz. of water, and simmer until peppers become tender. Drain the fat from the sausage links, and add the sausages to the peppers. Add salt and pepper to taste, and let simmer for another 10 minutes, adding a bit more water if necessary.

Salsicce e Friarielli
(Sausages and Broccoli Rapa)

Ingredients:
- 1 and ½ bunches broccoli rapa
- 8 links sausage
- 2 tbsp. olive oil
- 4 cloves garlic
- Salt and pepper to taste
- 1 cup chicken broth or water

Preparation:
Wash broccoli well, drain and put aside. Place sausage links in broiling pan, prick few holes on each link, lightly baste with olive oil and broil for 12 minutes. Drain excess fat from pan to prevent splatters. Turn over and broil for 12 more minutes.

In a large pot, brown garlic in olive oil, add broccoli, salt and pepper and chicken broth. Cover and cook for 5 minutes, turning broccoli over once or twice. When sausages are done put them in the pot with broccoli and let simmer for few minutes, pushing the links at the bottom of the pan.

Zuppa di Friarielli, Riso e Patate
(Broccoli Rabe Soup with Rice and Potato)

Ingredients:
- 1 and ¼ lbs. broccoli rabe
- 4 garlic cloves, peeled and left whole
- 3 tbsp. olive oil
- 6 cups water
- Salt and freshly ground black pepper, to taste
- 2 potatoes, peeled and diced in about ½" pieces
- 4 oz. rice, parboiled

Preparation:
Wash broccoli rabe really well, drain and shake out excess water, and then chop them to about 1" pieces. In a deep pot, brown the garlic in the olive oil, add the chopped broccoli, toss, add water and cover. Once it comes to boil, add salt and pepper, cover, reduce the heat and let it simmer for about 15 minutes. Add the potatoes, cover and let cook until potatoes are just about done. Then add the rice and when rice is cooked, turn off the heat and let the soup stand for few minutes before serving.

Minestrone
(Vegetable Soup)

Ingredients:
4 potatoes, peeled and diced to ½" to ¾"
2 stalks celery, diced
1 large onion, peeled and diced
1 large carrot, peeled and diced
2 cloves garlic, peeled and left whole
1 large ripe tomato, diced
1 lb. string beans, cut into 1" pieces
4 tbsp. olive oil
2 qts. water
1 lb. package frozen peas
Two 16 oz. can cannellini beans
1 tsp. chopped fresh Italian parsley
Salt and freshly ground pepper, to taste
Freshly grated Parmigiano, for serving (optional)

Preparation:
Using a large pot, over medium heat, place the first 8 ingredients along with 2 qts. water. Bring to a boil, reduce the heat, and simmer for 1 & ½ to 2 hours, stirring occasionally. Add the remaining ingredients and cook for approximately one more hour. Add parsley and taste for salt and pepper before removing from heat. Once served, sprinkle with Parmigiano, if desired.

Salsicce Pizzaiola
(Sausage Pizzaiola Style)

Ingredients:
   1 oz. vegetable oil
   3 large red bell peppers, washed and sliced
   3 oz. white wine
   8 links Italian sausage
   3 cloves garlic, peeled and left whole
   1 oz. olive oil
   28 oz. can imported Italian peeled tomatoes, mashed by hand
   1 tsp. chopped fresh Italian parsley
   ¼ tsp. dried oregano
   Salt and freshly ground black pepper, to taste

Preparation:
In a skillet, heat the vegetable oil, and when oil is hot, add the sliced peppers, cover and reduce heat. As peppers begin to get mushy, add half of the wine, cover and simmer. Continue process of adding wine until peppers are fully cooked. Drain out the liquid and set the peppers aside. Place the sausages in a baking dish and poke a few holes on both sides of the links so that fat can be shed and eventually discarded. Bake them for 30 minutes at 400 degrees. Drain the fat off and set the sausages aside for a minute. In a separate skillet, lightly brown the garlic cloves in olive oil, add the baked sausage links and quickly brown them on both sides, being careful not to burn the garlic. Once sausages are browned, add the tomatoes, parsley, oregano, salt and pepper. Simmer for about 15 minutes, add the peppers, and simmer for three or four more minutes before serving.

Zuppa di Fagioli
(Cannellini Bean Soup)

Ingredients:
1¼ lbs. dried cannellini beans (soaked overnight in 3 qts. water)
1 small celery stalk, peeled and very finely sliced
3 garlic cloves, peeled and finely sliced
1 tsp. chopped fresh Italian parsley
6 fresh basil leaves, torn
1 oz. extra virgin olive oil
Salt and freshly ground black pepper, to taste
Toasted Italian bread

Preparation:
It is always good to sort through the dried beans to make sure to remove tiny pebbles and any foreign objects. Rinse. Soak the beans overnight in a pot with 3 quarts water. In the same water, cover pot and bring to a boil. Reduce heat and cook the beans until tender, approximately 2 hours. Put the pot aside. In a separate pot, over medium heat, sauté the celery, garlic, parsley, and basil in the olive oil. When the celery softens, pour in the beans and some of their soaking liquid, making sure to add enough liquid to obtain a dense soup. Bring to a boil, add salt and papper, reduce the heat and simmer for 20 minutes. Toast few slices of earthy Italian bread (two per person), place the bread in individual bowls, and submerge with bean soup.

There is another version of making bean soup:
Soak the beans and bring to boil as directed, and when beans are fully cooked, drain from water. In a pot, pour 1 quart of fresh water and add the drained beans, chopped fresh parsley, chopped fresh garlic OR red onion very finely chopped, the juice of a fresh lemon and salt and pepper to taste. Then pour it over toasted bread as above.

Pesto alla Genovese
(Pesto Genova Style)

The aromatic basil from Liguria is what a very long time ago must have inspired the locals to come up with this exquisite concoction made up mainly of basil leaves, extra virgin olive oil and garlic. Of course, over the years so many variations have been made, and in many parts of the world today, we see pesto sauce on many things—sandwiches, dips, and so on. Each summer when the basil grew in abundance, this concoction was made in a mortar and pestle. ("Pesto" derives from the verb "pestare" which in English translates to "crush"). Before the discovery of electricity, this process took a lot of elbow grease, by placing fresh basil leaves, garlic and pine nuts in a mortar and crushing these ingredients together until it became a paste and adding olive oil. Pesto was kept at room temperature through the winter and spring. In some households that is still the one and only way of making pesto. An easier way is to use a food processor or a blender, especially if a large quantity is being made. In my restaurant, we would prepare pesto once a year, at the end of July or at the beginning of August, because that is the peak time to harvest basil in the New York/New Jersey area. Spaghetti is one type of pasta commonly used. Pesto goes well with potato gnocchi or a thick pasta like rigatoni or penne.

Pesto alla Genovese
(Pesto Sauce, Genoa Style)

Ingredients:

2 good size bunches of fresh basil (the total amount of all washed and dried leaves should fill a 2 qts. container lightly packed)

2 garlic cloves, peeled

1 oz. pine nuts (pignoli)

3 oz. extra virgin olive oil

1/8 tsp. sea salt

Preparation:

Remove basil from its the roots and soak it in a large bucket of cold water for a few minutes, remove the basil, discard the dirty water and refill the bucket with clean cold water. Continue this step three times, until all dirt and sand has been removed. Hang the basil to dry overnight. For a successful outcome, make sure that no water or sand is present. When ready to process, remove every stem and any bad/blackened leaves, and place ¼ of the basil, ½ clove of garlic and ¼ of the pine nuts in a blender and blend at low speed. Drizzle in ¼ of the oil very slowly, add a pinch of salt, and repeat, starting with basil and so on until every ingredient is finished. Pour this paste-like mixture into a bowl and mix with a wooden spoon. Pesto can be held in mason jars and refrigerated for a long period of time, without having to freeze it. If a small quantity is made that day for that evening's meal, it can be left at room temperature. However, if the intention is to use it the next day, it is best to refrigerate it overnight.

Spaghetti al Pesto con Patate
(Spaghetti with Pesto and Potatoes)

Ingredients:

2 medium-size potatoes, washed and peeled

A pinch of salt

1 lb. spaghetti *

4 tbsp. pesto (see previous recipe)

2 tbsp. freshly grated Parmigiano

1 tbsp. butter

2 oz. hot water from boiling spaghetti

Preparation:

Cut the potatoes into 1/3" cubes. In a small pot, bring water to a boil, add salt and add the potatoes, and when the potatoes are soft, drain them and set aside. Meanwhile, cook the spaghetti, and while it is cooking, put the remainder of the ingredients into a large bowl, including the diced cooked potatoes. When the spaghetti is al dente, just before draining it, ladle off and reserve about 2 oz. of the hot pasta water, and add this to the large bowl with all the ingredients. Add the drained spaghetti and toss the mixture well.

For conventional Spaghetti al Pesto use same recipe as above without potato.

---

* Follow the cooking instructions for the brand of pasta you are using, as every brand is different as far as the cooking times are concerned, but check through the cooking process to ensure that the doneness is al dente and to your liking.

Spigola alla Livornese
(Striped Bass Livorno Style)

Ingredients:
  1 tbsp. lightly salted butter
  2 tbsp. caramelized onions
  3 oz. white wine
  1 tbsp. marinara sauce
  4 filet of striped bass, about 6 oz. each
  20 pitted Gaeta or kalamata olives
  20 pitted green olives
  1 tsp. nonpareil capers
  1 tsp. chopped fresh parsley
  Black pepper to taste

Preparation:
Place butter, caramelized onion, wine and marina sauce in a skillet over low to medium heat. As soon as it begins to boil, place fish with skin side down, cover, lower the heat to low and simmer. After seven or eight minutes turn fish over and add olives and capers, parsley and a touch of black pepper and cook for seven to eight more minutes. If it seems too soupy, bring up the flame and cook for another one or two minutes, until satisfied.

Pollo alla Paesana
(Chicken Country Style)

Ingredients:

    4 boneless chicken breast, cut about 1" cubes

    2 tbsp. flour, to coat chicken cubes

    4 tbsp. vegetable oil

    4 sweet Italian sausage links

    2 tbsp. olive oil

    4 oz. white wine

    1 tbsp. lightly salted butter

    4 sweet vinegar pepper hulls cur into ¾" pieces

    12 medium size mushrooms; washed, sliced and blanched

    2 boiled potatoes, cut into ¾" cubes

    2 garlic cloves, peeled and lightly mashed

    4 oz. chicken broth

    ½ medium onion, peeled, sliced and caramelized

    Salt and pepper to taste

Preparation:

This dish requires many separate steps, but it is definitely worth it. Flour the chicken cubes lightly. In a large skillet, pour vegetable oil, when oil is hot (at least two minutes) add chicken and brown all sides, drain and set aside. Broil sausage for ten minutes, turn over and broil for ten more minutes. Cut sausage into 1" pieces and set aside.

Final step. In a large skillet, add olive oil, quickly brown chicken cubes and sausage together, drain excess oil, add wine and let cook for thirty seconds, add butter and all the other ingredients. Cover an let simmer for five to six minutes.

Vongole Oreganate
(Baked Clams)

Ingredients:
6 oz. plain breadcrumbs
3 garlic cloves, peeled and finely chopped
1 tsp. dried oregano
1 tbsp. chopped fresh Italian parsley
Salt and freshly ground black pepper
Enough olive oil to make a paste-like substance with the crumbs
2 dozen littleneck clams on the half shell (save the juice)
Juice of 2 lemons, optional

Preparation:
Put the breadcrumbs in a bowl and add the chopped garlic, oregano and parsley, salt and pepper, then add olive oil, a bit at the time, and mix well. Continue adding the olive oil until this bread mixture become like a paste. Open the clams on the half shell (or let the fish market do it), but save the juice. Add clam juice to the bread mixture and mix it in. Using a teaspoon, spoon the mixture onto each clam, spreading it evenly to a thickness of ¼". Place the clams on a baking dish, and on the bottom of the baking dish put a bit of water, and when all the clams are filled with bread mixture, bake them at 400 degrees until the tops are really browned. Before serving, squeeze a bit of lemon juice over the clams (optional).

Fettuccine Alfredo
(Egg Noodles in Cream and Parmigiano Sauce)

Ingredients:
   8 oz. package egg noodles
   3 tbsp. butter
   1 pint heavy cream
   4 tbsp. freshly grated Parmigiano Reggiano
   Salt, to taste
   Freshly ground black pepper, to taste
   2 egg yolks

Preparation:
Boil the noodles until very al dente (approximately 3 minutes). Drain and put them into a skillet over medium heat. Immediately add butter and heavy cream, and cover. When the cream comes to a boil, reduce the heat, add the Parmigiano and the salt to taste. Grind some fresh black pepper over the noodles, and keep mixing gently. When the sauce reaches a creamy consistency, turn off the heat and add the egg yolks, mixing gently but swiftly. Serve immediately.

Scaloppine al Marsala
(Veal Marsala with Mushrooms)

Ingredients:
8 slices veal scaloppine, pounded to about ¼" thick
2 tbsp. flour to dredge the scaloppine
2 oz. vegetable oil
2 tsp. caramelized chopped onion
1 tbsp. butter
2 oz. Marsala wine
2 oz. white wine
1 lb. fresh mushrooms; washed, sliced and blanched
3 oz. chicken broth
1 tsp. chopped fresh Italian parsley
Salt and freshly ground black pepper, to taste

Preparation:
Flour the veal scaloppine, shake off any excess flour, and using a large skillet, heat the vegetable oil over medium to high flame, and sauté the scaloppine until golden-brown on both sides. (Do not over cook the meat.) Drain off the oil, add the caramelized onion and the butter, and toss for 30 seconds until the butter melts. At this point, add the Marsala, white wine, sliced mushrooms and chicken broth. Cover the skillet and simmer until the sauce becomes a bit thick. Add the chopped parsley, salt and pepper.

Carciofo Farcito
(Stuffed Artichokes)

Ingredients:

    4 large artichokes, each about 3" in diameter

    6 garlic cloves, peeled and chopped

    2 tbsp. finely chopped fresh Italian parsley

    2 oz. olive oil

    Salt and freshly ground black pepper, to taste

    2 garlic cloves, peeled and mashed

    30 Gaeta or kalamata pitted olives

    2 tsp. nonpareil capers

    A few fresh basil leaves

    8 oz. chicken broth

    Artichoke cooking water

    1 cup croutons, preferably homemade (toss Italian bread cubes with olive oil, dried herbs of choice, salt and freshly ground black pepper, and bake in oven until lightly browned).

Preparation:

Choose the type of artichokes that are thin and pointed, not the well-rounded ones. Wear plastic gloves, as artichokes will leave your fingers with a grayish stain. With a large knife, cut the stems at the neck of the artichokes and place the stems in a large bowl partially filled with water. Cut off ¼ from the top of each artichoke, and discard, placing the body of the artichoke in the bowl with the water and stems. This is done to prevent the artichokes from becoming discolored.

    Dealing with one artichoke at a time, using a pair of scissors, trim the pricks from each leaf, and with the tip of your fingers remove the smallest leaves that are close to the base. With your thumbs, stretch the center of the artichoke, creating a well by removing some of the tiny hard leaves from the center, and place the artichoke back into the water. Continue this process with the rest of the artichokes.

Using a paring knife, trim the skin and the first 1/3" from the stem, at the side that was farther from the base of the artichoke. Cut each stem lengthwise and place back into the water. Using a cutting board, finely chop 6 garlic cloves and parsley and stuff the artichokes evenly, spreading out from the center. Place the artichokes upright tightly in a pot, and drizzle the tops of the artichokes with half of the olive oil. Add the stems and fill the pot with cold water up to about 1/3" from the top of the artichokes. Cover the pot and bring water to a boil. Uncover, reduce the heat, and add salt and pepper. 15 minutes in, start testing for doneness by piercing the bottoms of the artichokes with a fork, until they are tender but not soft. Turn off the heat and let stand until you can handle the artichokes comfortably. Remove them from the pot and set aside. Do not discard the cooking water, save for next step.

Mash the remaining 2 garlic cloves and brown lightly in a skillet with the remaining olive oil. Add the olives, capers, basil, chicken broth, and about 8oz. of the cooking water. Bring to sizzle and let simmer for 3 or 4 minutes, then taste for salt and pepper. Meanwhile, reheat the artichokes in their water, turn off the heat, remove them one by one, and place them individually in dinner bowls. Sprinkle the croutons on the artichokes and pour the garlic and olive/caper mixture over them.

Pollo Margherita
(Chicken Cutlets topped with Mozzarella)

Ingredients:

4 breasts of boneless chicken, pounded to about ¼" thickness

Salt and freshly ground black pepper, to taste

1 tbsp. flour

1 egg, beaten

3 oz. vegetable olive oil

1 tbsp. lightly salted butter

Small onion, sliced and caramelized

4 oz. white wine

8 medium-size mushrooms, sliced and blanched

3 oz. chicken broth

2 oz. tomato sauce

4 slices of prosciutto

4 slices of mozzarella

1 tsp. chopped fresh Italian parsley

Preparation:

Season the flattened chicken breasts with salt and pepper and coat them in flour and egg. Heat oil in a large skillet, place the chicken breasts and cook them slowly on both sides to a golden brown. Drain off oil and add butter and onion to the chicken. Two minutes later, add the mushrooms and the wine and cover. When the wine is reduced, add the chicken broth and most of the tomato sauce, holding about one 1 tbsp. to decorate the tops of the cutlets, then cover and simmer for 5 minutes. Meanwhile, turn the broiler on. Remove the cover from the skillet, top the chicken with the prosciutto followed by the mozzarella and just a touch of the tomato sauce in the center as decoration. Place in the broiler for 2 minutes or until the mozzarella is slightly melted but not burned. Sprinkle with chopped parsley.

Scaloppine alla Sorrentina
(Veal Cutlets, Sorrento Style)

Ingredients:
8 eggplant round slices about ¼" thickness
2 to 3 tbsp. flour, to dredge the scaloppine and eggplant slices
8 slices of veal scaloppine, pounded to about ¼" thickness
About 3 oz. vegetable oil, for frying the eggplant and scaloppine
3 oz. white wine
1 oz. beef gravy
Salt and freshly ground black pepper, to taste
1 tbsp. tomato sauce
8 thin slices of mozzarella
1 tsp. chopped fresh Italian parsley

Preparation:
Flour the eggplant slices, fry and set aside. Flour the veal scaloppine, shake off any excess flour, and sauté in a large skillet until golden-brown on both sides, (do not over cook meat). Drain off the oil, add the wine, gravy, salt and pepper. Simmer until sauce is reduced to a semi-dense consistency, top the scaloppine slices with the eggplant slices, spread a bit of tomato sauce on each and then top with mozzarella. Broil for 2 or 3 minutes until the mozzarella is slightly melted. Serve the scaloppine with some of the sauce spooned over it and onto the plate. Sprinkle with chopped parsley.

Rigatoni alla Ennio
(Ennio's Rigatoni)

Ingredients:

1 medium onion, peeled and thinly sliced

2 tbsp. olive oil

4 links sweet Italian sausage, meat removed from casing

1 tsp. chopped fresh parsley

2 oz. white wine

12 oz. white mushrooms, washed and diced to half-inch pieces

6 oz. frozen peas, cooked separately according to package

Salt and fresh ground black pepper to taste

1 lb. rigatoni *

2 tbsp. salted butter

4 oz. heavy cream

4 tbsp. tomato sauce

3 tbsp. grated Parmigiano

Preparation:

In a skillet, over medium to low heat, lightly sauté onion in olive oil. Add sausage meat and brown well. Add parsley and half of the wine. When wine evaporates add remaining half and bring to simmer. Add mushrooms, cover skillet and lower the heat. Once the mushrooms are tender, add peas and allow to cook for two or three more minutes. Add salt and pepper, remove from heat. Drain off all the liquid and set aside.

Meanwhile, in salted water cook rigatoni al dente. While pasta is cooking, in a separate skillet place butter, cream, tomato sauce and sausage/mushroom mixture and simmer gently. Drain rigatoni, put it back into the same pot and add part of the creamy Ennio sauce. Stir well, add Parmigiano and stir again.

Dish it out, adding the remaining sauce.

---

* Follow cooking instructions for the brand of pasta you are using, as every brand is different as far as the cooking is concerned. Check through the cooking process to ensure that pasta is al dente and not over cooked.

Funghi Portabello alla Griglia
(Grilled Portabello Mushrooms)

Ingredients:

4 medium-size portobello mushrooms
1 tbsp. olive oil, for brushing the mushrooms
2 cloves garlic, peeled and left whole
1 tbsp. olive oil, for sautéing
2 tbsp. white wine
2 tbsp. water or chicken broth
1 tbsp. brown gravy
Salt and freshly ground black pepper, to taste
1 tsp. chopped fresh Italian parsley

Preparation:

Turn the mushrooms upside down, and with a spoon, remove the dark flaky pulp. Using a dry, clean kitchen towel, clean all sides of the mushrooms. Brush tops and bottoms of mushrooms with the olive oil, place them on a baking sheet, and broil for 2 minutes on each side. In a skillet, brown the garlic in olive oil, add mushrooms, wine, chicken broth, brown gravy and salt and pepper, cover and simmer for 2 to 3 minutes. Serve the mushrooms topped with chopped parsley.

Melenzane alla Parmigiana
(Eggplant Parmigiana)

Ingredients:
1 and ½ lb. eggplants, possibly thin ones as they contain less seeds.
2 oz. flour for dredging
2 or 3 eggs
Pinch of salt
4 oz. vegetable oil
1 pint Marinara sauce
¾ lb. fresh mozzarella cut into small pieces
2 tbsp. grated Parmigiano cheese

Preparation:
Remove skin from eggplants and slice them into ¼" round pieces. Flour all pieces, remove excess flour.

In a bowl beat eggs, add a pinch of salt. Soak floured eggplant slices into egg.

In a skillet, heat oil. Wait three or four minutes until oil is hot and fry eggplant slices to a golden brown on both sides. Remove from oil and place eggplant on absorbing paper to remove excess oil. Let cool.

Using the same method of making lasagna, make layers of eggplant, marinara sauce and mozzarella and grated cheese. Bake at 325 degrees for about 30 to 40 minutes.

Melanzane con Pomodorini
(Eggplant with Cherry Tomatoes)

Ingredients:
 2 lbs. Italian eggplants
 5 oz. vegetable oil
 4 cloves garlic, mashed
 1 oz. extra virgin olive oil
 14 oz. can cherry tomatoes, partially drained
 6 fresh basil leaves, chopped
 ¼ tsp. dried oregano
 Salt and freshly ground black pepper, to taste

Preparation:
Wash and dry the eggplants, do not remove skin, and cut in ¾ inch cubes. Put the vegetable oil in a skillet over medium flame, allow the oil to heat, add the eggplant and fry for about 15 minutes, stirring often. When the eggplant pieces become soft, drain and set aside. Complete this step until all pieces are fried. In a separate pan, brown the mashed garlic in the olive oil, and add the tomatoes and some of their liquid. Once it starts to sizzle, add the eggplant and the remaining ingredients, and let it simmer for 5 minutes over low flame.

Calamari alla Luciana
(Squid in Wine Sauce)

Ingredients:
   1½ lbs. fresh squid, cut in 1/3" thick wheels
   4 cloves of garlic, peeled and lightly smashed
   1 tbsp. olive oil
   2 oz. white wine
   1 tsp. butter
   4 oz. clam juice
   1 tsp. chopped fresh Italian parsley
   salt and freshly ground black pepper, to taste

Preparation:
Cut off the tentacles/heads from the squid, wash and set aside. Wash the squid bodies/tubes really well, turning them inside out to remove sand. Feel for any thin hard cartilage in the tubes, pull it out and discard. Slice the squid tubes into 1/3" wheels. Boil squid slices and tentacles in lightly salted water until tender. Drain and set aside. Brown garlic in olive oil, add squid, and brown for 1 or 2 minutes, add wine, let simmer for ten minutes. Add the rest of the ingredients except the butter. Simmer for about 10 more minutes until the sauce gets a bit consistent, add the butter and mix well until the butter is totally melted. Serve topped with few parsley leaves.

Note: This dish may also be served over pasta. Just cook your favorite pasta according to package instructions.

Cozze al vino bianco
(Mussels in White Wine)

Ingredients:

    6 cloves garlic, peeled and left whole
    2 tbsp. olive oil
    2 lbs. fresh mussels, cleaned and washed
    3 oz. white wine
    3 oz. clam juice
    8 leaves fresh basil, torn
    1 tsp. chopped fresh Italian parsley
    Freshly ground black pepper, to taste
    Pinch red pepper flakes, optional

Preparation:

Brown the garlic in olive oil. Add rest of ingredients at once, including the mussels, and cook until most of the mussels are open. Remove those that refuse to open and discard them. Let the mussels simmer for a couple of minutes. Many times this recipe is paired with linguine. Cook the linguine in salted water and until al dente, drain and place in separate bowls, then pour mussels and sauce over the pasta, being careful not to empty the pan all the way, as many times a bit of sand will be at the very bottom.

Note: By adding two tbsp. Marinara sauce you make another delicious recipe known as Posillipo Sauce.

Pollo, Aglio e Rosmarino
(Chicken with Garlic and Rosemary)

Ingredients:

8 oz. vegetable oil

One whole 3 to 4 lbs. chicken, cut into 8 equal pieces

3 tbsp. flour, for dredging the chicken

4 garlic cloves

2 oz. olive oil

½ tsp. fresh rosemary

1 oz. red wine vinegar

3 oz. white wine

1 cup chicken broth, plus a bit more if needed

1 tbsp. butter

Salt and freshly ground black pepper, to taste

Preparation:

In a large skillet, pour the vegetable oil and heat. Lightly flour the chicken pieces and fry them on all sides until nice and brown. Remove the chicken and drain out the vegetable oil. In the same skillet, add garlic and olive oil for few minutes until garlic becomes lightly brown. Add fried chicken, rosemary, vinegar and wine. Cover for 30 seconds, and then add the broth, butter, salt and pepper, and let it simmer until the juice thickens, approximately 10 minutes. Poke the thickest chicken pieces to make sure that they are fully cooked, and if not, add a bit more broth and follow same step until done.

Luganiga Peperoni e Patate
(Thin Italian Sausage with Peppers and Potatoes)

Ingredients:
 1½ lbs. coiled luganiga sausage
 2 potatoes, peeled and left whole
 1 small onion, thinly sliced
 2 tbsp. olive oil
 3 red bell peppers, washed and sliced about ¾" thick
 2 oz. chicken broth
 1 tsp. chopped fresh Italian parsley
 Salt and freshly ground black pepper, to taste

Preparation:
Broil the luganiga for 8-10 minutes, turn the coil over and broil for an additional 8-10 minutes, then set aside. Boil the potatoes for a few minutes, remove them from water midway done, and set them aside to cool. Sauté the onion lightly in olive oil, then add the peppers, and fry them in the oil and onion until soft. Meanwhile, slice the luganiga into 3" pieces. When peppers become a bit soft, add the luganiga and potatoes, mix well, and then add chicken broth and the rest of the ingredients. Simmer until most of the broth is evaporated.

Insalata di Cannellini
e Finocchio e fette di Arancia
(Cannellini Bean Salad with Fennel and Orange slices)

Ingredients:

    1 lb. dried cannellini beans
    Salt and freshly ground black pepper, to taste
    3 oz. baby arugula
    1 large fennel, washed and thinly sliced
    1 small red onion, peeled and sliced finely
    2 oranges peeled, separate the wedges and slice each lengthwise
    1 tbsp. chopped fresh Italian parsley
    Extra virgin olive oil, to taste
    Balsamic vinegar, to taste

Preparation:

It is always good to sort through the beans to make sure to remove tiny pebbles and any foreign objects. Soak beans overnight in water. Rinse beans and place in deep pot with 2 qts. water and salt, and cook for 30 to 40 minutes over medium heat until tender, but not mushy. Drain and put aside to cool. In a large bowl, add baby arugula, sliced fennel, sliced onion, orange wedges, parsley, and cooked beans. Mix well, drizzle olive, add balsamic vinegar, salt and pepper. Toss and serve.

Salmone al Cartoccio
(Salmon in Aluminum Foil)

Ingredients:

Four 1 and ½" thick salmon filets, about 6 oz. each
One piece of heavy-duty aluminum foil, 18" wide by 24" long
Butter or olive oil (or Pam with olive oil), for brushing the foil
4 garlic cloves, peeled and mashed
1 oz. olive oil
3 oz. white wine
5 oz. clam juice
10 sprigs fresh Italian parsley
Salt and freshly ground black pepper, to taste

Preparation:

Trim the salmon filets of most of the fat at both ends, and remove any bones. Brush the center of the aluminum foil with butter or olive oil; in some cases, you may even use Pam with olive oil. Line up the salmon filet next to each other on the greased center of the foil. Fold over the foil as if to make a package, and roll and squeeze the joined parts very tight so that no juices will leak out. Do the same to one end of the package, leaving one side open. Make sure you have enough foil on the open end so that you will be able to close the third side as tight as the first two. Place the package on a cookie sheet, with the open side tipped upwards, taking care not to accidentally pierce the foil.

Preheat the oven to 450.

In a skillet, over medium heat, lightly brown the garlic in the olive oil, add the rest of the ingredients, simmer for a few minutes, and remove from heat. Pour this juicy sauce into the foil package, and carefully close the opening by tightly crimping the ends. Check all the sides to make sure they are sealed tightly, without ripping the foil. This is why heavy-duty aluminum foil works best.

Place the just made foil bag (on a cookie sheet) and bake for 15 minutes. The foil bag will inflate. To serve, cut an opening on the top of the package and spread open, so that you may easily remove each filet, Using a thin spatula in each hand will help to remove the filets without tearing the foil and not losing any sauce. Scoop out the sauce to pour over each filet.

Fagiolini Marinara
(String beans with Marinara sauce)

Ingredients:
1 lb. fresh string beans
3 cloves garlic
1 tbsp. olive oil
4 oz. peeled tomatoes
1/8 tsp. dry oregano
Salt and pepper to taste

Preparation:
Remove ends from String beans and rinse them. In a pot, boil about a qt. of cold water. Cook for 5 minutes, drain and put on the side.

In a skillet, brown garlic in olive oil, while garlic is browning, with your hand mash the peeled tomatoes and add to oil and garlic, (to prevent splattering, turn off heat for a few seconds before adding tomatoes.)

Let simmer for two minutes, add oregano salt and pepper, stir and add string beans. Continue to simmer for another 5 minutes. Once in a while check that the sauce is not too dry, if that happens, add 1 tbsp. water.

Peperoni rossi e gialli con olive e capperi
(Red and Yellow peppers with Gaeta olives and capers)

Ingredients:
   3 large red peppers
   3 large yellow peppers
   4 cloves garlic
   3 tbsp. olive oil
   4 oz. water or white wine
   1 tsp. chopped fresh parsley
   Salt and pepper to taste
   20 pitted Gaeta olives
   1 tsp. capers

Preparation:
Cut up 1" wide by the length of the pepper, remove seeds and stems. Wash and put aside.

In a large skillet, brown garlic in olive oil. Temporarily turn off heat, add peppers and all the other ingredients with the exception of olives and capers. Turn heat to simmer, cover, and cook for about ten minutes, stirring frequently. At this point add olives and capers, stir and simmer for two more minutes.

Fegato alla Veneziana
(Calf Liver, Venice Style)

Ingredients:
1 lb. calf liver, cut into thin slices approximately 2" x 1/3"
2 tbsp. flour
2 tbsp. olive oil
1 medium onion; peeled, sliced, and caramelized
2 tbsp. balsamic vinegar
3 tbsp. white wine
Salt and freshly ground black pepper, to taste

Preparation:
Flour the pieces of liver and set aside. In a skillet, heat the olive oil until very hot (make sure not to burn yourself as this step can be very tricky), place the liver pieces in the skillet and separate the pieces with a long fork, until the liver is browned on all sides, watching out for hot spatters. Discard most of the olive oil from the skillet, and add the caramelized onion. After 1 or 2 minutes, add the vinegar and wine, stir quickly, and add salt and pepper. Simmer for 2 or 3 more minutes or until it is cooked to your taste.

Torta di Ricotta
(Italian Cheesecake)

Ingredients:
    1½ cups sugar
    4 tbsp. flour
    1¼ lbs. ricotta cheese
    8 oz. whipped cream cheese (See Note 2)
    7 large eggs (See Note 1)
    1 tbsp. pure vanilla extract
    16 oz. sour cream

Notes:
    1) Take the eggs out of the refrigerator about one hour before starting this recipe and leave them at room temperature. Separate the yolks from the whites, leave the yolks at room temperature, but refrigerate the whites until ready to use.
    2) Whipped cream cheese is necessary because it incorporates smoothly with the ricotta.
    3) Pre-heat the oven to 350 degrees one hour before baking.
    4) Not all ovens are the same, for best results, the top of the cake should be a golden-brown color.

Preparation:
Butter and flour the sides and bottom of a 10" spring pan, and place it in refrigerator. Pre-heat oven to 350 degrees.

In a large bowl, mix sugar and flour together with a whisk, add ricotta and cream cheese. In separate bowl, mix egg yolks, and vanilla, then add to bowl with ricotta, cream cheese, sugar and flour. Add the sour cream and beat again. Take the egg whites out of the refrigerator and beat them with an electric beater until soft peaks form, and then fold them into the mixture, gently to preserve the batter's fluffiness.

Pour the mixture into the spring pan and bake for 1 hour and 15 minutes until the top becomes golden brown. Turn off the oven and leave the cake in for another 15 minutes. Remove from oven and allow the cake to cool and then refrigerate overnight. For best taste, serve at room temperature.

Gelato con Zabaglione
(Michael's Special Dessert)

Ingredients:
2 scoops hazelnut gelato
1 oz. dark chocolate, chopped into chunks
2 medium-size strawberries, cut in pieces
Cold zabaglione (see below)

To make zabaglione you will need a double boiler and a large bowl of ice water.

2 egg yolks, beaten
1 tbsp. sugar
1 oz. Marsala wine
1 oz. fresh whipped cream

Preparation of zabaglione:
Prepare a large bowl of ice water and set it aside. In a double boiler over medium heat, add the egg yolks, sugar and Marsala wine, and whip it with a constant beat until the mixture is fluffy. Remove the pan from the double boiler, and place it over the bowl of ice and water, and continue whipping until the fluffy cream is cool. Then fold in the fresh whipped cream, gently to preserve the zabaglione's fluffiness.

Final serving step:
In a glass bowl, spread the gelato, followed by the zabaglione, then the strawberry pieces, and finally sprinkle with the chunks of chocolate. Serve immediately.

Zeppole Di San Giuseppe
(St. Joseph Pastry)

Ingredients:
- 4 oz. butter, plus a bit more for greasing the pan
- 8 oz. water
- Pinch of salt
- 8 oz. flour
- 4 eggs, lightly beaten
- 1 oz. granulated sugar
- ½ teaspoon grated lemon zest

Preparation:

Grease a large baking sheet and set aside. Pre-heat the oven to 400 degrees. In a saucepan over medium heat, combine butter, water and salt and bring to a boil. Add the flour little by little, and whisk well continuously until the dough separates from the sides of the pan. Remove the pan from the stove and let cool. Once the dough is cooled, add the eggs, little by little, making sure to mix each egg well before continuing with the next one. Add the sugar and lemon zest and mix well. Drop the dough by spoonfuls onto the greased baking sheet, leaving a space of 3 inches between them. Bake the zeppole for 10 minutes at 400 degrees, then reduce heat to 325 degrees and bake for approximately 30 minutes more until golden-brown. Let the zeppole cool, make a slit on the side of each, and fill them with one of the fillings listed below.

Crema Pasticciere
(Custard Filling)

Ingredients:
3 oz. granulated sugar
3 egg yolks
3 oz. flour
Rind of half a lemon
½ teaspoon pure vanilla extract
16 oz. whole milk

Preparation:
Place all ingredients except milk in a saucepan, over low heat, and mix well. In a separate pan, scald the milk and pour it into the mixture, little by little, and, beating constantly with a whisk or electric beater, continue cooking and beating over low heat, making sure that no little balls form in the mixture. Cook for 3 or 4 more minutes, stirring with a wooden spoon. Remove the mixture from the stove, and continue to stir occasionally until it is cool. Remove the lemon rind. Place the custard in a bowl, continuing to stir occasionally to prevent a skin from forming on top (you can also take a piece of plastic wrap, and push it down to lay it directly on top of the custard surface to prevent a skin from forming). Once cooled, the custard is ready to be used. If not being used right away, refrigerate.

Crema di Ricotta
(Ricotta Filling)

Ingredients:
   1 lb. ricotta
   1 oz. confectionary sugar
   1/8 tsp. pure vanilla extract
   2 tbsp. candied fruits, finely chopped
   1 tbsp. mini chocolate chips (optional)

Preparation:
Place the ricotta, sugar and vanilla extract in a bowl and mix well until creamy and the sugar has completely dissolved. Fold in the rest of the ingredients. Refrigerate for a minimum of 2 hours.

Tortano Dolce
(Easter Sweet Treat)

This is a two step process.

Step #1) Ingredients:

   5 eggs (removed from the refrigerator for one hour before using)
   1 & ½ cups granulated sugar
   2 oz. limoncello (Grand Marnier or Cointreau May be used instead)
   1 tbsp. pure vanilla extract
   1 packet baker's yeast (dissolved in 4 oz. of lukewarm water)
   1 & ½ stick butter (removed from the refrigerator to soften)
   Zest from one whole lemon
   1 lb. all purpose flour

Preparation:

In a large bowl, beat eggs well, add all ingredients except the flour and mix well. Slowly fold in flour and mix well. In order to achieve the proper consistency, it should look and feel slightly thicker than ice cream.

Butter the inside of a 10" Anger Food pan, pour mixture, cover with Saran Wrap and place it on the side until it rises to double the height. Meanwhile pre-heat oven 30-40 minutes at 325 degrees and bake until golden brown. Approximately 35 minutes.

Step #2) Ingredients:

   2 egg whites removed from refrigerator as above
   ½ cup confectionary sugar
   1 oz. nonpareil cake sprinkles

Meringue Preparation:

Use a small stain steel bowl, place it in the freezer until ready to use. When the Tortano is ready, remove from oven, but keep the oven *on*.

Remove bowl from freezer. With an electric beater, beat the egg whites for a couple of minutes until you begin to see peaks forming. Add sugar a little at the time and continue to mix until it reaches smooth consistency and peaks have formed.

Spread meringue evenly on top of Tortano and loosely sprinkle with cake sprinkles.

Return Tortano in the oven for another 12 to 15 minutes until meringue hardens.

Made in the USA
Coppell, TX
29 November 2019

12068938R00176